THE PLEASURE
OF WRITING

Purdue Studies in Romance Literatures

Editorial Board

Floyd F. Merrell, Series Editor
Jeanette Beer
Paul B. Dixon

Howard Mancing
Anthony Julian Tamburri
Allen G. Wood

Associate Editors

French
Paul Benhamou
Willard Bohn
Gerard J. Brault
Germaine Brée
Mary Ann Caws
Gérard Defaux
Floyd F. Gray
Michael Issacharoff
Milorad R. Margitić
Glyn P. Norton
Allan H. Pasco
Gerald Prince
David Lee Rubin
English Showalter

Italian
Fiora A. Bassanese
Peter Carravetta
Benjamin Lawton
Franco Masciandaro

Luso-Brazilian
Fred M. Clark
Mary L. Daniel

Marta Peixoto
Ricardo da Silveira
    Lobo Sternberg

Spanish and Spanish American
Maryellen Bieder
Catherine Connor (Swietlicki)
Ivy A. Corfis
Frederick A. de Armas
Edward Friedman
Charles Ganelin
David T. Gies
Roberto González Echevarría
Patricia Hart
David K. Herzberger
Emily Hicks
Djelal Kadir
Lucille Kerr
Alberto Moreiras
Randolph D. Pope
Francisco Ruiz Ramón
Elżbieta Skłodowska
Mario Valdés
Howard Young

PSRL   volume 20

THE PLEASURE OF WRITING

Critical Essays on

Dacia Maraini

Edited by
Rodica Diaconescu-Blumenfeld and
Ada Testaferri

Purdue University Press
West Lafayette, Indiana

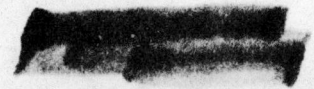

Copyright © 2000 by Purdue Research Foundation. All rights reserved.

04   03   02   01   00   5   4   3   2   1

∞ The paper used in this book meets the minimum requirements of American National Standard for Information Sciences—Permanence of Paper for Printed Library Materials, ANSI Z39.48-1992.

Printed in the United States of America
Design by Anita Noble

Library of Congress Cataloging-in-Publication Data
The pleasure of writing: critical essays on Dacia Maraini / edited by
   Rodica Diaconescu-Blumenfeld and Ada Testaferri.
       p.   cm. — (Purdue studies in Romance literatures ; v. 20)
    Includes bibliographical references and index.
    ISBN 1-55753-197-8 (cloth ; alk. paper)
    1. Maraini, Dacia—Criticism and interpretation. I. Diaconescu-Blumenfeld, Rodica. II. Testaferri, Ada. III. Series.

PQ4873.A69 Z84 2000
858'.91409—dc21   99-089306

Contents

vii **Editors' Preface**
ix **Acknowledgments**

Part 1
Preliminaries

  3 Rodica Diaconescu-Blumenfeld
     Introduction

21 Dacia Maraini
    Reflections on the Logical and Illogical Bodies of
    My Sexual Compatriots

Part 2
Demythicizing Genre: Issues of Representation
and Language

41 Ada Testaferri
    De-tecting *Voci*

61 Corrado Federici
    Spatialized Gender and the Poetry of Dacia Maraini

77 Elisabetta Properzi Nelsen
    Écriture Féminine as Consciousness of the Condition of
    Women in Dacia Maraini's Early Narrative

Part 3
Poetics and Practices of Liberation

103 Virginia Picchietti
     Symbolic Mediation and Female Community in
     Dacia Maraini's Fiction

121 Giovanna Bellesia
     Variations on a Theme: Violence against Women in
     the Writings of Dacia Maraini

135 Daniela Cavallaro
     Dacia Maraini's "Barricade Theater"

Contents

Part 4

Historiographies

149 Giancarlo Lombardi
A memoria: Charting a Cultural Map for Women's Transition from *Preistoria* to *Storia*

165 Maria Ornella Marotti
La lunga vita di Marianna Ucrìa: A Feminist Revisiting of the Eighteenth Century

179 Paola Carù
Vocal Marginality: Dacia Maraini's Veronica Franco

Part 5

Reclaiming the Body in the Construction of Subjectivity

195 Rodica Diaconescu-Blumenfeld
Body as Will: Incarnate Voice in Dacia Maraini

215 Gabrielle Cody
Remembering What the Closed Eye Sees: Some Notes on Dacia Maraini's Postmodern *Oresteia*

232 Pauline Dagnino
Revolution in the Laundry

246 Áine O'Healy
Toward a Poor Feminist Cinema: The Experimental Films of Dacia Maraini

265 List of Contributors

269 Index

Editors' Preface

Dacia Maraini is one of contemporary Italy's best-known writers. An active participant in the dialogue concerning the status of women, she has never wavered in her position. Her struggles on behalf of women have made her a figure of controversy as author and as cultural critic. A prolific writer, she has been the recipient of numerous literary awards. Yet in spite of, or perhaps because of, her stature, Maraini's work has not received the sustained critical attention it deserves. She has been effectively excluded from the Italian critical canon, depriving her of a voice and limiting the impact of her message. *The Pleasure of Writing* demonstrates the currency of Maraini's thought and argues for a revision of the canon.

The present study covers the whole range of Maraini's production, including novels, plays, poetry, and films. Anchored by a piece Maraini herself has contributed, these essays by an international group of Italianists advance the critical discussion of a writer who has received inadequate attention from the scholarly community.

Dacia Maraini has prepared, specifically for this volume, "Reflections on the Logical and Illogical Bodies of My Sexual Compatriots." The author draws on an earlier rendition of this text, "Riflessioni sui corpi logici e illogici delle mie compagne di sesso," which formed the introduction to *La bionda, la bruna e l'asino: con gli occhi di oggi sugli anni settanta e ottanta* (The blonde woman, the dark woman, and the donkey: looking at the seventies and eighties with the eyes of today), Maraini's 1987 collection of meditations on women in Italian society. Even in its earlier form, this essay has never before been published in English. In its revised and expanded version, it reflects on Maraini's own critical reception as well as on the relationship that female writers have with language, patriarchal society, and the canon.

The introduction that opens the volume provides an overview of Maraini's work and significance. The thirteen essays that form the body of the volume utilize a wide spectrum of interpretive perspectives, from semiotics to psychoanalysis. Part one comprises the introduction and Maraini's meditation. Part two examines segments of Maraini's work in relation to literary

Preface

traditions, aiming at recontextualizations for which gender forms a primary category. Part three highlights Maraini's signifying practices—whether contextual or formal—concerning the idea of women's freedom. History, the subject of part four, is a privileged territory for feminism, and several of Maraini's texts that draw on historical figures of women are here explored. Finally, in part five, the issues of the body and the construction of subjectivity are discussed, including a rarely examined aspect of Maraini's production: her films.

The studies in this volume offer access to the complex pleasures of reading Dacia Maraini. *The Pleasure of Writing* emphasizes the enduring cultural values of her work, which it presents as a politically committed art. Maraini's work stands as an answer to those who question the value of such an art.

Acknowledgments

The editors wish to thank, above all, Dacia Maraini. Thanks are also due to Lucia Lermond for both financial and editorial support and to the Vassar College Research Committee for its generous contributions toward the preparation and the publication of this work. They also thank Anthony J. Tamburri for his commitment to the publication of this collection and Susan Y. Clawson for her skillful copyediting. The editors are also grateful to all the contributors, who supported this project with their expertise and enthusiasm.

Rodica Diaconescu-Blumenfeld offers personal thanks to John Ahern for constant encouragement, and to Lisa Paravisini for advice in the process of coediting.

Ada Testaferri thanks Sebastiana Marino for her intelligent and sensitive translation of "De-tecting *Voci*," which appears in this volume.

"Reflections on the Logical and Illogical Bodies of My Sexual Compatriots," by Dacia Maraini, first appeared, in different form, as "Riflessioni sui corpi logici e illogici delle mie compagne di sesso," the introduction to *La bionda, la bruna e l'asino: con gli occhi di oggi sugli anni settanta e ottanta* (Milan: Rizzoli, 1987). The editors express their thanks to Rizzoli Editore for permission to include the revised and translated version in this volume.

Part 1
Preliminaries

Rodica Diaconescu-Blumenfeld
Introduction

Dacia Maraini
Reflections on the Logical and Illogical Bodies of My Sexual Compatriots

Dacia Maraini. Photograph courtesy of Dacia Maraini and Fotoarchiv Romanischer Autoren. © Heinz Willi Wittschier.

Rodica Diaconescu-Blumenfeld

Introduction

Dacia Maraini is a controversial figure. She is controversial in the context of Catholic Italy, and even that of the Italian left, where women had been secondary, then fought for emancipation, then for sexual difference, and are now being reabsorbed in a "postfeminist" complacency. While Maraini does not, normatively, use the term *feminist* to describe herself, preferring the adverbial phrase "dalla parte delle donne" ("on the side of women"), this volume celebrates Dacia Maraini in her life and art as in the fullest sense feminist, a feminism that is humane, complex, and uncompromising.

A committed activist, Maraini fights as a woman "on the side of women." Unrelenting in her opposition to gender roles that repress women and render them vulnerable to abuse and violence, Maraini listens to the voices of women and gives voice to their silences. Attentive both to the discourses of theoretical feminism and to the experiences of women, she keeps up with the changing forms of oppression. Maraini's art, in particular her continuous engagement with writing, bears witness to her struggle *dalla parte delle donne* as to the lived intelligence that nurtures this into poem and story.

It is for this reason that the lack of sustained critical attention to the work of an author so widely read in Italy must be understood in its full political force. Interpretation is not merely the affectation of isolated academics and intellectuals; it is a crucial mode of either reinforcing or remaking a lived cultural canon.

In this introduction, I propose first to give a brief overview of Maraini's oeuvre for readers unfamiliar with her work, in order to record her productivity and range; then to analyze

Introduction

Maraini's exclusion from the Italian literary canon, relating this issue to those of signature and sexed voice.

***

Born in Florence in 1936, to an anti-Fascist family, Maraini spent part of her childhood in Japan, where she was eventually imprisoned with her family in a concentration camp toward the end of World War II. Maraini started her career in 1962 with the novel *La vacanza* (*The Holiday*), followed by *L'età del malessere* in 1963 (*The Age of Malaise*), works that may be termed proto-feminist. The second of these novels details the dreary life of Enrica, a working-class young woman whose actions are at first subordinated to and determined by male presences and narratives but whose gradually awakening self-consciousness marks the possibility of an independent agency. The novel won the international prize Formentor. From 1963 to 1967 Maraini established her place in Italian culture by participating in contemporary debates, especially those of the neo-avant-garde Gruppo '63. Living in Rome during this period, she developed close friendships with many of Italy's leading artists and intellectuals, including Pier Paolo Pasolini and Alberto Moravia. In 1966 the volume of poetry *Crudeltà all'aria aperta* (Cruelty in the open air) appeared. In 1967 she published the novel *A memoria* (By heart) and started the experimental theater company Il Porcospino.

The next year, 1968, marked the beginning of Maraini's feminist activities and activism: she conducted sociological inquiries (e.g., on conditions in women's prisons), published articles, wrote and produced plays. In this year she started another experimental theater, La compagnia blu, and published *Mio marito: racconti* (My husband: short stories).

From 1969 to 1973 Maraini wrote, produced, and published plays, and directed her first and only feature film, *L'amore coniugale* (Conjugal love). Her play *Il manifesto* dates from these early years. In 1972 Maraini published *Memorie di una ladra* (*Memoirs of a Female Thief*), a novel based on the "adventures" of a convicted thief, Teresa, whom she had met during her prison investigations. She shared the royalties from the novel and the resulting movie with her collaborator. In *Memorie*

Introduction

Maraini investigated the dynamics of the underworld, shown to be quite as damaging as those of Teresa's supposed rehabilitation. In 1973 the author published *E tu chi eri? Interviste sull'infanzia* (And you, who were you? Interviews on childhood), a collection of interviews with well-known figures in Italian cultural life such as Roberto Rossellini, Carlo Emilio Gadda, Alberto Moravia, Pier Paolo Pasolini, and, most importantly, Anna Maria Ortese, Liliana Cavani, Natalia Ginzburg, and Rossana Rossanda. In 1974 Maraini published the collection of feminist poetry *Donne mie* (Women of mine), and *Fare teatro: materiali, testi, interviste* (Making theater: materials, texts, interviews), a mixed set of plays, interviews, and other texts on theater. She also composed the play *La donna perfetta* (The perfect woman).

The following year, 1975, saw the publication of *Donna in guerra* (*Woman at War*), her first major feminist novel. The trajectory of the protagonist Vannina, from a housewife subjected to a life of routine and male domination to an independent agent possessed of a feminist consciousness, is still one of the most powerful accounts of the conflicts and ideologies (patriarchal or feminist, conservative or left-wing terrorist) of the troubled 1970s. A second volume of poetry, *Mangiami pure* (*Devour Me Too*), appeared in 1978.

In 1976 Maraini shot the experimental film *Mio padre amore mio* (My father my love), and three documentaries: *Aborto: parlano le donne* (Abortion: women speak out), *Le ragazze di Capoverde* (The young women of Capoverde), and the three-part series *Ritratti di donne africane* (Portraits of African women).

From 1976 to 1980 Maraini wrote and produced many plays, among them *I sogni di Clitennestra* (*Dreams of Clytemnestra*), performed in New York at the Judith Anderson Theater in 1989, and *Maria Stuarda* (*Mary Stuart*), produced first in Rome, and subsequently translated and performed in more than twenty countries. This play was staged in the United States at La Mama Theater, New York, in 1987. In particular, *Dialogo di una prostituta con un suo cliente* (*Dialogue between a Prostitute and Her Client*), which articulates the physical and psychological subjection of women through the ubiquitous institution of prostitution, was widely produced in such countries as France, Belgium, England, and the U.S. In 1980, Maraini began directing plays.

Introduction

In 1981 Maraini published *Lettere a Marina* (*Letters to Marina*), a story of lesbian love whose ending in madness is seen as inevitable in a repressive society. *Dimentacato di dimenticare* (Forgot to forget), her third volume of poetry, appeared in 1982. From 1982 to 1985 she continued to write many plays that were presented in various Roman theaters. She also directed a short super-8 film, *Lo scialle* (The shawl). In 1985 *Isolina: la donna tagliata a pezzi* (*Isolina*), an essay in "investigative-reporting" style, marked Maraini's growing interest in historical fiction. The book won the Fregene prize and was published in five countries. In the period from 1986 to 1990 the author continued to write plays, among them *Norma '44* (Norma '44), staged in Montevideo and Buenos Aires, and *Stravaganza* (Extravagance), also performed in many cities around the globe. In 1987 Maraini published *La bionda, la bruna e l'asino: con gli occhi di oggi sugli anni settanta e ottanta* (The blonde woman, the dark woman, and the donkey: looking at the seventies and eighties with the eyes of today), a collection of essays on the culture and society of the 1970s and 1980s.

In 1990 a major historical novel, *La lunga vita di Marianna Ucrìa* (*The Silent Duchess*), was published. The protagonist is a noblewoman who has lost both her hearing and the power of speech. Her physical restriction embodies her alienation, but also the possibility of resistance and even freedom. This novel earned two of Italy's celebrated prizes, Campiello and the Libro dell'anno, and was published in eighteen countries. The spring of 1997 saw the release of the film *Marianna Ucrìa,* directed by Roberto Faenza. In 1991 a collection of poetry, *Viaggiando con passo di volpe* (*Traveling in the Gait of a Fox*), was published (recipient of two prizes, Premio Mediterraneo and Premio Città di Penne), and the following year the play *Veronica, meretrice e scrittora* (Veronica, prostitute and female writer) came out. In 1993, Maraini published *Bagheria* (*Bagheria*), an autobiographical text (recipient of three prizes and published in five countries), and the book-length feminist essay *Cercando Emma* (*Searching for Emma: Gustave Flaubert and Madame Bovary*). The same year saw the publication of an important and controversial essay on abortion, *Un clandestino a bordo: le donne: la maternità negata, il corpo sognato.* The English translation of this volume, *Stowaway on Board,* was prepared for publication by one of our contributors, Giovanna Bellesia, in cooperation with Victoria Offredi Poletto.

Maraini's latest major novel, *Voci,* was published in 1994 (*Voices*). This work explores the issue of violence against women in a society whose contempt for women is systemic. It received the Premio Napoli and the Sibilla Aleramo prize, and was published in ten countries. In 1995, she published the play *Camille,* which was presented at the Spoleto theater festival of that year. In 1997, an epistolary novel, *Dolce per sé* (Sweet by nature), was published and won three prizes (Agrigento, Brancati Zafferana, and Città di Salerno '97). As our book was being finished, Maraini's latest work, *Buio* (Darkness), a collection of short stories inspired by acts of violence against women in the new, multiethnic Italian society, came out in January 1999, and won Italy's single most prestigious literary prize, the Strega.

From the battles for the legalization of abortion in the 1970s to her involvement in activist groups fighting for the rights of Bosnian rape victims and current debates about the reassimilation of the female body by enduring patriarchal discourse, Dacia Maraini has also been, throughout her long career, a constant presence in the contemporary Italian public sphere as social critic, engaging in media discussions on current issues. She writes regular columns for the leading newspapers *Corriere della Sera, L'Unità,* and *Il Messaggero;* she publishes frequently in such journals as *Panorama, L'Espresso,* and the feminist *Noidonne,* and participates in televised cultural debates.

***

Despite the numerous literary prizes she has received, Dacia Maraini has not broken into the Italian literary canon. Maraini and other women writers, writing as women in a new way, are a priori excluded from this canon because they write outside the spaces where the canon does its work. Sexed voices, not only do they write the scandal of women as desiring subjects, but further, they write difference into dimensions that the canon cannot recognize. Maraini's exclusion from the canon devalues her as a writer and deprives her of critical attention.

In an interview, Italian feminist writer Lidia Ravera remarks on the abundance of works by women in bookstores:

Introduction

> [w]omen writers appear commercially useful, but they remain less respected than their male colleagues and are considered with such paternalism by literary critics that the critical apparatuses dedicated to them are infinitely inferior to those on male writers, even of more modest quality. (Sorbo, paragraph 4).[1]

Maraini herself comments on this subject in her essay "Reflections on the Logical and Illogical Bodies of My Sexual Compatriots" in our volume. To suggest the relation between critical attention and canonicity, let it suffice to note that in one of the most recent histories of Italian literature, Maraini is extended the space of five lines.[2]

In order to clarify the importance of Maraini's acceptance in the literary canon, I want to examine the nature of canons, both in their inherent conservatism and in their capacity for change. In so doing, I demonstrate the reason the canon necessarily resists female sexed voices, whose signatures bear contingency, historicity, non-metaphysical difference into a cultural order that constitutes itself as transcendent. Finally, I return to Maraini's passionate production of texts as working against the canon's work of foreclosure, to raise those questions of interpretation at the heart of our homage to Dacia Maraini.

Like all traditional institutions, canons maintain their hegemony on the basis of the self-proclaimed objectivity and transhistoricity of their operations. But the deconstructive practices of critical theory, feminist and postcolonial studies have challenged this.[3] Over time, canons are malleable, they can be expanded and revised. More importantly, what is being radically contested today are "the traditional aesthetic and cultural values that create the canon," as Laurie Finke states (154). These values, rooted in a Western tradition that allows for the possibility of self-differentiation only through domination and the naturalizing of domination, are eminently contingent in nature. Canons are not universal and transhistorical, rather they are sites of discourse, where various cultural forms, ideologies, and processes intersect and conflict.[4] To the claims of universality, monumentality, homogeneity, and non-ideological aestheticism of the canon, feminism opposes a heterogeneous, materialist dynamic of lived meaning.

A pluralizing "counter-canon," or better, "counter-canons," are in the process of being formed. These counter-canons reclaim from history forgotten texts by women and dislocate the Great Atlantic axes of interpretation. These counter-processes of reading and writing construct new technical means for new subject matters and new perceptions. Engaged in various representational strategies, from a subject position, women writers are rewriting the classic patriarchal masterplots, are transforming the rules of genre. Their chosen narrative forms, bound up with social identities and ideologies, are acts of resistance and of creativity.[5]

Eve Kosofsky Sedgwick writes of the "vision of an exploding master-canon whose fracture would produce, or at least leave room for, a potentially infinite plurality of mini-canons" (50), but sees "the most productive canon effects" issuing from the interaction of this pluralizing and from "a reading rebelliously within the master-canon" that *names* and hence particularizes the canon as *a* canon (50). Sedgwick specifically notes the institutional endurance of the master canon despite current movement toward its destabilization. This endurance of literary canons makes Maraini's inclusion matter, since what is at issue is the endurance of her voice in Italian and world literature.

Maraini has spoken of the absence of artifacts testifying to the many years of collective work in women's theater. Why did we not save them, she asks. Likewise, much current women's writing will be ephemeral, without commitment to its continued presence in Italian cultural life.[6] A canon, as Finke argues, is "forged in the classroom, in syllabi, anthologies, textbooks, literary journals, and reviews" (158), and from our experience as teachers, we know this.

Canons can change, but they also resist change. The master canon is not for nothing master. Historically, the very concept of canon has contained within itself a pretension of some sort of ultimate high culture. Two related qualities of Maraini's production, hence, contest canonicity. She is a woman, writing herself as woman. She writes with humility, against esotericism.

Maraini's own *Veronica, meretrice e scrittora* demonstrates that to criticize a woman writer has traditionally meant to criticize her as woman. As woman she is identified with her body,

Introduction

and her work is looked on as obscene, breaking the decorum, an instance of self-exposure. Women writers writing as women, however, necessarily write the body, source of signification of lived difference. Women as sexed subjects write the disruption of the canon of the same.

***

Perception itself is structured by the body, according to Italian feminist Patrizia Violi. Following the Irigarayan assimilation of knowledge to sexual difference, Violi advocates a differential cognitive "point of view" between men and women (Bono and Kemp, *Italian Feminist Thought* 18–19). Thus feminist theories posit the need for a different articulation of the body, away from patriarchal significations.[7] Discussing the relationship Italian feminism develops between "women, bodies, and writing," Sandra Kemp and Paola Bono state that for such theorists as Nadia Fusini and Viola Papetti "there is no figurative model of the female body's pleasure embedded in tradition" (Kemp and Bono, *Lonely Mirror* 14). Adriana Cavarero and Silvia Vegetti Finzi make this claim also. The body is the foundation of subjectivity, an overdetermined site of the history of oppression and struggle, where "those few degrees of freedom [are] stolen, little by little, from a biological and social destiny," as Vegetti Finzi writes ("The Female Animal," in Kemp and Bono, *Lonely Mirror* 150). The female body as subjectivity is Maraini's ultimate concern. She affirms that "in the words of the woman, there must be her body" (Badt).

The well-known French feminist literary practices of "écriture féminine" (as represented in vastly different modes by such writers as Monique Wittig, Hélène Cixous, Xavière Gauthier, Annie Leclerc) and the equally well known feminist/psychoanalytic theories of Luce Irigaray—from the late 1960s to the present, but with special force in the 1970s—have had a lasting influence on Italian feminist writers and activists.[8] "Writing as a woman" was envisioned as subversive, both in its refusal to submit to a social and symbolic order constituted by the phallus, and in its exercise of experimental narrative modes. Sharon Wood's introduction to *Italian Women Writing* offers a most valuable investigation of the relationship between feminism, literature,

Introduction

and politics in postwar Italy, describing how Italian feminist writers "explore ... the 'textuality of sex'; the weaving of gender through a range of discourses, experiences and institutions" (15).

***

In the quest for a theoretical structure for Italian feminism, moving away from the political struggles for emancipation of the early 1970s—which culminated with the legalization of divorce in 1974, and of abortion in 1978—the preeminent concept elaborated by Italian feminist philosophers was that of sexual difference,[9] first formulated by French feminist philosophers. Deeply influenced by Irigaray's 1984 *Ethics of Sexual Difference,* the concept of sexual difference in Italy was, in Teresa de Lauretis's description, envisioned not as "difference constructed from 'biology' and imposed as gender," but as a difference "of symbolization, a different production of reference and meaning" (de Lauretis, "The Practice of Sexual Difference" 13). For Luisa Muraro, feminism is the elaboration of a new, nonphallocentric, symbolic order ("Narrow Door"). A "general cognitive and interpretive category" (Bono and Kemp, *Italian Feminist Thought* 16), sexual difference, with its emphasis on the body, constitutes a revolutionary revision of Western ontology. It reclaims the body as the material foundation of knowledge. The philosophy of sexual difference is troubled, however, by the threat of essentialism, an affirmation of woman that falls into the naturalizing discourse of same and other. Dacia Maraini is able to avoid this. She states, "as a woman ... I am a participant in women's *history* and in the feminine unconscious that I carry with me, even if it's not my own; it's mine, but it belongs also to all the other women ... behind me" (qtd. in Anderlini, "Prolegomena" 150; emphasis added). For Maraini, being a woman entails a specific, contingent, material configuration of perception, and her writing is structured accordingly.

Maraini does not call herself a feminist writer, but neither does she invoke the dream of androgyny of both earlier and more recent Italian female narrative.[10] Her textual practice is "dalla parte delle donne" insofar as her production carries her signature. Within American gynocriticism, the "continuum ...

Introduction

perceived between author, narrator and character" foregrounded "female signature" as mark of authority and authenticity (Wood 14).[11] A concept made famous by Jacques Derrida in his analysis of signifying acts as necessarily context bound, signature cannot be an essence ("Signature, Event, Context"). It does not guarantee an unmediated relation between author and text. Still, it needs to be posited as a temporal trace, a discursive practice.[12]

The notion of sexed authors and gendered texts has been recently problematized by, among others, feminist philosopher Elizabeth Grosz. Using Derrida, she does recognize that "there are ways in which sexuality and corporeality of the subject leave their traces or marks on the text produced," but she argues that "the sex of the author has . . . no direct bearing on the political position of the text" (21). That neither the sex of the author, nor the sex of the reader, nor yet the content of the text can ever be presumed as absolute guarantor of meaning is unquestionable. Indeed, beyond the vicissitudes of transmission and reception, all agency remains a compromised being. Yet authors like Maraini, whose entire production carries a conscious intentionality as to gender, affirm the impossibility of an ultimate deconstruction of signature. To deny the relevance of signature would be an apolitical, obscurantist gesture, negating Maraini's relentless concern with historical specificity. Her work *is* context bound, and that context is *essere-donna* ("being-woman"), a practice of gender in culture.

Moreover, signature is tied in with the issue of style. Maraini does not believe in a "female style"; instead she speaks frequently of a "point of view, a historical subjectivity" (Maraini and Gaglianone 12). One may contend that to a certain extent, *écriture féminine,* although politicized, is constituted by a denial of its stylistic origins. In this respect, Maraini's writing is profoundly historical (and not only in its prevailing realism), and as such, constitutes an antidote to *écriture*'s ahistoricism. Consistent with her interest in history and historicity, Maraini's work does not make the mistake of identifying sexed writing with stylistic features,[13] but always with the specificity of gendered experience.[14]

When she first started to write, Maraini confesses, she believed that "literature must be above all else integrity and subtraction" (Maraini and Gaglianone 25), that it must possess

Introduction

a "chastity of style," and a "narrative modesty" (Maraini and Gaglianone 27). Later she understood that "style could be a prison," and her work became organized by a greater attention to sensuality. Moreover, from her original fear of "an explicit or didactic writing" (Maraini and Gaglianone 25), Maraini arrived at the kind of courage that was unthreatened by the charge of schematism, for indeed what some call schematic or ideological is in fact a profound commitment: she gives life to insights of feminist politics. Though initially interested in the neo-avant-garde of the early 1960s, she later rejected the aestheticism which denies that there are very simple things that can be said about honor to a woman. It takes political courage to express this, and genius to give it a life.

***

We entitled our collection *The Pleasure of Writing,* thinking first of Maraini's description of writing as "weaving in silence, listening to the profound reasons of the pleasure of telling stories" (Maraini and Gaglianone 40). Our title also echoes Roland Barthes's *The Pleasure of the Text,* since Maraini quotes his well-known idea of writing as "playing with the body of the mother" ("Reflections," see p. 29 in this volume). Maraini, however, unlike Barthes, does not play with the mother's body "in order to dismember it" (Barthes 37). This is not the writer's desperate need for mastery of *his* mother's body (Barthes 37), but writing as "profoundly feminine and maternal" ("Reflections," see p. 29 of this volume). Again and again Maraini's images associate writing and the act of giving birth. Her textual play desires the mother's body whole, and she takes her pleasure in giving life.

Dacia Maraini writes against the representation of women as monstrous site of mutilation, powerless in the world, "chopped to pieces," and severed from language and its institutions. Rejecting the mortuary practices of phallocentric culture, she fights for some sort of plenitude for woman, an intactness, not phallic, or pre-Oedipal, but one made up of bodies and psyches, wounded and bearing the marks of their history, but nonetheless alive, expressive, voiced, articulating their sorrows but also their pleasures. We cannot separate in Dacia Maraini's continuous

Introduction

engagement with writing an aesthetic from a political imperative. Given life and life-giving, her texts unfailingly contest the master canon's disavowal of sexual difference.

Notes

1. Unless otherwise indicated, all translations are mine.
2. Giulio Ferroni's *Storia della letteratura italiana* remarks Maraini's "overabundant ideological engagement" in feminism, and describes her as occupying "a place all her own" (709) (a place in which she is obviously expected to stay). In comparison, one might look to the nine lines afforded Pier Vittorio Tondelli, born in 1955, a generation later than Maraini, and whose production was cut short by his death of AIDS in 1991. (The reader of Ferroni's *Storia* may well note that neither Tondelli nor Aldo Busi are described as gay, unless Busi's "narcissismo frenetico" ["frenzied narcissism"] be taken as a code.) Even in some texts on the history of Italian political feminism, Maraini is not acknowledged, the most conspicuous example of which is Bono and Kemp's *Italian Feminist Thought*. By contrast, the Italian-American historian Lucia Chiavola Birnbaum gives Maraini's activism and literary production ample space in her *Liberazione della donna* (113–14; 147–48; 178–81).
3. John Gillory offers a good exposition of the issues involved in canon formation, among which he includes recent critiques. While giving serious consideration to gender as category in the revisioning of the canon, his is a rather conservative account. Although otherwise appreciative of the need to resist the "homogenizing pressure of the canon," and instead to historicize it, Gillory's remarks on the "forgotten works"—by women, nonwhites, and the lower classes—reveal a faulty logic, in which cause and effect have been reversed. Invoking the paucity of the forgotten works, Gillory questions the validity of ideologically grounded canon critique; he assumes that there must be something wrong with the view of canonization as a process of exclusion. He thus elides the historical operations of dominant interests that overdetermine the "disappearance" of texts.
4. For a thorough discussion of canon formation and the various feminist critiques brought to bear on the debate, see Laurie Finke's "Theories of Value and the Dialogics of Culture." The literature in this field is enormous, but I will mention here the classic *gynocriticism* promoted by Elaine Showalter's "Feminist Criticism in the Wilderness," Naomi Schor's *Breaking the Chain: Women, Theory, and French Realist Fiction*, and two useful recent studies, Susan Lanser's *Fictions Of Authority: Women Writers and Narrative Voice*, and *Ambiguous Discourse: Feminist Narratology and British Women Writers*, edited by Kathy Meizei.
5. On Maraini's oppositional literary practices, see JoAnn Cannon's "Rewriting the Female Destiny: Dacia Maraini's *La lunga vita di Marianna Ucrìa*"; and Carol Lazzaro-Weis's *From Margins to Mainstream: Feminism and Fictional Modes in Italian Women's Writing, 1968–1990*.

Introduction

6. To maintain in print the work of women writers is the mission of Feminist Press, which recently issued a translation of Maraini's *Silent Duchess* (1998). It is no accident that the 1995 edition of *Prego*, the popular first-year Italian text that describes Maraini together with Calvino as "ormai classici" ("already classic"; 328), is the product of American Italianists.

7. Maraini stated in an interview that "the female body is the locus of male imagination and violence.... Historically, man has tried to control it, to possess it, to annihilate its tremendous energy. This is the great project of patriarchal culture" (Rossi 3).

8. For a discussion of this issue, see de Lauretis's "The Practice of Sexual Difference and Feminist Thought in Italy: An Introductory Essay." For accounts of the rise of Italian feminism in the late 1960s, and its relation to Marxism, the Communist Party, the antiestablishment students' revolts, see Wood, Bono and Kemp (*Italian Feminist Thought*), and Birnbaum.

9. I will not discuss here sexual difference's chronological precursor, *la pratica dell'inconscio* ("practice of the unconscious"), nor the later practice of *affidamento* ("entrustment") of the group Diotima and The Milan Women's Bookstore Collective. For the chief texts of these categories, see Diotima, *Il pensiero della differenza sessuale* (with contributions by Adriana Cavarero et al.) and *Oltre l'uguaglianza: le radici femminili dell'autorità*; Libreria delle donne di Milano, *Non credere di avere dei diritti: la generazione della libertà femminile nell'idea e nelle vicende di un gruppo di donne,* and its English translation *Sexual Difference: A Theory of Social-Symbolic Practice*, by The Milan Women's Bookstore Collective, with an introductory essay by Teresa de Lauretis; *La differenza non sia un fiore di serra*, of the group Il filo di Arianna; Luisa Muraro, *L'ordine simbolico della madre*. For accounts, analyses, and critiques, see Bono and Kemp, *Italian Feminist Thought*; de Lauretis, "The Essence of the Triangle or, Taking the Risk of Essentialism Seriously"; Rosi Braidotti, *Soggetto nomade: femminismo e crisi della modernità*; Renate Holub, "Between the United States and Italy: Critical Reflections on Diotima's Feminist/Feminine Ethics"; and Serena Anderlini-D'Onofrio, "I Don't Know What You Mean by 'Italian Feminist Thought.' Is Anything Like That Possible?"

10. Wood writes at length about "post-feminist" Italian women's fiction, and correctly asks "whether the group of writers who reject the term 'scrittrice,' in assimilating themselves to the neutral (masculine) form, have lost more than they have gained" (23). She locates this move in the last decade's loss of ideological commitment to protest, grounded in social and political disaffection (18). Maraini has spoken on the related subject of young women's contradictory complacency and cynicism, for whom feminism has both won and is dead—what I would call the aporia of an assimilated struggle. See Simona Wright, "Intervista a Dacia Maraini: Pescasseroli, 13 luglio 1996" (74–75).

Introduction

11. See on this, the discussion about the narrating I, marked by "il segno femminile," in "Immagine e figura" by Paola Colaiacomo et al. (*Come nello specchio*), which precedes a collection of essays by Italian feminist critics on American and English women writers. This volume, of 1981, is representative of the "curious" phenomenon Wood notes of Italian women critics privileging foreign literatures long before turning to the exploration of local production (Wood 14). The same is true of the 1982 "Le madri di tutte noi" (The mothers of us all), published by the Milan Women's Bookstore Collective and discussed in *Sexual Difference* 108–13), where only one Italian woman is named, Elsa Morante (109). See also the essays by Italian women scholars (among whom Nadia Fusini, Patrizia Magli, Ida Camboni) included in Kemp and Bono's *The Lonely Mirror*, which examine such women writers as Woolf, Stein, and Colette.

12. Derrida here uses a historicist perspective, which is why he played a role for feminist theory, though nowhere in this text is that preeminently historical category of women's sexual difference present. See also Derrida's "Signéponge" and his discussion of Genet in *Glas*.

13. Theorists of *écriture féminine* would reject the idea that feminine writing can be identified by stylistic features: it is defined by its very uncodability, its evasion or undoing of codes. Yet in practice we do find in *écriture* the privileging of stylistic features of the high modernist avant-garde.

14. While crucial to feminist theory, the category of experience has been lately under attack on grounds of essentialism. See on this Scott 777–79, Fuss 118, and Freeman 149n.

Works Cited

Anderlini, Serena. "Prolegomena for a Feminist Dramaturgy of the Feminine: Interview with Dacia Maraini." *diacritics* 21.2–3 (1991): 148–60.

Anderlini-D'Onofrio, Serena. "I Don't Know What You Mean by 'Italian Feminist Thought.' Is Anything Like That Possible?" *Feminine Feminists: Cultural Practices in Italy*. Ed. Giovanna Miceli Jeffries. Minneapolis: Minnesota UP, 1994.

Badt, Karin. "Personal Interview with Dacia Maraini." Unpublished ms., 21 Mar. 1993.

Barthes, Roland. *The Pleasure of the Text*. Trans. Richard Miller. New York: Noonday, 1975.

Birnbaum, Lucia Chiavola. *Liberazione della donna: Feminism in Italy*. Middletown, CT: Wesleyan UP, 1986.

Bono, Paola, and Sandra Kemp. *Italian Feminist Thought: A Reader*. London: Blackwell, 1991.

Braidotti, Rosi. *Soggetto nomade: femminismo e crisi della modernità*. Rome: Donzelli, 1995.

Cannon, JoAnn. "Rewriting the Female Destiny: Dacia Maraini's *La lunga vita di Marianna Ucrìa.*" *Symposium* 49.2 (1995): 136–47.

Colaiacomo, Paola, et al., eds. *Come nello specchio: saggi sulla figurazione del femminile.* Turin: La Rosa, 1981.

de Lauretis, Teresa. "The Essence of the Triangle or, Taking the Risk of Essentialism Seriously." *differences* 1.2 (1989): 3–37.

———. "The Practice of Sexual Difference and Feminist Thought in Italy: An Introductory Essay." *Sexual Difference: A Theory of Social-Symbolic Practice.* By The Milan Women's Bookstore Collective. Trans. Patricia Cicogna and de Lauretis. Bloomington: Indiana UP, 1990. 1–21.

Derrida, Jacques. *Glas.* 1974. Trans. John P. Leavy, Jr., and Richard Rand. Lincoln: Nebraska UP, 1986.

———. "Signature, Event, Context." *Glyph* 1 (1977): 172–97.

———. "Signéponge." *Francis Ponge: Colloque de Cérisy.* Paris: Union générale d'éditions, 1977. 115–51.

Diotima. *Il pensiero della differenza sessuale.* Milan: La Tartaruga, 1990.

———. *Oltre l'uguaglianza: le radici femminili dell'autorità.* Naples: Liguori, 1995.

Ferroni, Giulio. *Storia della letteratura italiana.* Vol. 4. Milan: Einaudi, 1991.

Il filo di Arianna. *La differenza non sia un fiore di serra.* Milan: Cisem/Quaderni, 1991.

Finke, Laurie. "Theories of Value and the Dialogics of Culture." *Feminist Theory, Women's Writing.* Ithaca: Cornell UP, 1992. 148–90.

Freeman, Barbara. *The Feminine Sublime: Gender and Excess in Women's Fiction.* Berkeley: U of California P, 1995.

Fuss, Diana. *Essentially Speaking: Feminism, Nature, and Difference.* New York: Routledge, 1989.

Gillory, John. "Canon." *Critical Terms for Literary Study.* Ed. Frank Lentricchia and Thomas McLaughlin. 2nd ed. Chicago: U of Chicago P, 1995. 233–49.

Grosz, Elizabeth. *Sexual Subversions: Three French Feminists.* Sidney: Allen, 1989.

Holub, Renate. "Between the United States and Italy: Critical Reflections on Diotima's Feminist/Feminine Ethics." *Feminine Feminists: Cultural Practices in Italy.* Ed. Giovanna Miceli Jeffries. Minneapolis: Minnesota UP, 1994.

Kemp, Sandra, and Paola Bono, eds. *The Lonely Mirror: Italian Perspectives on Feminist Theory.* London: Routledge, 1993.

Introduction

Lanser, Susan S. *Fictions of Authority: Women Writers and Narrative Voice*. Ithaca: Cornell UP, 1992.

Lazzaro-Weis, Carol. *From Margins to Mainstream: Feminism and Fictional Modes in Italian Women's Writing, 1968–1990*. Philadelphia: U of Pennsylvania P, 1993.

Maraini, Dacia. *A memoria*. Milan: Bompiani, 1967.

———. *Bagheria*. Milan: Rizzoli, 1993. Published in English as *Bagheria*. London: Peter Owen, 1995; distributed by Dufour.

———. *La bionda, la bruna e l'asino: con gli occhi di oggi sugli anni settanta e ottanta*. Milan: Rizzoli, 1987.

———. *Buio*. Milan: Rizzoli, 1999.

———. *Cercando Emma*. Milan: Rizzoli, 1993. Published in English as *Searching for Emma: Gustave Flaubert and Madame Bovary*. Chicago: U of Chicago P, 1998.

———. *Un clandestino a bordo: le donne: la maternità negata, il corpo sognato*. Rome: Gabriele e Mariateresa Benincasa, 1993. Milan: Rizzoli, 1996. Published in English as *Stowaway on Board*. Trans. Giovanna Bellesia and Victoria Offredi Poletto. West Lafayette, IN: Bordighera, 2000.

———. *Crudeltà all'aria aperta*. Milan: Feltrinelli, 1966.

———. *Dialogue between a Prostitute and Her Client*. In *Only Prostitutes Marry in May*. Ed. Rhoda Helfman Kaufman. Toronto, Montreal, and New York: Guernica, 1994.

———. *Dimenticato di dimenticare*. Turin: Einaudi, 1982.

———. *Dolce per sé*. Milan: Rizzoli, 1997.

———. *Donna in guerra*. Turin: Einaudi, 1975. Published in English as *Woman at War*. 1981. New York: Italica, 1988.

———. *Donne mie*. Turin: Einaudi, 1974.

———. *La donna perfetta*. 1974. In *Il cuore di una vergine*. Turin: Einaudi, 1975.

———. *Dreams of Clytemnestra*. In *Only Prostitutes Marry in May*. Ed. Rhoda Helfman Kaufman. Toronto, Montreal, and New York: Guernica, 1994.

———. *L'età del malessere*. Turin: Einaudi, 1963. Published in English as *The Age of Malaise*. New York: Grove, 1963.

———. *E tu chi eri? Interviste sull'infanzia*. Milan: Bompiani, 1973.

———. *Fare teatro: materiali, testi, interviste*. Milan: Bompiani, 1974.

———. *Isolina: la donna tagliata a pezzi*. Milan: Mondadori, 1985. Published in English as *Isolina*. London: Peter Owen, 1994; distributed by Dufour.

———. *Lettere a Marina*. Milan: Bompiani, 1981. Published in English as *Letters to Marina*. London: Camden, 1987. Freedom, CA: Crossing, 1988.

———. *La lunga vita di Marianna Ucrìa*. Milan: Rizzoli, 1990. Published in English as *The Silent Duchess*. London: Peter Owen, 1992. New York: Feminist, 1998.

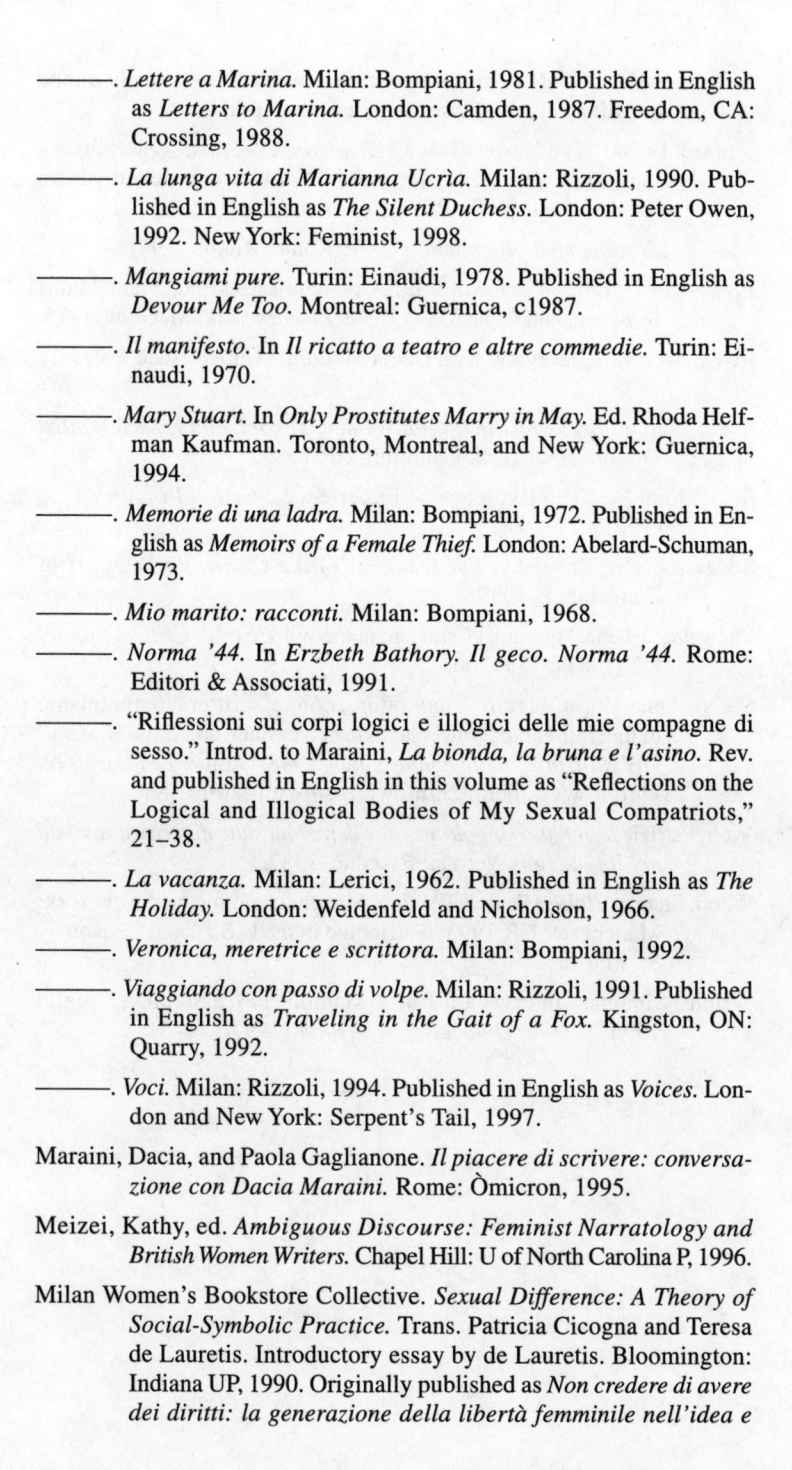

———. *Mangiami pure*. Turin: Einaudi, 1978. Published in English as *Devour Me Too*. Montreal: Guernica, c1987.

———. *Il manifesto*. In *Il ricatto a teatro e altre commedie*. Turin: Einaudi, 1970.

———. *Mary Stuart*. In *Only Prostitutes Marry in May*. Ed. Rhoda Helfman Kaufman. Toronto, Montreal, and New York: Guernica, 1994.

———. *Memorie di una ladra*. Milan: Bompiani, 1972. Published in English as *Memoirs of a Female Thief*. London: Abelard-Schuman, 1973.

———. *Mio marito: racconti*. Milan: Bompiani, 1968.

———. *Norma '44*. In *Erzbeth Bathory. Il geco. Norma '44*. Rome: Editori & Associati, 1991.

———. "Riflessioni sui corpi logici e illogici delle mie compagne di sesso." Introd. to Maraini, *La bionda, la bruna e l'asino*. Rev. and published in English in this volume as "Reflections on the Logical and Illogical Bodies of My Sexual Compatriots," 21–38.

———. *La vacanza*. Milan: Lerici, 1962. Published in English as *The Holiday*. London: Weidenfeld and Nicholson, 1966.

———. *Veronica, meretrice e scrittora*. Milan: Bompiani, 1992.

———. *Viaggiando con passo di volpe*. Milan: Rizzoli, 1991. Published in English as *Traveling in the Gait of a Fox*. Kingston, ON: Quarry, 1992.

———. *Voci*. Milan: Rizzoli, 1994. Published in English as *Voices*. London and New York: Serpent's Tail, 1997.

Maraini, Dacia, and Paola Gaglianone. *Il piacere di scrivere: conversazione con Dacia Maraini*. Rome: Òmicron, 1995.

Meizei, Kathy, ed. *Ambiguous Discourse: Feminist Narratology and British Women Writers*. Chapel Hill: U of North Carolina P, 1996.

Milan Women's Bookstore Collective. *Sexual Difference: A Theory of Social-Symbolic Practice*. Trans. Patricia Cicogna and Teresa de Lauretis. Introductory essay by de Lauretis. Bloomington: Indiana UP, 1990. Originally published as *Non credere di avere dei diritti: la generazione della libertà femminile nell'idea e

Introduction

    nelle vicende di un gruppo di donne. By Libreria delle donne di Milano. Turin: Rosenberg & Sellier, 1987.

Muraro, Luisa. "The Narrow Door." *Gendered Contexts: New Perspectives in Italian Cultural Studies.* Ed. Laura Benedetti, Julia Hairston, and Silvia Ross. New York: Lang, 1996. 7–17.

———. *L'ordine simbolico della madre.* Rome: Riuniti, 1991.

Prego: An Invitation to Italian. Ed. Graziana Lazzarino, Mara Mauri Jacobsen, and Anna Maria Bellezza. New York: McGraw, 1995.

Rossi, Monica. "Interview with Dacia Maraini." Unpublished ms., July 1995.

Schor, Naomi. *Breaking the Chain: Women, Theory, and French Realist Fiction.* New York: Columbia UP, 1985.

Scott, Joan M. "The Evidence of Experience." *Critical Inquiry* 17.4 (1991): 773–97.

Sedgwick, Eve Kosofsky. *Epistemology of the Closet.* Berkeley: U of California P, 1990.

Showalter, Elaine. "Feminist Criticism in the Wilderness." *Critical Inquiry* 8.2 (1981): 179–206.

Sorbo, Anna Maria. "Teatro e letteratura: donne, scrittura, femminismo di fine millennio: conversazione non casuale con Lidia Ravera." *DW Notiziario delle donne* 3 Nov. 1998. Online. 22 Mar. 1999. <http://www.mclink.it/n/dwpress/dww148/rub1.htm>.

Violi, Patrizia. *L'infinito singolare: considerazioni sulle differenze sessuali nel linguaggio.* Verona: Essedue, 1987.

Wood, Sharon. *Italian Women Writing.* Manchester, Eng., and New York: Manchester UP, 1993; distributed in the U.S.A. and Canada by St. Martin's.

Wright, Simona. "Intervista a Dacia Maraini: Pescasseroli, 13 luglio 1996." *Italian Quarterly* 34.133–34 (1997): 71–91.

Dacia Maraini

Reflections on the Logical and Illogical Bodies of My Sexual Compatriots

I am in the countryside. In a house without a telephone. Five kilometers away from the nearest village. On a hill called Cava del Bruciore.[1] In fact, there is something burning: a fragrance of dry grasses, the crackling of air so taut that it seems about to splinter and crumble.

I am here to think about the relation between women's writing and criticism. How, when, and why was that distrust born, that unconscious bias that too often accompanies the reading of texts written by women?

Recently I happened to take part in a meeting of a jury of which I am a member, called for the purpose of assigning an important national prize. Counting us, I see that there are two women and seven men. Each of us had to present ten books that had appeared during the course of the year. And, naturally, each had to do it as a critic, recounting them and judging them publicly.

I presented six books written by women and four by men, but not even one of the novels was taken into consideration by the other members of the jury. I asked why; they answered in a chorus: "We don't make distinctions between men and women; for us they are all authors; we have not chosen on the basis of gender, but quality; if there aren't any women on the list, it means they didn't deserve it."

The books to be read were, however, many, more than sixty, and the time frame was two months. Is it possible to read sixty books in two months? Obviously not. Thus, some books had been only skimmed. I started to ask, book by book, what they thought, and I quickly discovered that the books by

---

[1] *Bruciore* means "burning."—*Trans.*

women had been approached from the beginning with less interest and attention. Other books, written by men, among which was the autobiography of a famous journalist, had been given prominence and had been read by all the other jurors.

The debut novel of a young woman writer, five hundred pages long, had been read by no one, and, despite my favorable presentation, it was summarily dismissed. Not because it was bad, but because it had not been taken into consideration.

And yet I'm certain that none of the board members, among whom there was a female literary scholar, was conscious of having done feminine writing an injustice. If among these books there had been a famous female name, perhaps it would have attracted more attention, but since most of the female authors were little known, or neophytes, the members had not considered them worthy of consideration.

Of these small, invisible defeats is made the history of female literature. How can we forget the paternalistic letters of the critic Thomas Wentworth Higginson to Emily Dickinson, who was asking for his opinion? The critic, with much goodwill and gentleness, advises her decisively against writing. Yet, this great literary man, I'm certain, did not think he was a victim of sexist prejudice. His mind was enlightened; his judgment was severe but just. It was simply that the poetry was not praiseworthy; that it was written by a man or a woman did not matter at all. It was solely a question of quality, not of gender. This was certainly his thinking, and it still is today the concept that many critics bring to bear on texts by women.

Now here I am, immersed in the pale green landscape that trembles on the horizon like a mirage. I realize that I am closed inside an unknown silence, with my ideas and my papers, as if alarmed by a quiet rhythm I sense pressing me. On second thought, it's not even a silence. There are many sounds that ring in my ear, but there's something different: these sounds are linked one to the other like stitches in the same piece of needlework.

In the city, sounds are isolated, without connection among them, and they first strike the eyes rather than the ear. If it is possible to hear sounds through the eye, then in the city, every noise has the neatness of a daily image, polished and deprived of mystery.

But in the country, noises are fused together and form a current, a wave, which enters and exits through the window with a lazy and obsessive movement.

It is a silence to which I am so little used that it seems painful, troubling. My fingers go to the little radio, the color of mint, which I keep on the table. I'm looking for an end to the skein, a rope that might give me back the thread of things.

I hear a strident voice, industrious and optimistic, of a foolish and vulgar optimism. I turn it off at once. But somebody from afar is pressing me: "What is vulgarity, Signora Maraini?" It resembles the voice of so many opponents I face in public debates, in public meetings around the country. It is this voice that took the shape of an indictment in no less than five trials for obscenity, of which, fortunately, I was cleared, but after how much trouble and expense!

"How can you condemn vulgarity, you who constantly use curse words, stark and crude subjects?"

Is it the usual grasshopper who jumps up when one talks about pornography and sex? How to explain that words are not noble or ignoble, there are no pure words and impure words, beautiful words and ugly words?

Vulgarity for me is simplification—let's put it this way: when reality is cut through with an ax, when the person is divided into useful and useless parts, when the complexity of a thought is reduced to a broth to be stuffed down the throats of the greedy, when one falsifies, dresses up, consoles, embellishes, simpers, when distances are taken priggishly, when it's decided a priori what's right and what's not, when one sweetens, gentrifies, in order to reduce waste, in order to reassure, when the gaze is calcified, when . . . I realize that I'm giving vulgarity a moral sense. It isn't a question of taste any longer.

But who said that taste is not a matter that raises the question of what should or should not be done? Writers, if we read them closely, have always started to dance because they had been bitten by the tarantula.

The much-discussed escapist literature, in fact, is not at all escapist. Romance novels drip with morality, teachings, messages, prohibitions, codes, exhortations. Their success comes precisely from this. The Harmony love stories want, first of all, to teach, not to distract.

Dacia Maraini

Commercial novels want to shape inchoate thought, they want to enter the belly of the world with their ideas, their moral suggestions. Their cleverness consists in combining their ideological certainties with a taste for adventure, exoticism, psychological folklore. Their characters will fall prey to grand sentiments, will always make juicy things happen, will fuss a lot to demonstrate that they exist. And, in the end, the plots will reveal a well-defined design, recognizable and of assured morality.

The noncommercial author does not have to make his characters "act"; rather, he follows them in awe, almost as if asking what they're up to. Sometimes, they're up to nothing; they simply hang around.

The vulgarity of so-called escapist literature lies precisely in proposing a distraction that does not exist. It lies in promising what it will never offer: consolation, beauty, love, joie de vivre, pleasure.

Vulgarity, dear sir, for me, is nothing but one of the many forms of willful intervention in the imagination of another. That this intervention is wrapped in the pretense of entertainment, of consolation, of leisure for the tired mind, makes no difference. It remains an act of authority.

And the euphemisms are often worse than the things "by their true names." As Nora Galli De' Pratesi accurately notes in her book *Le brutte parole* (Ugly words), euphemisms belong, above all, to those social groups who least want to expose themselves, who most hold dear the idea of decorum and the apparent stability of life relationships. Usually, the nostalgia of stability hides the desire to maintain a position of power over those in a state of subjection and inferiority.

Almost always, the idea of vulgarity refers to the use of certain words, considered obscene. But the border of this obscenity changes from moment to moment, from place to place. It's hard to keep up with it. Books, even yesterday rigorously banned, are suddenly read as innocuous.

But the accusation of obscenity is not limited to "ugly words." Often it attaches itself to the raw and pitiless mode in which many authors look at things.

Because of bad habits, taken on from "fancy-dress literature" and through an innate fear of what is hidden behind the door, the simplest and the least cultivated readers ask for a

Reflections on the Bodies of My Sexual Compatriots

systematic sweetening of reality. They want it made gracious, purged, refined, rendered innocuous.

Crudity makes people suspicious, even if it also attracts. There has always been, toward authors considered pornographic, an attitude of attraction, morbid curiosity, and repulsion, condemnation. Think of Henry Miller, Bataille, and, going back in time, Lawrence, and further back, Belli and Boccaccio.

In the case of women, though, few people are inclined to accept obscenity. Neither the use of forbidden words nor too raw a vision of the world. Where are they gone, the smiling grace, the innate seductive sweetness, the feminine modesty?

And here, another voice, another question on the surface of the evening, flies in like a mosquito to sting the skin: "But is there a difference between *scrivere donna* and *scrivere uomo?*"[2] And if so, in what does it consist?

I saw that Nadia Fusini, in her last book on great women writers, *Nomi* (Names), has eluded the question. She pushed it slightly to the side with a delicate movement of her hand. As the fine literary scholar that she is, as if it were inappropriate and somewhat ill-timed.

Yet I like her elliptic style of critical writing, all full of closely crafted joinings and understanding of language. I'm only sorry that she looked on the other side of the Alps, according to an old teaching of Arbasino's, forgetting unjustly the great mothers on this side of the mountains, those extraordinary women like Anna Maria Ortese, Elsa Morante, Lalla Romano, Anna Banti, Natalia Ginzburg, who have taught us to write as women.

Nadia Fusini does not answer the question on female writing, but she does choose a group of women writers, not male authors, almost as though suggesting that difference exists but is taken for granted.

Usually, female writing meant or used to mean something sentimental, delicate, imprecise, crepuscular. A plot made of fragrant and affected "sensibleries," a vortex of fireflies and spores that the wind of criticism would take care to sweep away from the world of literature as transient matter, simply cumbersome.

---

[2] *Scrivere donna* and *scrivere uomo* refer to gendered writing: writing as a woman/man.—*Trans.*

Dacia Maraini

It is clear that, faced with such a restrictive view of female writing, many women novelists have denied being *scrittrici*.[3] They redefine themselves as simply *scrittori*,[4] reinforcing the idea that literature is genderless.

"But is writing really genderless?" asks another harassing voice. Other shining eyes look at me from a crowded hall, searching in me for the sense of being a woman and of writing, of being a woman and using instruments, by tradition—male.

Writing, with its roots that stretch out lazily into the deep soil of collective imagination, feeds on ancient habits of thought, on secret aspirations, on swollen fears, on unconscious desires.

But almost always these desires, these aspirations, these habits, when they become ordinary plot, have characterized the interests of man, with no concern for woman, and often even against woman. It is enough to look at the most common symbols in fairy tales, in myths, in ancient and modern cosmogonies. The fact is that in order to accede to writing, one must learn to maneuver three types of instruments: the more mechanical ones, like the typewriter, the computer, the printer, to which the male hand is guided lovingly from infancy, by teachers, fathers, tutors; then, the instruments determined by the specific events of a country, of a people, like language with its dowry of idioms, dialectal forms, jargons, expressions, etc.; and finally, the more profound and delicate instruments purported to be equal for everybody, like philosophy, psychoanalysis, religion, politics, anthropology, literature. In sum, the whole history of thought of one's time, to which in various ways the writer makes reference.

It is happily repeated that literature is pure imagination, and imagination can't have a sex. It is by definition free, intolerant of constrictions, ties, corsets, belts that constrain and limit it. If one learns to manipulate it, one makes it one's own, whether one is a man or a woman.

This is what traditionally is said to ingenuous young girls, who bend their heads over textbooks and stain their fingers with ink: Imagination is yours. Writing is learned like any other skill. It's up to you to make it into a manageable and perfect tool. It's up to your will, your talent.

---

[3] In Italian, *scrittrice* means "female writer."—*Trans*.

[4] The masculine *scrittore* stands for the more general category, ostensibly genderless, of "writer."—*Trans*.

Reflections on the Bodies of My Sexual Compatriots

Nobody tells her that imagination is not at all that seagull with great white wings soaring innocent and in an empty sky. Nobody reminds her that imagination is born loaded with archetypes, emotional stratifications, recurring loci of the mind, verbal meeting places, mythologies, which exclude her as fantasizing subject.

But the illusion of being in the same boat is very strong. It is sufficient to glance through the many recently published books on woman's erotic imagination, to understand the depth of the laceration. Just like a prisoner who, after a life of segregation, cannot distinguish freedom from constraint, she ends up falling turbidly in love with her prison and her own tribulations.

Imagination, more even than ideology, is totalizing. The part assigned to personal inspiration is small. For the rest, it belongs to a "here and now" of profound historical immediacy. The imagination of a country, of a people, of a social milieu, of an era, of a situation, requires complete adhesion to its most audacious constructions, to its projects for the future, to its enthusiasms, to its limitations; all enterprises of an androcentric character.

We'll listen without even realizing, above all, to that voice that speaks to us, if only in a secret place of consciousness, with deep and strong tones, charged with ancient authority.

The other voice, the light one, the keen, leaping one, the voice that smells of kitchen, of bedroom, does not convince even women themselves because of its total lack of prestige.

Writing is tongue, and the tongue is not limited to moving in the mouth, producing, as if by a miracle, sounds more or less beautiful, more or less bold. There are tongues that have lain like little corpses in the tombs of their mouths, and if we believe that the dead are capable of thought, we might imagine a thought made of torn phantasms, of buried and gangrenous desires.

In the end, one writes with the body, and the body has a sex, and sex has a history of separations, of distancings, of segregations, abuses of power, violences, aphasias, fears, mortifications, of which we preserve an atavistic memory.

Well, what is to be done? Deny the segregated fantasy or "dip your bread,"[5] as they say in Sicily, in that soup that has become ours through long practice and love, whose scent and taste we know profoundly?

---

[5] This saying means "Give flavor to the morsel that you have."—*Trans.*

Dacia Maraini

I would say that at this point it is impossible to distinguish what is ours from what we have swallowed with paternal blessing. Perhaps it isn't even important. Whoever fishes inside herself will find all sorts of things, and it isn't necessary to be shocked.

This is why many women have taken up the trumpet. To make themselves heard in spite of their consignment to silence. With a courage sometimes precipitous, which renders them suspect to other women.

The majority of women writers, to cross these moats, have become refined acrobats, equilibrists of thought and senses. They have walked gracefully on the edge of the division, not caring about the danger of falling into schizophrenia; often estranged from themselves, sometimes to the point of desiring their own destruction.

The suicide of so many women writers, is it not perhaps the sign of a deep laceration, of a heart so cracked by pain that in the end it gives up altogether?

There was in the malaise of these women artisans, in these female dragons of the mind, the consciousness of having to use instruments not their own, weighed down with rigorous and very ancient taboos.

It seems easy to violate these taboos. Reason requires it, and everybody agrees in theory that it must be done. But that part of ourselves that extends into the past, those pale phantoms that continue to inhabit the darkest corners of our brains, rebel, asking for justice against those who infringe on the prehistoric rules of a bearded and intolerant god to whom we have promised devotion and obedience.

In their passion for literary invention, they did not realize, our mother novelists and poets, that writing means holding in the hand not a pen but a scepter, not a pencil but a sword. The scepter and the sword belong to kings and warriors. When were women ever kings and warriors? True, there was Joan of Arc. Significantly, she described herself as guided by God's voice because she considered herself to be the executrix of the will of another.

The greatest confusion is created, however, by that strange fact that readers have always been more female than male, and that writers knew how to open their peacock plumes to a world of languid eyes who would decipher lovingly, bent over an oil lamp, in a silent room, the last of the black marks on the page.

Reflections on the Bodies of My Sexual Compatriots

Strange, isn't it? Readers, but never writers, or almost never. Passive even in the place of intellectual exchange. They were thrown spicy morsels—the eternal stories of betrayed love, of jealousy, of tormented passions, the quarrels of everyday life—while the writers kept to themselves the ultimate secrets and the final meaning of the whole.

It is the male architect who decides on paper how to make the house in which we'll live as prisoners for life, the mothers and the daughters who will choke each other, with love.

So, in the great house of literature, the one who holds the pen in hand is the father, who lovingly pours for his beloved daughter the juices of truth, of beauty, of desire.

From this patient and hirsute head of Zeus, inhabited by solemn, divine whims and ingenious creativities, have sprouted the Sapphos, the Austens, the Bröntes, the Sands, the Deleddas: a small procession of women who had the courage, with the father's kind permission, to take in hand the pen, the scepter, the spear, and throw themselves into the battle for artistic survival.

But what can she say of herself, of the experience she shares with her sisters, her cousins, her women friends, this woman with the helmet covering her face, her arm bearing the shield, and the sword held tightly in her fist?

In fact, many intellectual women felt this. The pride of their own difference drove them toward an arrogant literary society, made them share often in its misogynist attitudes.

Only in the moment in which they bent over their vegetable gardens, did these warrior women instinctively abandon the helmet, the suit of armor, the sword.

They found themselves, for love of truth, coming to terms with their own childhood fantasies, the stupors, and the bitternesses of female adolescence, the indelible love for the father, the conflicts with the mother, the envy of male freedoms, the shared habit of looking at the world from the window instead of going down into the street to face the enemy or simply to loaf.

Because after all, with its wandering through daily minutiae, its insistence on the ever fresh foolishness of love, its feeling of language as food, its everyday heroes, writing is profoundly feminine and maternal. This is especially true of the novel—tied as it is to the sense of becoming, which reminds us of what Roland Barthes says: "to write means to play with the body of the mother."

Dacia Maraini

The body of the mother means the flesh and the milk of every spoken language. But, and here comes a surprising thing: language, born female, growing up becomes, through an unexpected reversal of the parts, male. It puts on muscles and hair and professes the absolute priority of its spiritual interests.

So the body of the mother who gives nourishment and caresses transforms itself into the body of the father who requires subjection in exchange for security, who asks for faithfulness in exchange for greatness.

At this point it is useless to pretend we are different, to put on whiskers, to say that now everything has changed, to get rid of difference with a shrugging of the shoulders. I'm not falling in, I'm not falling in, she said while she was already inside the trap up to her hair. But her eyes were looking proudly into the distance.

Passing/transvestitism, besides, serves only to delude oneself. The world will not be tricked, much less the critics. In the world of letters, nobody will ever take a woman who writes for a *scrittore*.

You see it when looking for critical material on women writers in libraries. Articles, yes, and as many as you want, but true and really challenging essays, studies in depth, extremely few.

The fact is that writing an essay is like falling in love, or even more, like taking a wife. It is rare that a prestigious critic would wed himself to the imaginary world of a woman. He would consider it a wrong marriage, a *mésalliance,* something to be ashamed of.

In fact, discrimination does not occur at the moment of writing (nobody forbids a woman to write, except herself), nor at the market relations point (we know that women writers constitute the majority and that editors do not censor; they only want to sell).

The crucial moment of selection, the great sieve that starts to work in order to separate the wheat from the chaff, comes afterward and sanctions the passage from one generation to the next.

The selection will be made in the school anthologies, in the collections of the most authoritative critics, in the arrangements, put together little by little by the Great Systemizers that every generation chooses as guardians of its literary estate. It will be made by the university professors, the librarians, the literary historians, the critics specializing in "objective overviews" of our national letters, by those who establish the classifications, the surveys, the lists, the currents, the schools.

In this way every generation loses its women intellectuals, its women poets and novelists. In a free market, they are tolerated while alive, but rarely accepted, once dead, among the great, to be honored, studied, taken as models.

Even when they are present in anthologies, women writers are never at the center of the picture. Theirs is always a "case," an "exception," a "phenomenon," which, it is suggested, has something extraordinary about it. I remember that Pier Paolo Pasolini, thinking to pay me a compliment, used to say: "You are not a woman, you're a man, you have the brain and the character of a man." I kept trying to make him see that he was offensive, but he couldn't see it.

In sum, women writers, even the most gifted, generally die when their bodies die. The very few who save themselves will be kept there like beautiful flags, precisely in order to demonstrate that there is no literary discrimination. But for every one who survives, how many disappear unjustly!

Sometimes thirty years suffice. Weren't the traces of Anaïs Nin, to give one example, already lost, when they were pulled from oblivion by feminist publishing houses?

In Italy, that is what has happened with Sibilla Aleramo, Cristina Belgioioso, Veronica Franco. And even Grazia Deledda, though she was the recipient of the Nobel prize, is sliding gently out of the picture. Is there anyone anymore who studies her?

A woman writer may sell very well, may be much loved by her women readers, may even receive some praise from the critics. What is denied her is that prestige that every great male writer has and that produces imitators, schools, currents, and most of all, a body of criticism with which every student will have to come to terms.

From the window, a prolonged howling reaches me. It must be Mulino, the dog that has lived with me for fifteen years. For days now he has been lying on the wooden floor of the terrace. The flies land on his muzzle insistently, but he doesn't drive them away. His eyes are open, but he doesn't see. Every so often, he gets up, walks around, following a light, a smell. It's painful to see him, immobile before a wall, with eyes wide open and dark, as if asking himself if these are the last frontiers of his world.

I can't take him inside, because he has become incontinent. He does his business wherever he is. During the last few months I was in Rome, he drove me mad: I used to spend the day cleaning where he had soiled.

I ended by confining him to the foyer, covering the floor with a plastic sheet, but I still had to clean up. And he was very offended that I had excluded him from the bedroom, from that lair under the night table where he slept for years. I even tried to put him in Pampers, like a newborn, but he kept tearing them up with his teeth.

My friends ask me, "Why don't you put him down?" I don't know why, when people talk about a cow, a dog, a bear—how terrible, that bear in the Rome Zoo, dying of infection because the vet was on vacation—they say "put down."

It sounds like the Nazi "final solution," a euphemism, an attempt to refine things. One says "put down" so as not to say "kill." A habit that's spreading. Don't we call the garbage man an "ecological operator"? Don't we call maids "domestic collaborators"? Don't we say "visually impaired" for blind?

Pretentious ways to camouflage reality, mask it and make it more pleasant. This doesn't cause the blind to stop being blind, the garbage men to stop sweeping the streets, the maids to stop cleaning houses.

As for Mulino, I can't "put him down." He will die a natural death when he must die. Why take away from him the experience of agony? His body has its own slow, deep way of getting close to death. To cut this process in half seems to me a sin of impatient technology in the face of the capricious delays of illness.

Only in the case of terrible pain that drives the sick themselves to ask to be "helped to die" can I understand it. But in that case, they're capable of speech, of expressing their will, something a dog cannot do.

While Mulino laboriously begins his journey toward death, a little cat, minuscule, black as a raven's wing, laboriously begins his journey toward life. I called him Carbone ("charcoal"), because of his nocturnal color. As soon as he was born, he was dumped into a garbage bin. From there, a friendly hand pulled him out and nourished him.

But he has remained minute, with a neck like a chicken's, fanlike ears, and yellow eyes avid for life. He already knows he can only count on his own powers. The games he plays are animated by a sort of festive despair. Having lost the body of the mother, he looks for warmth here and there, sticking his head under the paw of the sick dog, or rubbing against a human ankle. But he never lets himself go. He is vigilant, with those ears stretched out, the wretched neck, the eyes that rummage diabolically in hidden corners.

The days in the country pulsate with circular time: one is much more aware of the alternating of night and day, of cold and hot. Every event is repeated with the sweetest monotony, accompanied by the uninterrupted, maniacal chant of cicadas by day and of crickets by night.

The repetition is interrupted by short, fulminating episodes of death. The shepherd killed a dog because it was barking at his sheep; the cowherd butchered three cows to sell for meat; a fox devoured six chickens at the neighbor's house. The spider behind the window caught a hornet last night, and now is enveloping it in its threads, immobilizing it like a mummy.

I too feel part of this general feeding. Have I not swallowed the meat of those beautiful cows with broad, lyre-shaped horns whom I encounter during my walks in the woods?

This morning I was surprised to find a story of mine in *Corriere della Sera*. It was a strange experience. Many years ago, perhaps fifteen, I remember sending a story to the *Corriere* and the publisher of the time answering, "In my newspaper, I want neither faggots nor women." He didn't say it directly to me, but he sent word, without any shame.

The story that came out today is called "Amparo's Horse" and was inspired by the story of an old circus horse that was to be "put down" and that I took with me to the country.

The text is accompanied by the critical comments of Antonio De Benedetti. It is he who made this choice for the "Roman page" of the *Corriere,* mixing, with journalistic intelligence, unknown writers with intellectuals and with politicians who had never written fiction.

De Benedetti maintains that I am a "naturalist" writer. "In Dacia, there is a conscious, deliberate refusal of what is abstract, complicated, and inexplicable. Her plain prose avoids preciosity and archaisms like sin. Absolute and total refusal of lyricism is also hers" (*Corriere della Sera,* 13 July 1986).

Dacia Maraini

"But why is that?" De Benedetti asks: "Behind everything Dacia writes, there is obviously a project, that of expressing herself literally while expressing reality. But what reality?"

And here he cites a phrase I uttered à propos of my investigative-report novel *Isolina:* "For me, writing means putting myself in women's place."

From this, De Benedetti deduces that "This affirmation serves as an indication of method and of poetics: to put oneself in the place of others, women and also men, who have historically existed, means to accept an essentially naturalistic idea of storytelling . . . it means precisely to recount a story for the sake of recounting, by means of lived experience, that is, by means of denunciations, everything that is not right with the world and that might be better."

Unfortunately, we know that in the Italian literary world of today—which is in love with the poetics of artifice, ambiguity, dream, unreality, delirium—the title of "naturalism" brings an immediate exclusion.

To be "naturalistic" means, according to this poetics, to be on the other side of the river, on the flat side of things said, against the bristling of things alluded to, on the stupid side of clarity, against the suggestive shadow of uncertainty. In sum, the word carries a suspicion of "socialist realism," something inconvenient and inferior, absolutely out of fashion.

But doesn't naturalism presuppose a faithful reconstruction of nature, which maintains the fragrance of things without the intervention of feeling or reason?

The writer who wants to intervene upon reality, as De Benedetti maintains that I do, the writer who "wants to change the world," how could she at the same time abstain from judging it?

Paradoxically, it was, above all, the avant-garde that proposed new forms of naturalism. With the difference that the naturalism of the nineteenth century was copying faithfully, as in a mirror, a reality supposedly "objective," in which one recognized oneself as part of a universal machine whose key was to be found in scientific awareness. Today's naturalism, on the contrary, just as uncritically mimics a reality that has become incomprehensible. A senseless world that produces in its observers those effects of malaise, of loss, of delirium that are considered essential for the modern artist.

Reflections on the Bodies of My Sexual Compatriots

But we're still talking about naturalism. About abstaining from moral and political judgment. The writer, in brief, declines to intervene upon narrative matter, declines to offer a subjective angle on things. The writer simply gives back the disorder, as is. The writer's work consists in miming, through verbal and syntactic irregularity, the irregularity of the real.

At any rate, I must thank De Benedetti for having sketched out, even if only in a newspaper, a critical assessment of my prose. Little has been written about my books, and that little was done in a hurry, with no desire for depth, unwillingly and distractedly.

Just recently, the critic Angelo Guglielmi, one of the most prestigious and coherent theoreticians of the avant-garde, has recognized publicly his "mistake" about me. He confessed candidly that he had taken me "lightly," not giving my writing enough credit. Only now, after many years, after many books, has he declared that I am a "serious and capable" writer.

I must say that he showed courage, because many other critics, who also have become more attentive to my writing, still do not dare acknowledge that they acted with prejudice in the past.

Many times young women come to me because they have to write theses and find themselves disconcerted by the scarcity of critical material about my work.

Unfortunately, this same condition applies to women writers more prestigious than me, from those of long ago to the most recent. No matter how much one rummages through libraries, how much one pokes into books, all that is to be found on women's books is thin stuff and of little interest.

Women themselves are loath to produce a history of/for female writing. Italian universities are full of intelligent and daring young women who lose sleep over the books of some unknown male author of centuries past. Very few of them wish to dedicate themselves to the study of a female author. They too would feel that they were "marrying beneath" themselves if they chose a female rather than a male writer. And then, often, their professors discourage them (I have direct knowledge of at least five cases) from such an enterprise.

The many female students, graduate students, and even teachers themselves find nothing wrong with this. This is the way history goes. We are so good at receding, forgetting, destroying, that we are more active and efficient than that old friend with the scythe and black robe.

The memory of women does not preserve, does not treasure. It is prodigal to the point of destruction. It grinds, it gathers, and then it disperses what it has to the wind.

In order to build memories, one needs to love one's own past and thus in some way oneself. But women prefer to die rather than demonstrate tenderness and indulgence toward themselves. They are acquainted with narcissism, of the closed kind, which brings them to self-denial in the name of love, but they do not know the scope of their own thought, with its reasons and its needs. Feminine memory is wounded, mutilated. It prefers not to turn around: it's afraid of becoming a pillar of salt, like Lot's wife. Speaking of Lot, I have looked in various versions of the Bible for the name of the young woman transformed into a statue, but I have not found it. Only Lot is entitled to a name; neither the wife nor the daughter, with whom the man will lie, have access to that first of human recognitions: a proper name.

Yet feminism wagers a lot on memory. And much has been done to recuperate events and people, female names and models, buried by androcentric history. But today, in the nineties, everything seems already forgotten. And while in the United States at least, Women's Studies programs have been created to preserve feminine history, in Europe we keep counting only on the will of certain groups to accomplish this end, certain female scholars who have to fight against the enormous force of collective inertia. And then, many women consider feminism dead, buried, and unpleasantly "out of fashion." They close their eyes to the renewed manifestations of social and artistic misogyny.

But how much of this talent for self-flagellation—derived from a history of suffered flagellations—should be considered a patrimony of female history to be conserved, and how much should be rejected as dangerous inclination to self-annihilation? How much is part of a tendentious teaching, and how much has been transformed into a virtue we might acknowledge as our own? Should we be proud of this entirely feminine talent for suffering, for sacrifice, for self-punishment?

Is it more important for women to know the defeat, even if heroic, even if glorious, of their martyrs, or to know the thought

Reflections on the Bodies of My Sexual Compatriots

and the victorious body of a mother or a daughter who, notwithstanding the call to sacrifice, has not sacrificed herself, but has fought to make herself visible and strong?

It's hard to answer. Doesn't enthusiasm for the honesty and the strength of our negative "heroines," the many martyrs, the saints, the sacrificial mothers, condition our judgment of women's destiny?

These things come to mind when I look at the rubble that surrounds us: eviscerated collectives, abandoned places, lost friendships, fragmented solidarities, unfinished dialogues.

And as a symbol of this disintegration, I cannot but think again of the theater La Maddalena, where I worked for more than eighteen years, with its floors that are water-soaked and cracked, its empty archives, the humidity that devours the walls. The posters of the shows? Lost. The pictures of the sets? Disappeared. The tapes? Gone. The letters? Who knows. A void, a chasm, a black hole into which precipitates our past with everything that it has cost us in terms of efforts, experiments, pains, conflicts, inventions, and night watches.

But can we resist the ruin of things, of environments, of memories, of experiences? Isn't it a sin of presumption to think of preserving a place that had belonged for so long to women while everything around us disintegrates, transmutes, dies?

Is it legitimate to swim against the current, against fashion, against the new explosive realities that enter your throat like a pitiless and lacerating wind?

Perhaps it is not legitimate, not normal, no matter how common it seems? Yet in this lake of disaffection, in this flurry of women toward the threshold of the home, in this dazzling use of black stockings and silk garters, in this rediscovery of marriage and of the splendors of love, it seems necessary to leave behind, like Tom Thumb, little white stones to mark the way toward self-recovery.

If I look around, I see young women who could care less about anything and set out for adventure without a moment's thought. I see girls who put on mustache and beard and mount motorcycles as if they were new centaurs with breasts cut off. There, in this wind of new certainties, it seems to me that my obstinacy is somewhat demented. Wearing mountain boots, they go on those streets full of stones and thorns, toward that gate that opens on female happiness. But does it really exist? What flavor does it have? What meaning, what stability, what force? Is not the bittersweet and familiar taste of subjection and self-denigration more flavorful? We have become so used to it that we consider it an innate taste, known by now to our senses.

The very young, especially today, wear light little shoes and do not like to feel on their necks the breath of another woman who pressures them, interrogates them, troubles them. They do not like understanding gazes and requests for solidarity. They have found the happiness of dressing up like oriental dancers, with that little bit of detachment that makes them daring and assured. They have the illusion of equality, which, in fact, they are able to practice in school and in the first experiences of love.

The troubles start afterward, with their entry into the work force, and with marriage. Even when the husband is of the most modern, willing to work together, respectful of their independence.

Discrimination comes from afar, it has deep roots. It comes from an ancient worldview in which the genders were divided along the lines of dominion and possession. And there is no beard in the world they could put on able to save women from work experienced as destiny: that of home, children, the sick, invalids, etc. There are twelve million full-time housewives in Italy still. It's hard to forget this. Twelve million women who do heavy labor, without schedules, without salary, without insurance, and, above all, without the respect of those who demand this work and who make use of it.

So, here I am, with my burden of reflections that have matured in so many years of practice with women, keeping that minimum of love for the past that saves me from crushing these thoughts under foot, calling them useless or antiquated. Rather, I defend them as the best that I have learned.

In times of serial killers and AIDS, I want to believe that public reflection on the logical and illogical bodies of my sexual compatriots still has a meaning.

Translated by Rodica Diaconescu-Blumenfeld. An earlier version of this article appeared as "Riflessioni sui corpi logici e illogici delle mie compagne di sesso," the introduction to La bionda, la bruna e l'asino *(Milan: Rizzoli, 1987). Reprinted with permission.*

Part 2
Demythicizing Genre: Issues of Representation and Language

Ada Testaferri
De-tecting *Voci*

Corrado Federici
Spatialized Gender and the Poetry of Dacia Maraini

Elisabetta Properzi Nelsen
Écriture Féminine as Consciousness of the Condition of Women in Dacia Maraini's Early Narrative

Ada Testaferri

De-tecting *Voci*

The novel *La vacanza* (1962; *The Holiday*) marked Dacia Maraini's official debut on the literary stage. She was greeted as a writer of promise and a disciple of neorealism partly because of Alberto Moravia's pronouncement in his introduction to the novel: "Dunque tu sei una scrittrice realista" (xii; "Undeniably you are a realist writer"; my translation), but also because at the time neorealism dominated the Italian cultural scene. Thus, with no misgivings, the literary establishment integrated feminine writing[1] into the mainstream, failing to recognize its distinctness. Besides, by Maraini's own account, *La vacanza* is not a true feminist novel, although its "existential" premise revealed an auspicious beginning. The expectations raised by that youthful oeuvre have been fulfilled by a long writing career. In the years following her debut, Maraini would attempt every form of contemporary writing, successfully blending literary constraints and pressing social needs, while focusing her interest on women, specifically on Italian women and their becoming.

With *Voci* (1993; *Voices*) Maraini tackles the detective novel, born in a literary milieu[2] but afterward an autonomous genre demoted to the rank of escapist literature and just recently given new credibility, in Italy as elsewhere, by critically acclaimed authors.[3] Notwithstanding the prominence of women within the international coterie of crime fiction writers (Murch 152), the narrative traditionally associated with the genre is culturally rooted in chauvinism.[4] This stems only in part from the fact that the victim is often a woman, while a male character is assigned the role of detective. It happens mainly because the classic detective novel tends to restore the order existing before a crime temporarily subverts the status quo. Structural constraints entail a writing plan leaning toward conservative, at times even reactionary, values (Porter 115–29; Priestman 36–55; Murch 67–83). The ending of a detective story supposedly validates an existing power structure, patriarchy in the case of *Voci*.

In this article, I intend to analyze how Maraini, fashioning *Voci* after the detective genre, lays claim to narrative structures that, measured by traditional standards, are typically androcentric, by making them comply with the demands of a woman writer and turning them into a harsh criticism of the present phallocracy. *Voci* reintroduces the subject of violence against women, a theme underscoring much of Maraini's output. In a sense it constitutes a rewriting of other works, some of which focus expressly on violence against women, a case in point being *Isolina* (1985), while others deal broadly with the subject, for example *Donna in guerra* (1975; *Woman at War*). The book also points, at times indirectly, to a series of intertexts in order to provide a contextual framework for the novel as a unique literary artifact. Thus, I will dwell upon some examples of intertextuality with specific reference to *The Secret Sharer* (1912) by Joseph Conrad (an author read by protagonist Michela Canova) and *The Murders in the Rue Morgue* (1841) by Edgar Allan Poe. Poe's work is not mentioned by Maraini but, I believe, is present at a deeper level insofar as it is unanimously acknowledged as the prototype of detective fiction. In the conclusion I will show that *Voci,* taking as a starting point women's ex-centric position, deconstructs the very concept of the detective genre as it questions and challenges the literary canon and its tradition, as well as other fiduciary institutions and the value judgments they entail.

Rewriting the Detective Novel: *Voci*

A set fixture of the detective novel is the threesome victim-detective-murderer.[5] The peculiarity of their being interchangeable and interdependent bonds them together. Within this network each character is endowed with essential narrative functions. Understandably, the victim is the causative agent. His/her role is extremely ambivalent: being the only true link between detective and murderer, the victim is at the core of the story, yet at the same time ex-centric, absent, usually dead at the opening

De-tecting *Voci*

or near the beginning of the novel. Paradoxically, the victim's presence is felt only through absence. The importance of the victim is confirmed by the fact that the roles of detective and murderer are defined by their association with the victim. Their relationship within the narrative is almost always antithetical, the detective standing for goodness, order, justice, while the murderer embraces the opposite values.[6] It is an irony that the primordial struggle between good and evil takes place over the silent corpse of the victim, who functions as a system of signs:[7] the detective reconstructs both the scene of the murder (the last episode in the victim's life) and the events prior to the crime. The story thus reconstructed via the investigation moves backward, from absence to presence, from the moment of death to the victim's existence. Concurrently the killer builds up a different account, an alibi. Moving in the opposite direction and starting from the victim's life, the assassin deletes any possible clues in order to sidetrack the detective by means of disinformation and misleading depictions of the events leading dangerously to the murder. The story told by the killer denies and voids the detective's account. This narrative pattern, twofold and contradictory, is a set device required by the structure of the genre. Detective fiction, consciously or not, threatens the concept of narration as a monolithic and objective act.

It may be inferred that the detective novel is characterized by a tension-driven narration, sustained by frequent delays that arouse the reader's anticipation and by the existence of unfinished stories and limited points of view. By juxtaposing and playing with the opposites "truth" and "lie," it stages a double crisis: in the particular, that of the subject-narrator in its authorial competence; in the absolute, that of the social subject in its authoritativeness.

At first sight *Voci* is a very accessible work, easy to read and digest like any popular thriller.[8] But in reality *Voci* is structured along the lines of a complex narration, which focalizes, by way of the narrative technique of mirroring, the artificiality and arbitrariness of narration as representation. The first case of double narration occurs when the readers follow the chronology of events in the life of Michela Canova, a radio journalist responsible for a reportage on unsolved crimes against women, while they keep up simultaneously with her investigative report concerning the murder of her neighbor Angela Bari. In this instance one can see the overlapping of two diverse narrative styles, belonging to different genres, the detective story and the diary, the latter a perfect vehicle for the novel of feminine self-discovery—two kinds of ex-centric writing that, according to the literary canon, are mutually exclusive, since they convey gendered points of view. However, within *Voci*—detective story and bildungsroman with a feminist perspective—these two dissimilar narratives come into contact and interact. The bidirectional narration of detective fiction runs counter to that, linear and univocal, of the novel of self-discovery and maturation. Nevertheless they both exhibit the same structuring narrative function, the quest. For Michela—the internal narrator of *Voci*—the quest expresses itself as self-searching, an issue built around the traditional motifs of identification and representation. At the same time for Michela—the character given the role of detective—the quest is realized as search for the murderer, in other words as search for the "other." This process of redoubling both the narrative voice and the actant of the search plays with the traditional conceptualization of "one" and "many," thus questioning the legitimacy of absolute values such as "similarity" and "difference." In addition *Voci* accomplishes further narrative duplications by stressing the phenomenon of multiple voices through the device of the investigation. During the investigation, the distinction between "truth" and "lie" is put into question time and time again by the murderer's deceitful account as well as by the ritualistic procedure of the witnesses being interrogated and giving evidence. A web of many diverging and contradictory stories shrouds Angela Bari's lifeless body. The stories told point to the illegitimacy and arbitrariness of narration as a method of representation.

This very fact allows the readers to question some fundamental concepts of Western culture: the meaning of history, creativity, subjectivity, sexuality, and family. Maraini indeed capitalizes on the antagonism between detective and murderer in their narrative roles by relocating this conflict to the sphere of sexuality. In the role of amateur detective,[9] Michela Canova reiterates the marginality engulfing ordinary and career women alike in present-day Italy. Michela repeatedly challenges this peripheral status by rejecting amateurism as an existential attribution of the feminine.[10] And by assigning the murderer's role to Glauco Elia, the stepfather, Maraini injects quite openly into the detective genre a feminist perspective whereby the indicting process of the woman detective and the denunciation of the abuses of paternal power coalesce.[11] References to the father are interspersed throughout the story disguised as dreams, myths, and fables. They foreshadow the final act of the book, the accusation brought against Glauco of prolonged violence leading at first to rape and incest and in the end to murder. The indictment points to a private reality inside the social microcosm of the family, but its scope extends metaphorically to the macrocosm of society at large. Police commissioner Adele Sofia and Michela often talk about fathers, albeit in different contexts. Michela detects an ambiguity in her relationship with her father that reveals the essential power structure within. Reminiscing about her father, Michela experiences opposing feelings: surrender and trust, rejection and suspicion. Her feelings mimic the customary oppressive relationship of patriarchy vis-à-vis women. Patriarchy takes on the proportions of an all-encompassing reality reaching beyond culture and history. The character of Angela Bari exemplifies women's victimization throughout history. Peculiar to the detective story is the narrative function of the victim, who in the instance of *Voci* sets off the real absence of women from society against their virtual presence. Angela Bari appears to Michela Canova as a complex yet decipherable system of signs that affords her a plausible, though incomplete, representation of the feminine. The women portrayed by Michela are necessarily very different from their counterparts constructed by the media. Michela unsettles the deep-rooted vision of women as passive victims by placing in its stead a representation, at the same time a self-portrait, of the feminine where women are positioned as the subject of meaning and of social reality.

Voci comes across as a "new" hybrid genre wherein two popular but ostensibly contradictory types of fiction coalesce. The author skillfully fuses social criticism, a feature of detective fiction, and feminist-inspired themes into a cohesive whole. But while the detective genre denounces the present, temporarily upset by the exceptional intervention of crime, and posits a return to the past, *Voci* deconstructs today's phallocracy and conceives a future where there exists a social-symbolic system compatible with gender difference and feminine inclusiveness. In the text all of this is foreshadowed by Michela Canova who, after solving the case and being fired from her job, is tempted by the perspective of becoming a writer, even though this prospect leaves her perplexed and hesitant. *Voci* does not close the Bari investigation by uncritically reverting to the status quo before the murder. At the end of the novel, the reader sees that through the murder inquiry the character of Michela has attained a critical outlook and her own identity.

Rewriting and Intertextuality

During her sleepless nights, Michela reads Joseph Conrad, the author central to the inspiration of another Maraini work, *Un clandestino a bordo* (1996; *Stowaway on Board*). In *Voci*,[12] he is mentioned three times and on two different occasions: first, when Michela thinks she is being followed by Nando, a suspect in the killing of Angela Bari; then, when she finds out about the relationship between Angela and Marco, her lover. On the second of these occasions, the reader learns that the book being read is called *The Secret Sharer*. In the topos of the double, Michela singles out something that applies to her:

> Mi sembra di riconoscere nella doppiezza del capitano di Conrad qualcosa della mia doppiezza, non sarei tanto incuriosita da Angela Bari se non riconoscessi in lei parte delle mie perdizioni e dei miei disordini, delle mie paure e delle mie abiezioni. (273)

> In the experience of Conrad's captain, I seem to recognize something of my own. I would not be so curious about Angela Bari if I did not recognize in her some of my own confusion, my fear and my lack of assertiveness. (224)

The Doppelgänger motif, originating with the German writer Jean Paul Richter (Hallam 5) at the end of the eighteenth century, has acquired through time and various writers several meanings.[13] The topos so appealed to Conrad that he made it the pivot of some of his works. Leggatt, the double rescued from the sea by a young captain, has given rise to diametrically opposed interpretations.[14] According to some, Leggatt likely represents the captain's alter ego, the hidden part of the self seen in negative terms, a kind of "shadow" of Jungian descent; or it is purported to be a resurfacing of subconscious influences, that is, in Freudian terminology, a return of the "repressed" (Hallam 1–4). Other critics view Leggatt as a positive model for the captain, some sort of idealized self, a dream of maturation and plenitude that may be attained only at the moment of separation from the double.

As a result of reading Conrad, Michela recognizes her double. What happens is a kind of double mirroring: at first she sees herself in the captain, then in Angela, just as the captain recognizes himself in Leggatt. This indirect identification is pointing at a negative image of the double, that of Angela as victim. Later on, after further consideration, Michela identifies herself directly with the captain. This encounter with an ambivalent Doppelgänger, considering the moral and psychological ambiguity of Conrad's character, carries mostly positive meanings inasmuch as it puts forward the theme of salvage/salvation:

> Anch'io sto facendo una manovra arrischiata per avvicinarmi il più possibile alle rocce, col pericolo di fracassare malamente il mio futuro, per deporre delicatamente in acqua la morta dalle scarpe di tela azzurrina, perché nuoti al sicuro, nel buio della notte e raggiunga qualche approdo, se non felice, per lo meno tranquillo. (273)
>
> I too am carrying out a dangerous maneuver to bring myself as close as possible to the rocks with the risk of shattering my future. To let down gently into the water the corpse of the blue canvas shoes so it can swim to safety in the darkness of the night and reach another landing place that will at least be tranquil even if not happy. (224)

In both instances of self-recognition, Michela ponders the motif of the Doppelgänger in Conrad's novel as if to explain by means of a fictional narrative the complexity of her own life. In short she is dealing with confrontations with the double that occur after reading a fictional text. This may explain why the encounter with a feminine Doppelgänger is replete with difficulty. First of all, it happens to be an encounter brought about by an intermediary, since it is depicted as the result of a double mirroring. Secondly, it is shown as a negative encounter, since Angela, who is seen as a woman/victim, is also Michela's alter ego. On the contrary, the second confrontation with the male Doppelgänger is direct and positive. Here *Voci* seems to evidence how gendered images, where the masculine is readily available and also characterized by generally positive traits, constantly bounce back at the reader from the pages of literature. Maraini seems to imply that the literary tradition clones one-sided representational patterns that are obviously gendered.[15]

The Doppelgänger motif is frequently found within the detective novel, where it often acts as a structure of mirrorlike *dédoublement* between narrator and detective.[16] This is unnecessary in the case of *Voci* since narrator and detective are the same person. Maraini prefers to play with a complex system of associative mirrorlike identifications that bear upon various relationships among women in their role as Doppelgängern. Michela identifies with Angela and vice-versa, Ludovica becomes one with Angela, Sabrina recalls Ludovica, Adriana looks like Angela, and so forth. These psychological look-alike doubles are not highlighted to arouse empathy with women's victimization but rather to fulfill an essential goal, to showcase the motif of solidarity among women. This motif finds a different expression in the practice of entrustment,[17] exemplified by numerous acts of cooperation among women, such as the friendship between Adele and Michela and the instant bonding between Rosa and Michela.[18]

The motif of the double in the detective novel structures the relationship between detective and murderer. They relate to each other at various levels, sometimes as opposites, at other times as accessories, especially when they are of the same gender. Actually the detective succeeds in understanding the murderer's mode of reasoning and in assuming the murderer's personality only by getting into the killer's head, to the point where detective and killer become one and the same. The interchangeability of the roles of victim, assassin, and detective is realized not without ambiguity: the murderer is in turn a victim; at the same time the detective may subsume all the roles, consecutively becoming the victim and, potentially, the murderer. In *Voci* the accessorial and oppositional relationship between detective and murderer is conveyed through the theme of artistic creativity.[19] Michela Canova shares her surname with the great sculptor, but to her regret he is not her forebear. This peculiarity denotes a shortcoming, a want, an "absence"; in fact, she is excluded from the art world,[20] unlike Glauco, who, though an architect by profession, is also a rather well known sculptor. Not fortuitously, a secluded villa in a bucolic country setting provides the stage where Michela calls on Glauco. The description of the villa, in stark contrast with that of the crime scene, is an indication of Glauco's privileged status. On the way to the villa—the whole route is paved with the symbology of the journey as quest—Michela finds a wounded turtle, which she picks up, looks after, and then sets free, albeit reluctantly in view of some impediments.[21] During the meeting, Michela and Glauco are respectively marked by a "branding" (Propp 52), signaling absence and presence vis-à-vis art. Paradoxically, Michela will discover that Glauco is the murderer by looking at one of his works, a statue representing the feminine, the female body as the object of desire. By appealing to that same creativity that simultaneously brings them close together and pulls them apart—not unlike the device of conflicting narrations and narrators who contradict each other in the detective novel—Michela, as the associative double of the architect, at this point of the story turns the initial situation upside down. As a matter of fact, in the detective novel the oppositional relationship between detective and murderer is maintained and reaffirmed through a significant functional displacement: at the end of the story the detective takes on the function of executioner, while the murderer becomes the victim. In *Voci*, given that Glauco and patriarchy are strictly correlated, the final victory of the detective—an ambivalent victory marred by Glauco's suicide—signals the triumph of the feminine.

Therefore, Maraini appropriates the motif of the Doppelgänger (whether derived from Conrad or an essential structural feature of the detective genre) and rewrites it. This rewriting addresses issues pertaining to the feminine, the themes of identification and resistance. Ultimately it reveals itself as a possible strategy of opposition to patriarchy, even though it may be ambivalent and fraught with doubts.

Edgar Allan Poe's *The Murders in the Rue Morgue* is the inspiration for the second occurrence of intertextuality, an

Ada Testaferri

inspiration surfacing perhaps from a deeper level of Maraini's consciousness. The reputation of *Murders,* in all likelihood the progenitor of detective fiction, may be due to the ingenuity of its inventions that, as often happens with a prototype, were destined to become part of the standard repertoire of the classic detective story. Relevant to the present analysis is Poe's accurate description of the crime scene. The room in question, locked from the inside and inaccessible to the killer, has nevertheless been the setting of an atrocious double murder. Inside the residence everything is in a shambles; the signs of destruction are everywhere. The two victims, an older woman and her daughter, have been viciously murdered. The devastation at the crime scene and the atrocity of the slayings leave the public and the police equally dismayed and convinced that an act of superhuman violence has been committed.[22] An overpowering sense of mystery surrounds the crime, which from the start the police deem unsolvable, given that the site is impenetrable. This sense of mystery, soon to become a fixed element of the genre, is often associated with the motive of the crime. Thus the unmasking of the motive and of the assassin is the object of the detective's search. In Poe's story the mystery resides in the physical features of the enclosed room, actually built like the box of a puzzle whose pieces Dupin must fit together in order to reconstruct the events of the crime in a logical time sequence.

In the detective story, the locale is an element of narration. It generally functions as a framework enfolding and revealing a series of clues that pertain—as every detective knows—to the crime itself but also to the Weltanschauung of the writer and of the society in which s/he operates. In Poe's case, the enclosed room suggests that crime is a form of deviation that can be quarantined and kept away from society. As such it is containable and must be contained. Dupin, with his profound intuitions and his outstanding reasoning faculties, is the only one capable of solving the mystery of the enclosed room. He embodies the positive categories of order and human genius prevailing over the mystery of crime and bestiality, the latter to be taken literally, since the perpetrator of the murders turns out to be an orangutan. Hence *Murders* is about a Subject conceived as the infallible interpreter of reality who gives order to the world.

Unlike Poe, Maraini describes the scene of the crime as a primarily "open" site. When Giovanni discovers Angela Bari's corpse, the door to the house is "open"; it is still open when Michela comes back from her trip. It remains persistently open even after the police cordon off the apartment. The locale must have indeed appeared "open," that is accessible, to Angela's murderer.[23] Unlike Poe's interior, everything is tidy inside: the sky-blue canvas shoes neatly aligned near the threshold, the victim's clothes painstakingly folded and laid on a chair, hardly any traces of blood. All these referents emphasize the ordinariness, the normality of the crime. The insistence on order and on the "openness" of the locale makes it difficult for both detectives, the amateur (Michela) and the professional (Adele Sofia), to solve the case. It is especially significant that the locale in *Voci* is no longer a referent of the extraordinary and of the separate. On the contrary, the dull familiarity of everyday things seems to encompass violence, specifically violence against women.

An enduring sense of mystery pervades the book. Maraini, however, cleverly shifts the mystery from the puzzlelike room to the woman as such. All of this is highlighted by the fabrications published in the press. These images of the feminine, arbitrary and offensive, crisscross day after day with the effect of disorienting the readers and of shaping public opinion. Angela Bari turns into a hypnotic mystery that feeds the morbid curiosity of a public hungry for news. It is an uncaring public that reads but does not want to know. Angela Bari, whose body has been stabbed twenty times, is literally sacrificed to the feeding frenzy of greedy and indifferent consumers.[24]

Regardless of whether it can be ascertained to which extent Maraini is conscious of rewriting Poe, and taking into account the historical and cultural gap that divides them, it must be pointed out how in the two texts under discussion gender difference brings forth distinct outcomes. The two detectives possess and display profound intuitive skills but it is striking that, unlike Dupin, Michela Canova does not rely too much on her reasoning powers; in fact she mistrusts the "logica geometrica dei signi scritti" (301; "the logical geometry of written signs"; 248). Moreover, Michela does not attempt, like her counterpart Dupin, to interpret and to regulate the reality surrounding her. While "covering," as a journalist, various cases of violence against women and "uncovering," as an amateur detective, Angela Bari's murderer, Michela cannot help but refer the whole ordeal to an experience of the "social" that is fundamentally an experience of the "personal," to an "understanding" that is also and foremost a form of "self-understanding." As such, these forms of understanding are, of necessity, extraneous in their intrinsic modality to Dupin's outlook and inward look.[25]

Both texts assign a central function to "voices," a motif warranting intertextual comparison. In *Murders* the voices heard by some passersby provide a key element that points toward the solution of the mystery, thus helping Dupin's investigation. In Maraini's novel the voices, filtered electronically by a Nagra recorder and by other means of modern technology, instead of helping with the investigation, baffle the detective and lead her astray. In Poe's story, the difficulty in identifying the "gruff voice" is one more blatant reference to "otherness." The "gruff voice" does not sound French, therefore it does not belong in the national context; nor does it belong to any of the major languages spoken in Europe, hence it intimates an agent totally alien to Western civilization. Once the crime is solved it is revealed that in fact that "voice" does not even belong to a human being. By means of referents pointing to a kind of horror that can only be classified as "other," Poe constructs the beastlike homicidal fury as a unique and deviant case of bestial insanity. It is not at all like *Voci,* where the voices, who talk and act out violence against women, are easily identifiable. Gathered within the bosom of the household, culled from the intimate privacy of the feminine, these voices talk about the decay of Roman society; through the Italian press and some Anglo-American studies consulted by Michela, they call attention to the violence within the nation and beyond, a violence that involves the cultural context of the whole West. Voices, all of them, talking about "truth" and "lies," demanding to be believed. Michela perceives them as "organismi viventi" ("living organisms") and, unlike Poe, ascribes human attributes to them, "belle o brutte, deboli o forti. . . . Sono percorse di vene lunghissime di azzurro" (301; "beautiful or ugly, weak or strong, they are criss-crossed by long veins"; 247).

For the woman narrator and the woman detective alike, the attempt to enter the Social-Symbolic is met by a hostility as old as history itself. Not being endowed a priori with heuristic means of knowledge, Michela is an outsider, yet she carries through the Bari investigation and solves the mystery. In lieu of Poe's cognitive process, where the "I" or Subject, rules reality by fiat, Maraini installs Michela and her methodical questioning.

Michela is a Subject that does not know, does not classify, does not judge a priori. For this ex-centric "I" there is no fiduciary agreement between questions and answers; to know consists in questioning and self-questioning. The outcome is transient knowledge and inconclusive answers: sequential stages of reverting afresh to renewed queries. This kind of questioning puts its own trademark on the whole society.

De-tecting *Voci* means covering, as in an investigative report, the totality of our reality, and uncovering first of all the mechanisms of representation, which inevitably lead to the many ways of exercising power. How is "difference" constructed and what are its sociohistorical consequences? What does "love" mean in the relationship with the other (Marco) and within the family? Which position does gendered division occupy within society (family, neighborhood, workplace, city, world)? How is the Social of history molded? Who appropriates economic power in the Social? What is creativity and who controls the terms of production? Maraini, pushing beyond the usual perimeters of her narrative, does not provide the readers with any definite answers. Michela, like many of Maraini's characters, cannot make up her mind. Will she continue her relationship with Marco, in spite of his lying, fully aware that she does not really know him? Will she go back to being a radio journalist and put up with daily abuse and being taken advantage of? Will she follow Adele Sofia's advice and write a book even though she mistrusts writing? Unlike other Maraini characters (Vannina of *Donna in guerra* being a case in point), Michela does not become alienated from the Social, does not withdraw categorically rejecting societal values. Michela, by insisting on being included, wants her own voice, Angela's, and all other women's, to be heard, and the feminine to be present, albeit as "otherness," in the production of meaning.

In a brilliant pairing of detective novel and feminine/feminist bildungsroman, Dacia Maraini builds a model of knowledge and cognition that, though somewhat unfathomable and unattainable, nevertheless is within women's reach. It is a double knowledge, full of ambiguity, in love with its own reflection and at the same time mirroring the phallocentric trademark of contemporary culture. This double knowledge, since it is manifold in spite of itself and because it is divided, constructs cognition as the very process of duplicity, imitating in its need to conceal and to conceal itself the narrative technique of the detective novel: a narration often incomplete, always multifaceted, and most of all, always ambiguously double.

Notes

1. I employ the term *feminine writing* in a broad sense, as found in Kristeva's work rather than as interpreted by Irigaray and partly by Cixous. Maraini's work on the whole does not come across as a writing of separation, in spite of the fact that the author highlights the difference resulting from specific conceptualizations of the masculine and of the feminine.

2. Most theorists of detective fiction agree in locating its literary sources in France and England. Among the authors most frequently mentioned as possible forerunners of the genre are Dickens, Fielding, Balzac, and Dumas. Priestman traces its origins as far back as Sophocles's *Oedipus Rex*. All of the critics I have consulted agree in recognizing Poe as the official founder of the genre.

3. The best known is Umberto Eco, formerly a scholar of Ian Fleming (a noted master of the thriller), subsequently author of the best-seller *The Name of the Rose,* which became a successful movie of the same title.

4. Many scholars concur with this assessment: among the studies devoted to the genre I call attention to Kathleen Gregory Klein, *The Woman Detective: Gender and Genre.* In this influential work the terms *woman* and *detective* are seen in a dichotomous relationship. On the same subject one may also refer to Dennis Porter, *The Pursuit of Crime: Art and Ideology in Detective Fiction.*

5. Although critics differentiate among subgenres, making a distinction between *murder story* and *thriller,* I use the general term *detective novel*, since the present analysis does not warrant such a subtle distinction.

6. In my review of the features specific to the detective genre, in addition to the aforementioned works, I have taken into account the following authors: Uri Eisenzweig, *Le récit impossible: Forme et sens du roman policier;* of equal importance, Jerry Palmer, *Thrillers: Genesis and Structure of a Popular Genre.* Also recommended are Jon Thompson, *Fiction, Crime and Empire: Clues to Modernity and Postmodernism;* Sally R. Munt, *Murder by the Book: Feminism and the Crime Novel;* and *Feminism in Women's Detective Fiction,* edited by Glenwood Irons.

De-tecting *Voci*

7. In Maraini's narrative, too, the absence of speech acts as "branding." But the woman/victim is read and represented mostly as a symbol of resistance: one needs only to think of the oppositional yet complementary connection between mutism and writing in *Marianna Ucrìa* (*The Silent Duchess*).

8. One might argue against Maraini's choice of the narrative structure of the detective novel as it seems to revictimize women. Instead, choosing popular fiction to deal with violence against women ensures, in my view, a large following of readers and a public that has not been preselected to represent a specific ideology. Thus by choosing a light and entertaining kind of fiction to showcase a theme so central to feminist thought, Maraini actually makes it easy for her readers to undergo various processes of identification.

9. Traditionally, the detective story builds up a major antagonism between murderer and detective alongside a minor one between the detective, whether an amateur or a private eye, and the police. Often the detective's movements are hindered by the police, either out of incompetence or rivalry. In *Voci* the official investigation is headed by police commissioner Adele Sofia, who at times curbs Michela's intuitions, but she also functions as a true helper of the detective: first, she hands Michela materials and data for the radio reportage; second, they have an amicable discussion concerning the Bari murder in the privacy of the commissioner's home. As her surname (Sofia) indicates, she possesses knowledge and acts as a guide. It is she who encourages Michela to become a writer. As with many other figures in Maraini's works, the police commissioner is described as a bundle of contradictions. Authoritarian and mannish, she toils behind a stove, cooking being her true passion. The irony of a stereotype being superseded by another is inescapable. She wears braces on her teeth, which add a touch of youthfulness and vulnerability to her character. Maraini also plays with clichéd portrayals of lesbian and heterosexual couples. Definitely the couple Sofia-Girardengo shows its own pattern of domination/subordination, but by comparison it also shows a mutual understanding not shared by heterosexual couples, neither married nor common-law. In a variation from traditional detective fiction, in *Voci* one finds cooperation between the police commissioner and Michela, made possible by their common status of marginality.

10. A recurring word in *Voci* is *imbranata,* an insult hurled without cause at Michela. The term appears for the first time when Michela succeeds, after countless maneuvers, in rescuing her Fiat 500 from a "Roman-style" parking spot. The owner of the Mercedes blocking Michela's exit (oblivious to the successful outcome of her maneuvering) rewards her with the classic derogatory remark, "imbranata come tutte le donne" (32; "can't get it right like all women"; 23). In the book this chauvinist cliché becomes an ironic badge of the feminine. Angela too is the recipient of the same slight. At first this appears to Michela as a possible reason to find a resemblance between herself and her neighbor, in spite of their differences. This graphic phrase is the vehicle chosen by Maraini to introduce into the novel one of the most debated topics of contemporary feminism. Originally a North American issue, it professes to identify within the abstract category "woman" real differences among women. Since the list of critics who theorize about "differences" and "feminisms" is almost endless, I will make reference only to three well-known names: bell hooks, Teresa de Lauretis, and Trinh T. Minh-ha.

11. From every point of view, Glauco is the quintessential repository of phallic power. Metonymically he represents all of the prerogatives of today's patriarchy. Glauco is endowed with many attributes of power. A series of connotations point to his status as a demiurge-like father figure. His name refers to the color of the sky (which is the dwelling of the deity), his surname recalls the Hebrew prophet Elijah, his profession alludes to the Masonic concept of God as architect of the world. Sociojuridical connotations that imply paternal authority: Glauco is Ludovica's and Angela's legal stepfather; he calls himself "father" and when he talks about himself he stresses his power as head of the family: the recent birth of his daughter Augusta attests to his official title of "father." Socioeconomic connotations that affirm his superiority: Glauco is a rich and famous professional. Connotations that draw on the power of art, a cross-reference to Lacan: Glauco is not a sculptor by profession (he does it as a hobby), but he has earned a national reputation and he is about to exhibit his works. Finally, as murderer-narrator he has the power to kill but also to create his own story of the sisters Bari, and his own alibi, which actually translates into a forgery of archival data, that is to say a falsification of History. Taking advantage of his power as narrator-murderer and acting counter to the rules of the genre, Glauco himself will provide the final version of the events, thus encroaching upon the detective's right to the final explanation.

12. For the English quotations, I have used *Voices*, translated by Dick Kitto and Elspeth Spottiswood.

13. Besides being essential to the structure of the detective novel, the Doppelgänger motif is fundamental to the overall production of both Conrad and Poe. In this instance again I refer to some basic texts I have consulted for my evaluation of the motif: John Herdman, *The Double in Nineteenth-Century Fiction: The Shadow Life;* Ralph Tymms's *Doubles in Literary Psychology,* still relevant. For the reading of *Secret Sharer* I have used the very fine edition prepared by Daniel R. Schwarz. For a general commentary I have consulted Jeremy Hawthorn, *Joseph Conrad: Narrative Technique and Ideological Commitment.*

14. Conrad and Poe use the motif as it was first conceived. The classic concept of the Doppelgänger draws on psychological and/or moral phenomena that have a special influence on individuals. In Maraini the motif acquires more of a collective significance as it benefits women as a community. *Voci,* therefore, bestows on the Doppelgänger a social function

De-tecting *Voci*

that traditionally was not its prerogative. Even when Conrad and Poe use the motif to signify a contrast of sociopolitical import, the encounter takes place from a modernist viewpoint, on the basis of a polarized differentiation. Maraini uses the motif to probe the complexity of the process of identification in all of its variants.

15. At the end of chapter 17, Maraini mentions Patricia Highsmith, remembered for her well-known misogyny and for her familiarity with the theme of murder. Lack of space prevents me from comparing the two authors, but I wish to comment briefly upon the meaning of this inclusion in *Voci*. Michela says that, in spite of her efforts, she has not been able to read any of the American writer's novels (94), not only because her mind is elsewhere, but clearly because the reading of fiction that victimizes women is neither pleasant nor suited to the psychological state she is in. Indeed Highsmith admits with no qualms that she prefers the male viewpoint in the representation of reality in general and of women in particular, and she writes in *Plotting and Writing Fiction,* "I prefer the point of view of the main character, written in the third-person singular and I might add masculine . . . I tend to think of women as being pushed by people and circumstances instead of pushing . . ." (88). This reference to the American author implies that Maraini, knowing that her own writing is typically subjective, wishes to distance herself (yet another problem, of identification/differentiation?) from a kind of writing that draws inspiration from the modality of objectivity associated with male writers.

16. The best known example is that of Sherlock Holmes and the inseparable Dr. Watson.

17. For an in-depth discussion of this practice, I call attention to *Sexual Difference: A Theory of Social-Symbolic Practice,* by the Milan Women's Bookstore Collective. The introductory essay is by Teresa de Lauretis.

18. In *Voci* the theme of friendship and solidarity among women is expressed by the presence of the linden tree. With its fragrant flowers, it promises rest and brings relief in a city, like Rome, overrun by cement. However, the linden flowers are used for a sleep-inducing herbal tea. The motif of the linden tree unites Michela and Angela, as well as Michela and Rosa.

19. Feminine creativity is represented metaphorically by the ceaseless weaving of a small spider. The spider's work in *Voci* also alludes to the constant weaving of the detective and to the unremitting interruptions of the murderer with the purpose of sidetracking the investigation.

20. To verify this, one should read the attributions given to Michela's character, which turn out to be the very antithesis of Glauco's (see note 11).

21. It is Michela who states that she recognizes herself in the turtle: this happens (as with the captain's double in Conrad) at the moment of separation. Setting the turtle free is not an easy undertaking given that the natural environment has been destroyed by man. "L'Italia brucia"

(246; "All Italy is burning"; 202), remarks Michela, obviously referring to her social habitat.

22. Poe's story is discussed in most of the texts consulted for the theory of the detective novel, particularly by Eisenzweig. I will also mention Eveline Pinto, *Edgar Poe et l'art d'inventer; The Purloined Poe: Lacan, Derrida and Psychoanalytic Reading,* ed. John P. Muller and William Richardson; and, lastly, Giorgio Ghidetti, *Poe: l'eresia di un americano maledetto.*

23. The symbology of open vs. closed refers to the different ways Poe and Maraini conceive female sexuality, undoubtedly as a result of their different places and times in history. But it also points to the availability of women in the family milieu, where as a rule the father figure engenders a fiduciary relationship centered around "openness."

24. The theme of woman as an object to be possessed, worse still, to be devoured, is typical of feminism in the 1970s and also present in Maraini's work. Here ironically it is teamed up with the subject of the representation of the feminine in art. Giulio Carlini remembers one of his youthful impressions, his first reaction to art and maybe to the nude female form. He is talking about "Paolina Borghese ritratta dal Canova ... mi sembrava fatta di zucchero, avrei voluto mangiarla" (95; "Canova's bust of Paolina Borghese. It looked as if it were made of sugar, I'd have liked to eat it"; 76).

25. Dupin is especially proud of his exceptional intellect, an attitude that brings to mind both Giulio Carlini and Glauco Elia. Because of the male-originated equation between woman and body/matter, they actually glorify the myth of man's spiritual/intellectual superiority and of woman's corresponding inferiority. I invite the reader to refer to Carlini's appraisal of art, partially discussed in the preceding note, and also to Glauco's statement after Michela has identified the nude created by him. Both of them, faced with a disquieting reality—disquieting because it is erotically charged—sublimate the experience of the real by turning to an abstraction (the kind described by Freud as the to and fro of a swing when referring to little Hans's game with *fort* and *da*). For both of them the great power of art—as practiced by man—resides in its ability to go beyond matter (marble for Canova, the female body for Glauco) to seize the ineffable. On the contrary, art for Michela is concretely anchored in reality and in society, in this case, in the female body, lusted after and defiled.

Works Cited

Cixous, Hélène. "The Laugh of the Medusa." Trans. Keith Cohen and Paula Cohen. *Signs* 1 (1976): 875–93.

Conrad, Joseph. *The Secret Sharer: Complete Authoritative Text with Bibliographical and Historical Contexts: Critical History and*

Essays from Five Contemporary Critical Perspectives. Ed. Daniel R. Schwarz. Boston: Bedford, 1997.

de Lauretis, Teresa. *The Practice of Love: Lesbian Sexuality and Perverse Desire.* Bloomington: Indiana UP, 1994.

Eco, Umberto, and Oreste del Buono. *The Bond Affair.* Trans. R. A. Dawnie. London: MacDonald, 1966.

Eisenzweig, Uri. *Le récit impossible: Forme et sens du roman policier.* Paris: Christian Bourgeois, 1986.

Ghidetti, Giorgio. *Poe: l'eresia di un americano maledetto.* Florence: Arnaud, 1989.

Hallam, Clifford. "The Double as Incomplete Self: Toward a Definition of Doppelgänger." *Fearful Symmetry: Doubles and Doubling in Literature and Film.* Ed. Eugene J. Crook. Tallahassee: UP of Florida, 1981.

Hawthorn, Jeremy. *Joseph Conrad: Narrative Technique and Ideological Commitment.* London: Edward Arnold, 1990.

Herdman, John. *The Double in Nineteenth-Century Fiction: The Shadow Life.* New York: St. Martin's, 1991.

Highsmith, Patricia. *Plotting and Writing Fiction.* Boston: Writer, 1981.

hooks, bell. *Yearning: Race, Gender and Cultural Politics.* Toronto: Between the Lines, 1992.

Irigaray, Luce. *An Ethics of Sexual Difference.* Trans. Carolyn Burke and Gillian C. Gill. Ithaca: Cornell UP, 1993.

Irons, Glenwood, ed. *Feminism in Women's Detective Fiction.* Toronto: Toronto UP, 1995.

Klein, Kathleen Gregory. *The Woman Detective: Gender and Genre.* Urbana: U of Illinois P, 1988.

Kristeva, Julia. *Desire in Language: A Semiotic Approach to Literature and Art.* Trans. Thomas Gora, Alice Jardine, and Leon Roudiez. New York: Columbia UP, 1980.

Maraini, Dacia. *Un clandestino a bordo.* 1993. Milan: Rizzoli, 1996. Published in English as *Stowaway on Board.* Trans. Giovanna Bellesia and Victoria Offredi Poletto. West Lafayette, IN: Bordighera, 2000.

———. *Donna in guerra.* Turin: Einaudi, 1975. Published in English as *Woman at War.* 1981. New York: Italica, 1988.

———. *Isolina.* Milan: Mondadori, 1985. Published in English as *Isolina.* London: Peter Owen, 1994; distributed by Dufour.

Maraini, Dacia. *La lunga vita di Marianna Ucrìa*. Milan: Rizzoli, 1990. Published in English as *The Silent Duchess*. London: Peter Owen, 1992. New York: Feminist, 1998.

———. *La vacanza*. Milan: Lerici, 1962. Published in English as *The Holiday*. London: Weidenfeld and Nicholson, 1966.

———. *Voci*. Milan: Rizzoli, 1994. Published in English as *Voices*.

———. *Voices*. Trans. Dick Kitto and Elspeth Spottiswood. London and New York: Serpent's Tail, 1997.

Milan Women's Bookstore Collective. *Sexual Difference: A Theory of Social-Symbolic Practice*. Trans. Patricia Cicogna and Teresa de Lauretis. Introductory Essay by de Lauretis. Bloomington: Indiana UP, 1990.

Muller, John, and William Richardson. *The Purloined Poe: Lacan, Derrida and Psychoanalytic Reading*. Baltimore: Johns Hopkins UP, 1988.

Munt, Sally R. *Murder by the Book: Feminism and the Crime Novel*. London: Routledge, 1994.

Murch, A. E. *The Development of the Detective Novel*. Port Washington: Kennikat, 1968.

Palmer, Jerry. *Thriller: Genesis and Structure of a Popular Genre*. London: Edward Arnold, 1978.

Pinto, Eveline. *Edgar Poe et l'art d'inventer*. Paris: Klinksiek, 1983.

Poe, Edgar Allan. *The Fall of the House of Usher and Other Writings*. Ed. David Galloway. Middlesex: Harmondsworth, 1967.

Porter, Dennis. *The Pursuit of Crime: Art and Ideology in Detective Fiction*. New Haven: Yale UP, 1981.

Priestman, Martin. *Detective Fiction and Literature: The Figure in the Carpet*. New York: St. Martin's, 1991.

Propp, Vladimir. *Morphology of the Folktale*. Trans. Laurence Scott. Austin: Texas UP, 1975.

Thompson, Jon. *Fiction, Crime and Empire: Clues to Modernity and Postmodernism*. Urbana: Illinois UP, 1993.

Trinh T. Minh-ha. *Woman, Native Other: Writing Postcoloniality and Feminism*. Bloomington: Indiana UP, 1989.

Tymms, Ralph. *Doubles in Literary Psychology*. Cambridge: Bowes, 1949.

Translated by Sebastiana Marino, York University.

Corrado Federici

Spatialized Gender and the Poetry of Dacia Maraini

In his *Poetics of Space,* Gaston Bachelard conducts a formal analysis of the aesthetics of spatial signifiers. He prefers to deal with what he refers to as "topophilia" or "images of felicitous space" and defers the task of examining the negative or apocalyptic dimension of the topic. He argues in favor of the interpretability of spatial structures in the context of a phenomenological discourse and spawns a number of semiotic analyses such as those of Juri Lotman and Angelo Marchese in the area of poetry criticism. In all of these cases the working premise is that specific physical locations are associated in the imagination of the poet with particular affective states. Although inspired to a degree by the theories of these critics, by a sensitivity to the polyphonic feminist discourse in general and concern for the "new spaces of female sociality" (de Lauretis 8) in particular, the present essay turns on an inverted premise. Instead of taking a given locus as a hermeneutical starting point and proceeding to ascertain the associations or connotations that it promotes in the imagination of the reflective subject, what is proposed is the notion that a hypothetical or virtual spatiality is constructed that houses and determines a set of gendered images corresponding more or less to Bachelard's "topography of our intimate being" (1).

In the poetry of Dacia Maraini, at least three significant spatial configurations emerge, operating through a complementary but sometimes oppositional dynamic in which the writer's ideology and aesthetics take form. The spatialization is the product of a metaphorizing process in that Maraini's images of men and women can be situated in two contiguous macro-spaces or parallel universes that are figurative grids or three-dimensional loci. This is where the poetic subject's impressions of the two

Corrado Federici

sexes tend to gravitate. In some cases actual physical space within which the protagonists of the poems operate or live is named. More often than not, the space exists by implication. Maraini herself makes this distinction in writing: "the oppressed take on the values of their oppressors" (Birnbaum 114).

The general scheme identifiable in the poetry of Maraini is that of two co-extensive but distinct ideological and emotional hemispheres: one male and the other female (S_1 and S_2 in figure 1). Each of these is subdivided into smaller conceptual areas (S_1A, S_1B, and S_2A, S_2B, S_2C). A third space, S_3, also begins to be delineated, though less forcefully. Incorporated within the male segment of the model are all references to images of the male as predator, aggressor, or patriarch (S_1A) and allusions to males as themselves victims of social pressures and norms (S_1B). The feminine portion of the figure is filled with characterizations of women as exploited, oppressed, and disenfranchised members of society (S_2A); as redeemed, liberated citizens of a truer democracy (S_2B); or as leaders of the women's liberation movement (S_2C). S_3 emerges as an ideological alternative to the main antithetical "spheres of influence" and can be considered in a sense as a stepping back from perhaps too clinical a polarization of male-female relationships.

Each of these paradigms is the product of the "productive imagination," as Bachelard might say, but in several illustra-

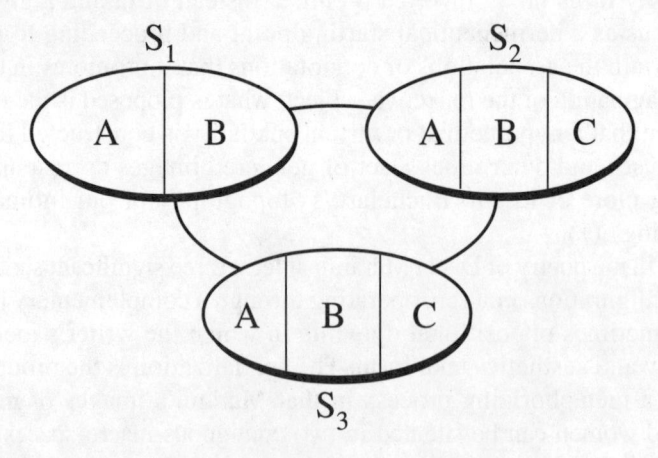

Fig. 1. Spheres of influence in Maraini's poetry.

tions a complex societal voicing can be detected beneath or within the voice of the poetic subject. The volume in which these categories are most compellingly articulated is *Donne mie* (1974; Women of mine).[1] In *Crudeltà all'aria aperta* (1966; Cruelty in the open air), the spatial-rhetorical paradigms are not as convincingly conceptualized, while in the later poetry of *Mangiami pure* (1978; *Devour Me Too*), *Dimenticato di dimenticare* (1982; Forgot to forget) and *Viaggiando con passo di volpe* (1991; *Traveling in the Gait of a Fox*), the categories tend to soften, and greater attention is given to elaboration of the S_3 interpretive model.

In the space designated as repository of terms that denote the male as visualized by the female poetic subject, the figure representing manifestations of the oppressor or despot, especially in *Donne mie,* takes shape around the noun *padrone* ("owner" or "boss"), which recurs six times. The word connotes possession of objects or property over which is exercised sanctioned dominion or authority. Such a function is reinforced by adjectival markers such as *legale* ("legal") or *mio* ("my"). On occasion, ownership is associated with family space, as when the speaker considers herself to have been treated by "il padrone, con paterna pazienza" (*Donne mie* 12; "the boss, with fatherly patience"). Usually the poetic persona uses the metaphor to indicate control exerted by the male over a determined space, which can be restrictive, as in the "anello nella / catena dolce-violenta della continuità patriarcale" (14; "ring in the / sweet-violent chain of patriarchal continuity"). This is ownership or authority over the female subject portrayed as an extensive entity; man can be viewed as "proprietario del vostro sorriso" (17; "proprietor of your smile"), "padrone del vostro animo / e del vostro ruvido cervello" (17; "owner of your soul / and of your primitive brain"). The poetic subject objectifies and spatializes the soul and the mind over which rule is exerted.

Representations of man in a commanding position in an explicitly or implicitly identified kingdom with female inhabitants are the images of man as king. Maraini's anthropological knowledge allows her to summon male authority figures from the earliest times, calling men "Dei paralitici e gessosi" (18; "paralytic gods of chalk") or "maschio faraonico" (38; "pharaoh male"). The poetic subject ironically and facetiously genuflects before the presumed "divine right" of men who claim that the "regole a cui si rifanno sono naturali ed eterne" (16; "the laws to which they defer are natural and eternal"). In all such images the speaker constructs an archetypal male figure who rules as a god and often with a distant imperialism, as when he is guilty of a "gelida tirannia" (39; "icy tyranny"). Metaphors such as these, situated in a political, historical context, are supplemented by a more distinctly modern sequence of characterizations of the male-female dialogue in the age of consumerism and technology. This is to say that for Maraini, woman can be visualized as a commodity. For instance, the companion of a woman is her "compratore" (21; "buyer") or there is the suggestion that the male is attempting to "usarti come userebbe / un'automobile" (20; "use you the way he would use / an automobile").

These categories are not fully developed in *Crudeltà all'aria aperta,* the volume that precedes *Donne mie,* and yet the spatial context in which the prototypical male figure operates is concretely identified in some verses where place and personality are interchangeable, such as: "le ampie piazze e i vicoli affollati / del tuo chiuso carattere di uomo" (59; "the spacious piazzas and the crowded avenues / of your closed male character"). There are also the "vasti uffici, le calde vetrine, / prefabbricato mondo del tuo ceto" (59; "the vast offices, the warm windows, / prefabricated world of your social class"). The first image is an interesting inversion of architectural functionality: the "offices" and "windows" imply openness and accessibility but the male personage is said to be "closed." What Maraini constructs is the disturbing portrait of an aloof, inaccessible male who takes in with his gaze the urban landscape that he has created and controls. The second image represents the post-industrial environment.

A comparable metaphor of physical and psychological partitioning occurs in *Viaggiando con passo di volpe,* where we find verses like "dietro quelle palpebre azzurre / un pensiero di fuga / un progetto di sfida / una decisione di possesso?" (37; "behind those blue eyelids / an urge to flee / an intent to challenge / a decision to possess?"). Here the male is envisioned as a personality concealed and yet readable behind the barrier of the eyelids that segregate the space occupied by the addressee from that occupied by the speaking subject—demarcating as well the arena of the authority figure who contemplates a metaphoric incursion into the vulnerable territory of the speaker who, in turn, presents herself as a state that cannot defend itself against invasion and occupation. She says: "aspetto un lupo / dai grandi occhi di agnello" (99; "I wait for the arrival of a wolf / with the large eyes of a lamb"). A parallel image is found in *Mangiami pure:* "ancora una volta mi lascerò depredare" (71; "once more I will let myself be pillaged").

Although the prevailing paradigm of male spatiality is the one represented to this point—namely, a sociopolitical sphere of influence wherein the archetypal male unreflectively applies his conditioned responses of virility and self-possessed pride to the world he is continually remaking in his own image— there is also room for a softer, less stark perspective. Maraini portrays a less aggressive male persona: an exploited figure himself, a victim of the same society that disempowers its women citizens. This is the S_1B zone, where we identify a much more sympathetic and comprehending stance on the part of the speaking subject. In *Donne mie,* Maraini makes several statements to that effect: "anche lui è vittima dell'oppressione" (16; "he too is a victim of oppression"). The source of these observations is the historical process itself. Maraini's subject intimates that the attitude that gives man the appearance of despot and predator is transmitted unconsciously from generation to generation: "la storia . . . vi insegna che il soggetto . . . è l'uomo" (39; "history . . . teaches you that the subject . . . is man"). Inside the process of social evolution, the male is seen as abusive or abrasive; however, these character flaws are to an extent excused on the basis of genetic and sociological determinism. The references to "la stoltezza ereditaria" (39; "hereditary stupidity") and to the "storia mimetica" (26; "mimetic history") indicate recognition of the formative and attenuating role played by behavioral norms in the production of the male self-image. In this more compassionate realm, the modern male can also be visualized as being "colonized" by other males and by the State: "lo sfruttamento dell'uomo sull'uomo" (18; "the exploitation of man by man").

From time to time, the tension between this portrayal and the dominant one discussed earlier leads Maraini to subvert or question her more generous view of the contemporary male. For example, she hints that he may be incapable of understanding his actual status as social victim and cannot reverse the historical impulse to dominate; we read: "non sai di non essere mai stato che / una falsa imitazione di te stesso" (*Crudeltà* 59; "you don't realize that you've never been anything / but a fake imitation of yourself"). This evokes a whole series of socially crafted and sanctioned images superimposed on each other as the male grows within his context. At other times, the subversion occurs at the hands of the male interlocutor himself, who is accorded considerably greater self-awareness than is the case in the preceding excerpt. There is, for example, the following remark: "sei una 'vittima di classe' an? / sei un 'oppresso senza speranze' an? / per questo mi violenti / mi strappi la carne / mi entri con le scarpe / nel ventre messo a nudo?" (*Crudeltà* 27; "you're 'a victim of class,' eh? / you're 'hopelessly oppressed,' eh? / is this why you violate me / rip my flesh / with shoes enter / my naked womb?"). The poetic persona believes that the male controls the male-as-victim mythology in order to excuse his aggression. In either case the notion of transgression of a private space applies in this forceful and stark image.

To sum up this portion of the thesis regarding the postulation of a "male hemisphere" expressed in ideological, psychological, emotional and linguistic terms, the poetic subject's main preoccupation is with images of the dominant male who controls his domain by means of privilege or power. A smaller area of concern is reserved for images of a less conspicuously self-willed being propelled by natural and societal forces he neither detects nor comprehends. Such a line of interpretation extends to some of the novels of Maraini in which one critic detects the tracing of a distinctly "prosperous male enclosure" (Merry 198).

The segment of the analogue dealing with the female figure as depicted by the poetic narrator is equally compartmentalized notwithstanding the views of Grazia Sumeli Weinberg, who argues that "women do not have a space in which to represent themselves" (461). The dominant construct is the passive equivalent or opposite of the male figure in S_1A, that is to say, the female victim of exploitation, the subservient figure pointed to in many references to servitude in its transhistorical dimension. There are the "servitù storica" (*Donne mie* 9; "historical servitude") and "destino servile" (8; "servile destiny"). This condition extends to the familial level as well as the social; there is talk of "dovere donnesco" (6; "womanly duty"), "dovere sociale" (6; "social duty"), and "dovere maritale" (45; "marital duty"). We can argue that gender is spatialized to the extent that the locus where these duties are performed is connoted by the adjective in each of the preceding phrases. In other instances, the locus where the exploitation or oppression occurs is explicitly identified, as when the speaker considers herself to be "crocifissa sopra un letto d'amore matrimoniale" (13; "crucified on a bed of matrimonial love"). The unusual position of the adjective *matrimoniale* (at least unusual in the original Italian version) gives rise to a certain ambiguity in the sense that it is displaced for the purpose of characterizing the relationship rather than the bed, thereby reinforcing the lack of spontaneity or romanticism in the union. More graphically depicted is the locus where the drama of female-male interaction takes place in a phrase like: "ti spingono come una / vitella di carne chiara verso la macellazione" (7; "they push you like a / calf with clear flesh toward the slaughter"). Here Maraini forcefully, even brutally, characterizes the places of woman's contact with men as the equivalent of the path to the slaughterhouse, where the soul, if not the flesh, of the female subject is seen to be destroyed. Antonio Porta finds a consistent depiction of women's humiliation in the male environment and regards the female sex as "always defeated and often humiliated, but certainly not tamed, by male power" (53).

Furthermore, in depicting the life of a typical woman in her social surroundings as a role that she is conditioned to recite, Maraini sets up an equivalency between each of the places where the woman resides and the stage. Although the stage is never explicitly mentioned, the ideal woman reader to whom the verses appear to be directed is frequently instructed to be mindful of the fact that there is nothing natural about her cultural roles as mother, daughter, lover or spouse. Some examples follow: "parte da recitare" (*Donne mie* 10; "a part to act out"); "recitare adesso un'altra parte, quella di moglie" (11; "play now another part, that of wife"); "recitare la scena della resa" (12; "act out the scene of surrender"). Maraini deliberately constructs the real spaces in the lives of contemporary women in terms of theatrical surroundings with the result of demythologizing the experience of living. Completing the display of imagery that unambiguously attributes artificiality and lifelessness to the addressees are the direct denunciations of the objectification or deprivation of personality and identity of women by an impersonal society: "siete una proprietà, un lusso / un oggetto prezioso" (39; "you are property, a luxury, / a valuable object"). Woman is to be thought of as "proprietà privata" (13; "private property") or "merce in vendita" (19; "merchandise for sale").

S_2A is the very same territory occupied by the males of S_1A and S_1B but observed from a different angle: that of the female poetic subject decoding the behavior of her female peers. From this perspective, all of society's geographic and psychological spaces are reduced to "prigionia" (*Donne mie* 18; "imprisonment"), a place of torment: "il mondo che ti opprime" (23; "the world that oppresses you"). It is not, strictly speaking, the "invisibilization of women" (Merry 61) that one critic finds in Maraini's novel *Isolina*. This particular quadrant does not receive much attention from Maraini in *Crudeltà all'aria aperta;* there is only one characterization of woman as object: "la nausea di essere la cosa che ero" (61; "the nausea of being the thing I was"). Similarly infrequent are citations of this sort in *Viaggiando con passo di volpe*. Two are especially noteworthy for their relevance to the argument at hand. In the first, a station stands for the marginalization of woman; indeed the theme of departure, in its physical and spiritual dimensions, emerges in "una donna ha perduto se stessa . . . in qualche stazione / con la valigia piena di libri / la lingua chiusa in bocca / come un bene senza valore?" (42; "a woman has lost herself . . . in some station / with a suitcase full of books / her tongue in her mouth / like a worthless asset?"). On the margins of the patriarchal space, woman is displaced and silenced—a view reiterated in the following lines: "le tue bugie . . . mi inchiodano la lingua al palato / mi seppelliscono l'intelligenza / da viva sottoterra" (84; "your lies . . . nail my tongue to my palate / bury my intelligence alive underground"). The station and burial place are conspicuous domains that Bachelard might well be inclined to label as "hostile space."

In *Mangiami pure,* spatialized gender acquires greater prominence in expressions such as: "ma la tenerezza è delle donne mi dici / la maternità la pace il latte la terra / luoghi comuni che ci portiamo in spalle / come bisacce" (21; "tenderness is for women you tell me / motherhood peace milk earth / commonplaces that we carry on our shoulders / like knapsacks"). For the speaker the archetypal, culturally manufactured, feminine myths are tangible landscapes: easily perceived and clearly marked. Also, the usual site of male-female sexuality, the bed, reappears as an arena of repressed violence, something of an altar: "abbiamo tagliato le teste dei / nostri mariti amorosi che si accingevano / ad immolarci come femmine docili / dentro il letto del dovere sociale" (46; "we have cut off the heads of our loving husbands who were about / to sacrifice us like docile women / on the bed of social duty"). An interesting locus of demarcation is also implied in the following quote: "dentro il nuovo medioevo borghese / che ci condanna come streghe sacrileghe / del pensiero scientifico dei padri" (52; "inside the new bourgeois Middle Ages / that condemns us like witches blaspheming against / the scientific thought of the fathers"). Several locations or areas are evoked here, setting up a stark psychological antithesis. The preposition *dentro* ("inside") effectively transforms the society around the speaker into a container or enclosure. Feminist discourse, aligned with the work of witches, evokes visions of burning stakes as the preeminent site of judgment of their activities.

Whereas the male spatial scheme is divided asymmetrically in the sense that S_1A receives considerably more authorial attention and is more conceptually intricate than subzone S_1B, the female matrix appears to be more balanced. Adjacent to S_2A, we find a second spatialized female gender, an S_2B that corresponds to the hypothetical space reserved for assertions relative to the potential of women. There the speaker locates her vision of woman as liberated from automatic behavioral patterns—in short, freed from the cultural stereotypes found in S_1A, S_1B, and S_2A. In this category, it is difficult to identify a specific concrete locus because S_2B is primarily a state of being encouraged in the imagination of the text's female ideal readers residing within the same social space occupied by the exploited and dehumanized women. Instead of designating particular sites where the new or real contemporary woman may reside, the speaker projects a utopia of the mind. She exhorts her addressees to recognize their stereotypical posture, visualize their genuine but latent qualities, and transform the oppressive space into something of an earthly paradise. The poetic subject urges her interlocutors to become aware of their "integrità umana" (*Donne mie* 7; "human integrity"), "integrità / di cuore" (15; "integrity / of the heart"), and "dignità di farfalla" (19; "dignity of a butterfly")—in a word, rediscover their pride, which has been neglected or buried beneath layers of conditioned responses.

Along the same lines, the speaker encourages the female reader to educate herself, to "conoscere la sua diversità" (*Donne mie* 19; "know her difference"), with the most fundamental aspect of this knowledge being the awareness that differences are historically determined and not innate; women are "diverse / dall'uomo per ragioni storiche e non naturali" (26; "different / from man for historical not natural reasons"). Expression of this diversity comprises a direct perception and image making on the part of women who operate independently of the image-forming impulses of male-dominated social structures. To this end the speaker constructs a series of animal metaphors that strongly suggest the true nature of feminine essence: "camelia affamata" (6; "starved camellia"), "agnello dolce" (21; "sweet lamb"), "colombe da cortile" (27; "courtyard doves"), "faina intossicata" (31; "poisoned marten"), and "leonessa che è stata / tenuta pecora" (29; "a lioness that has been / treated like a lamb"). Here, the spatialization of gender results from the selection of animal parallelisms that connote habitats, and from the use of adjectives such as *affamata* ("starved") and *intossicata* ("poisoned"), which connote either a polluted or an abusive environment. The noun *cortile* ("courtyard") has associations of urban enclosure as well as of a medieval aristocratic social code. Functioning as additional markers that designate the placement of the genuine woman beneath the socially manufactured personality construct are phrases denoting liberation: "libere infine di essere noi / intere" (40; "free to be ourselves / whole"). Though the word is often used in nonphysical contexts, *freedom* is a polysemic term that suggests movement not only out of the moral and psychological constraints imposed by the social order but also out of the spaces that Bachelard would identify as "hostile."

The garden, with its phenomenological value as refuge and place of nourishment or growth, serves as a metaphor in *Viaggiando con passo di volpe:* "quel malandato giardino / che viene chiamato cuore" (55; "that neglected garden / called the heart"). These verses indicate that the proper locus for the feminine sensibility has been figuratively closed off by cultural preoccupations that have denatured or falsified original thoughts and sentiments—displacing the subject from an intimate garden into a depersonalizing context. This image of the Garden of Eden undergoes geographical extension in *Mangiami pure,* where we find this exhortation: "il sangue lascialo / correre verso le rive dell'intelligenza / ne faremo bandiere e ventagli amorosi / per la gioia di tutte le donne" (29; "let the blood / flow toward the shores of intelligence / we will make of it flags and fans of love / for the happiness of all women"). The flag is an allusion to the concept of nationhood, as is the word *shores*—suggesting the establishment of a privileged domain where women can realize their potential and construct their ethics and ideology free from harsh male imperatives.

In the same volume, Maraini hints at the existence of a third, intermediate subcompartment of S_2: reserved for the leaders of the feminist movement. While acknowledging that she should share the same ideological space as the radical feminists, the speaker distances herself from them for the reason that they alienate a vast segment of the female population by their condescension. This is the population whom the speaker places in S_2A and S_2B and whom she considers "sisters." She states, for example: "è così difficile amarti, donna emancipata, / per te la casalinga è solo una che si è arresa" (*Mangiami pure* 31; "it is so difficult to love you, emancipated woman, / to you, a housewife is only someone who has surrendered"). The attitudinal distance between the emancipated, self-reliant woman and one who has yet to be emancipated is established without the evocation of a spatiality within which the attitude is translated into the pragmatics of daily living. However, other passages do point to such a domain. Two places, a circle and a harem, are phenomenologically associated with contrasting types of intervention on the part of feminist activists. The first appears in an "affirmative" action context: "dentro lo stretto giro dei coglioni ammantellati / hai piantato la bandiera rossa dell'onore" (32; "within the tight circle of well-dressed jerks / you planted the red flag of honor"). In the circle, the feminist is metaphorically staking out a new territory for her pioneers to settle. Another quote places the feminist in a less flattering posture: "eri il capo della banda, comandavi un harem / di mute bambine dalla gonna immacolata" (32; "you were the leader of the gang, you ruled a harem / of mute girls in immaculate skirts"). This is interesting from a semiotic point of view in that the leader of the women's movement is visualized as operating much the way the decried male despots of S_1A do.

Whereas the loci tend to be categorical and neatly delineated from a phenomenological or semiotic perspective and indicate an equally categorical consciousness on the part of the speaking subject, in the more recent poems there begins to take shape what we may call a "sphere of compromise" or "middle ground" symptomatic of a less confrontational and more conciliatory mentality. In these few but significant poetic statements, adversarial relationships are replaced or at least augmented by those of a different order: one according to which both males and females find themselves operating in a uniformly perplexing or enigmatic space, where knowledge of the self and of the other is extremely problematical. There is in these no exploiter-exploited dichotomy, no master-slave antithesis. For example, we read: "non ci conosciamo / due uccelli che volano / su cieli diversi / senza valigia / senza patente / senza neanche una idea gentile di sé" (*Viaggiando* 32; "we do not know each other / two birds flying / in different skies / without suitcases / without licenses / without the slightest idea of themselves"). The spatial differentiation indicated by the separate skies is more than offset or canceled by the common psychological or epistemic condition of the participants in the analogy. Similar contrast between physical distance and compatible psychologism can be noted in assertions such as: "il telefono chiama / ha la voce lunga il telefono / e lui l'altro, l'amato / non risponde, non fiata" (52; "the phone calls / the phone has a long voice / and he the other, my lover / doesn't answer, / doesn't breathe"). Normally phone lines stand for contact by the transmission of the voice, a synecdoche for the self, from one space to another. Rather than connect or bridge distances, the telephone line appears to emphasize rupture or emotional isolation. The silence encases both male and female within a single space of estrangement inside of which neither party has an advantage.

We also find spaces that unify the speaker and her male companion in "ci baciamo come due del cinema" (*Viaggiando* 74; "we kiss like two people in the movies"). That very same societal structure that in S_1 is a figurative battleground for the sexes, can be a space of commonality: "nella maldestra divisione di classe / che ci fa nemici anche se amanti e amate" (*Mangiami pure* 48; "in the clumsy division of classes / that makes us enemies as well as lovers and loved"). Responsibility and role differentiation are lessened along with the acidity of the speaker. A more compassionate disposition replaces or parallels the hostile one as the speaker appears to suggest that both sexes are equally exposed to cultural and genetic agents that determine the formation of the self. Perhaps the most dynamic imagery of this type is one in which the body itself functions as shared space. In a poem entitled "Lui lei e io" ("He She and I") we find the following two passages: "avendo convissuto senza saperlo per due anni / nello stesso liquido corpo d'uomo" (*Mangiami pure* 16; "having unknowingly cohabited for two years / in the same liquid body"), and: "senza quel corpo di maschio da cui io esco e tu entri" (17; "without that male body that I leave and you enter"). In these images the male body represents something of a locus wherein the female speaking subject establishes an intimacy with the other who becomes integrated with the self. This type of imagery appears to obliterate dividing lines and create shared experiences of affection. In these instances, idyllic or idealized though they may be and by nature inherently rare, affection causes the relationship to be visualized as occurring inside a single space where two bodies and two personalities coalesce. When the speaker's state of mind changes, the notion of separate existences returns, as in fact the second quote confirms.

We can find a third version of S_3 or shared space. In several cases Maraini positions her speaker within boundaries that do not unify, but instead distance the protagonists. Consider for example this reference to "io non credo . . . al tuo fiato che si innesta nel mio / dentro un gelido anello d'argento" (*Dimenticato* 5; "I don't believe in . . . your breath that becomes one with mine / within a cold silvery ring"). Here we have a compelling juxtaposition of unity and disunity within the same frame, characterizing two figures in an unresolved relationship. The fusion of breaths, symbolic of merged spirits, is opposed by the tension of the "cold silvery ring." In an analogous situation, we read: "la bocca cucita / a passo di lupo / torniamo verso casa" (30; "with mouths sewn shut / and walking like wolves / we head for home"). Apparently the couple is entangled in a conflict acted out in the shared space where they walk without communicating, repressing their anger and violent impulses.

In the dramas played out in this third sector, S_3, the actors have the same advantages and disadvantages. Both are subject to the unpredictability and inconstancy of their affective states. The male and female protagonists seem to be at the mercy of incomprehensible natural forces that provoke happiness and dejection alternately, if not simultaneously. Emphasizing this line of interpretation are additional assertions of the sort: "lui e io dentro la pancia / danzante del tempo eretico" (*Dimenticato* 47; "he and I inside the shaking belly / of heretical times"). The subject and her companion are again trapped in an enclosed space within a larger structure: the essence of contemporary malaise. Also depicting herself and her male companion as common exiles from an exponentially greater phenomenon that dwarfs the individual are the verses "ci siamo baciati leggermente / inghiottendo gas dolce / lì proprio lì ai confini della storia" (72; "we kissed each other lightly / swallowing sweet gas / precisely there on the border of history"). The vastness and the unknowability of spatialized destiny or the evolutionary process appear to erase the more localized or temporally specific S_1 and S_2 in considerations such as these.

In conclusion, the three major spatial schemes constructed by the Maraini poetic subject appear to be distinct and separate areas of activity: one occupied by males, one occupied by females, and another that serves as a common site for both sexes. The segmentation is quantifiable in the sense that it is possible to identify males that tend to exhibit primary attitudes that would relegate them to the S_1A or S_2B areas as well as women who could be placed in any of the subgroups slotted in the S_2 zone.

A smaller number of relationships would probably qualify for inclusion in the more moderate S_3. Upon reflection, it becomes apparent that the three spaces are actually the same space viewed or regarded with different standards and could be better displayed as shown in figure 2. S_3 represents the actual space shared by males and females facing common existential conditions.

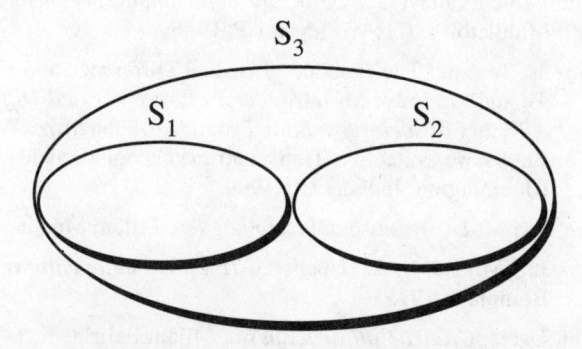

Fig. 2. Revised spheres of influence in Maraini's poetry.

Within this psychophysical sphere, certain situational factors draw individuals closer together, while others drive them apart. However, cultural and ideological forces combine with genetic markers to create gender and gender consciousness: hence the emergence of the ideological spaces S_1 and S_2 within the general societal space S_3. The margins are fairly well defined as far as collective or categorical forms such as patriarchy and subservience are concerned, but ill defined in particular terms. Stated differently, the categorization mechanism functions less precisely in individual or particular terms, as certain persons may exhibit traits that relegate them to the S_1 in one set of social circumstances and slide them into S_2 in another. While delineating the antagonisms that segregate men from women, Maraini suggests the need to reduce the value or applicability of figure 1 and to increase the value or applicability of figure 2 as a mode of interaction between the sexes, thereby promoting a more collaborative and compassionate mentality on both sides of the gender borderline.

Corrado Federici

Notes
1. All translations are mine.

Works Cited

Bachelard, Gaston. *The Poetics of Space.* Trans. M. Jolas. Boston: Beacon, 1969.

Birnbaum, Lucia Chiavola. *Liberazione della donna: Feminism in Italy.* Middletown, CT: Wesleyan UP, 1986.

de Lauretis, Teresa. "The Practice of Sexual Difference and Feminist Thought in Italy: An Introductory Essay." *Sexual Difference: A Theory of Social-Symbolic Practice.* By the Milan Women's Bookstore Collective. Trans. Patricia Cicogna and de Lauretis. Bloomington: Indiana UP, 1990.

Lotman, Juri M. *La struttura del testo poetico.* Milan: Mursia, 1972.

Lotman, Juri M., and B. A. Uspenskij. *Tipologia della cultura.* Milan: Bompiani, 1975.

Maraini, Dacia. *Crudeltà all'aria aperta.* Milan: Feltrinelli, 1966.

———. *Dimenticato di dimenticare.* Turin: Einaudi, 1982.

———. *Donne mie.* Turin: Einaudi, 1974.

———. *Mangiami pure.* Turin: Einaudi, 1978. Published in English as *Devour Me Too.* Montreal: Guernica, 1978.

———. *Viaggiando con passo di volpe: poesie 1983–1991.* Milan: Rizzoli, 1991. Published in English as *Traveling in the Gait of a Fox.* Kingston, ON: Quarry, 1992.

Marchese, Angelo. *Introduzione alla semiotica della letteratura.* Turin: SEI, 1981.

———. *Metodi e prove strutturali.* Milan: Principato, 1979.

———. *Visiting Angel: interpretazione semiologica della poesia di Montale.* Milan: SEI, 1977.

Merry, Bruce. *Women in Modern Italian Literature.* Townsville, Austral.: James Cook U of North Queensland, 1990.

Porta, Antonio, ed. *Poesia degli anni settanta.* Milan: Feltrinelli, 1980.

Sumeli Weinberg, Grazia. "All'ombra del padre: la poesia di Dacia Maraini in *Crudeltà all'aria aperta.*" *Italica* 67.4 (Winter 1990): 453–65.

Elisabetta Properzi Nelsen

Écriture Féminine as Consciousness of the Condition of Women in Dacia Maraini's Early Narrative

> La vie fait texte à partir de mon corps. Je suis déjà du texte. L'Histoire, l'amour, la violence, le temps, le travail, le désir l'inscrivent dans mon corps...
>
> Hélène Cixous
Entre l'écriture
>
> Life is a text beginning with my own body. I am already part of the text. History, love, violence, time, work and desire write it in my body...

There is a general consensus that Dacia Maraini's early literary production, including both her poetry and her novels from 1962 to 1974, represents one of the most original expressions of Italian feminist literature.[1] In a profile introducing the author to the general public in the 1976 anthology *Donne in poesia* (Women poets), editor Biancamaria Frabotta noted that Maraini had been extremely active in the public debate about women's liberation issues during those years and that her latest novel at that time, *Donna in guerra* (1975; *Woman at War*), was avowedly feminist (120).

Dacia Maraini began her career as a writer in 1962 with the novel *La vacanza* (*The Holiday*), followed by *L'età del malessere* (1963; *The Age of Malaise*), and *Memorie di una ladra* (1974; *Memoirs of a Female Thief*). During the same period she published two volumes of poetry, *Crudeltà all'aria aperta* (1966; Cruelty in the open air) and *Donne mie* (1974; Women of mine). Her literary activity also extended into the area of theater: she was founder and president of the Roman feminist theater association La Maddalena during the 1970s.

Elisabetta Properzi Nelsen

Given this body of work, one can see that these years were a period of active exploration of various types of writing for the author. The range of Maraini's output is indicative of her effort to master the tools of her craft and, at the same time, to introduce new forms of literary expression with respect to both content and style. The search for, and achievement of, these new ways of writing derived from an in-depth analysis of women's role in society, and consequently, of women's role as writers. In this context, we need to ask which novels by female authors could have served as models for writers seeking to create new modes of representing women in literature. We also need to keep in mind that the issue was not so much a question of themes as one of style and language.

Without a doubt, one of the earliest feminist works to appear in Italy was Sibilla Aleramo's *Una donna* (1906). Her autobiographical narration became a prototype of an exemplary and extremely topical literary genre: the firsthand account of women's conditions in Italy presented from the perspective of a rigorously Marxist ideological framework. Four decades later, the years after World War II were a period in which women writers flourished, and perhaps the three most significant works produced by them were Natalia Ginzburg's *É stato così* (1947), Anna Banti's *Artemisia* (1947), and Elsa Morante's *Menzogna e sortilegio* (1948). At the time of their publication, the prevailing literary climate in Italy was largely dominated by the interests of male literary traditions of the 1940s, which centered on the historical novel, *prosa d'arte,* and the increasingly influential neorealist movement in literature. These interests tended to inhibit, if not obscure, the widespread appreciation of the author's gender difference and of its literary representation. In addition, all three writers mentioned always rejected being labeled feminist authors, insisting instead upon the neutrality of the writer's role and psyche and on the "objectivity of every human experience" represented in a novel (Morante, "Nove" 23). The human drama of the novelist, however, can also include the drama of acknowledging one's own sex, and consequently, that of the woman writer's different frame of reference in her journey of exploration through the real world.

In Ginzburg's *É stato così,* the main character is perhaps the closest precursor of Enrica in *L'età del malessere* and Vanna in *Donna in guerra*. Through the device of an inner—and later written—confession, the narrator-protagonist in *É stato così* recounts the motives that drove her to kill her husband. In spare and somber prose, Ginzburg's petite bourgeoise, betrayed and rejected by her husband, affirms her identity by murdering him. Symbolically and paradoxically, this final act marks the dawning of her courage to write her own novel. But Ginzburg's anonymous heroine is unsettling: she is an anachronistic and idiosyncratic presence on the neorealist horizon of the postwar years and is certainly closer to the psychological portrayals of protagonist-authors in the French and Russian novel. In spite of this, she spawned a series of portraits of disturbing women by numerous Italian female authors.

I do not know if *É stato così* was ever a source of inspiration to Dacia Maraini, who began her writing career during the Italian economic boom of the sixties and matured as an author during a period of general political ferment and consciousness-raising: the first half of the seventies, which witnessed the birth of a highly organized feminist movement. The Italian women's movement has been more heavily influenced by French feminists' philosophical and psychoanalytical ideas than by Anglo-Americans' pragmatic focus, but Italian feminists have always been consistent in their commitment to radically change the status of women in society. In addition to demanding civil rights (such as divorce and abortion) and heightening political awareness of sexual violence against women, the Italian feminist movement focused on issues regarding Italy's government and on terrorism, which came to define the controversial "anni di piombo."[2] Italian feminism was also able to define a new women's role. The creation of this identity was not only a result of the social emancipation of women, but above all, of a reevaluation of sexual differences and of the intrinsic nature of femininity.[3]

Dacia Maraini's early novels constitute authentic and solid pieces of writing, and they are still an important record of the intellectual and political debate of those years: a product of the keen critical sensibility of a writer who sought to link together the crucial issues of gender, narrative discourse, and political stance. Hers is a way of telling a woman's story through provocative prose that portrays the female protagonists of her novels in a new light. The main female characters are given prominence by their isolation and marginalization, even though they are completely immersed in—and their existence determined by—the social class to which each one belongs.

In *L'età del malessere,* the protagonist Enrica lives in a squalid neighborhood in Rome with her mother, a routine office worker, and her father, a disillusioned old man and borderline schizophrenic who spends his time building elaborate bird cages that no one will ever buy. While still in high school, Enrica has an affair with Cesare, who is older, in college, and whom she considers more mature. He is not in love with her, but he keeps her around for sexual amusement when he is not preoccupied with his studies.

Vanna in *Donna in guerra,* like Enrica, belongs to an intermediate social stratum between the working class and the petite bourgeoisie. She is an elementary school teacher, and her husband, Giacinto, a mechanic, believes in the traditional values of the nuclear family and of the man as the paternalistic head of the household.

In *Memorie di una ladra* there is a shift downward in the choice of social class portrayed. Teresa belongs to the swarming lumpen proletariat of modern Rome, occupying an intermediate social position between the peasant and working classes. She comes from a broken home and a large dysfunctional family, and when her mother dies she is left on her own, despite the presence of her father and various siblings. She then embarks on a career of theft and fraud that results in her imprisonment. The "memoirs of a thief" are hence compiled from her own account of her life, including her escape attempts, lovers, and pregnancy. She reveals the sexual violence and abuse she suffered at home and in prison, and alternates between resolutions to change her life and periods of backsliding.

The lives of all three of the protagonists above constitute an indictment of women's extreme marginalization and exploitation, so prevalent in a rigidly Catholic culture that allows very few roles for women: invariably the guardian of the hearth and family (the wife, mother, servant, and nurse)—and her antithesis—the prostitute. Nonetheless, at the end of all three works, each protagonist manages to find her own ability to reason and judge and a personal way of weighing the experiences of the past. This is a hard-won freedom, and it constitutes a new consciousness that will lead her to make radical choices and to become, literally, "a woman at war."

The segregation, repression, and exploitation of women is asserted by Maraini through the adoption of her own feminine style. Although mainly forged as a result of the feminist political choices that she made when she was writing these three works, this style seems to anticipate *avant la lettre* later French feminist research and practice on women's writing by Julia Kristeva, Hélène Cixous, Luce Irigaray, and Monique Wittig. The concept of *écriture féminine,* developed during the late seventies and early eighties, postdates Maraini's early fiction by many years and is still evolving. Yet one can discern in those first novels an indication of a mode of writing that is subversive and deconstructive.[4] Moreover, Maraini's early works already raise the issue of the textuality of sex, which subsequently became the main focus of debate of much highly original French feminist criticism.

To analyze this aspect of Maraini's writing, it is important to examine certain recurrent structures and themes in the three novels mentioned above, which are handled through what could be defined as characteristic Marainian *écriture féminine.* These structures and motifs can be defined as follows: (1) The first-person narrative voice, the "I" that recurs in all three novels. Within the traditional genres of the private female diary and the personal letter, it creates a new language: the voice of the body, which expresses both physical and psychological levels of personality. This voice communicates in a raw language of disenchantment and repressed desire, and it expresses boredom, impatience, disgust, and rage. (2) Love as a deconstructed and unromanticized feeling that is experienced in an often tormented relationship between a woman and a man. In Maraini's works, such a relationship is typically accompanied by a dysfunctional family setting as well. (3) The liberated woman's attainment of consciousness. This results in her ability to speak in her own words and claim her own freedom of expression. In doing so, she provokes a break with the traditional and historically codified male mode of writing, and she thereby forges an unconventional new literature by and for women.

Elisabetta Properzi Nelsen

Women's Attainment of Self

Fundamental to Dacia Maraini's early work is the role of a narrator–main character who speaks in the first person. Accordingly, Enrica, Vanna, and Teresa all write their own stories and are, at the same time, protagonists of their plots. All feminist criticism recognizes the use of the first person as a constant in female narration. Indeed, the female predilection for autobiography (real and fictional) and for the diary as tools for gaining knowledge about one's own sex and role can intentionally reproduce forms of self-analysis.[5] In some instances, Maraini's story in the first person seeks to eliminate the distance between author and character, eschewing objectivity and intentionally expressing her own subjectivity. In this case, the personal story does not consist solely of a simple transcription of events experienced. The author also interweaves and superimposes her own personal identity in the telling of a series of facts. One could say that the "I" and the "she" disappear, having been subsumed in a dimension that is midway between autobiography and fiction. This particular relationship of the "I" and the "she" in Maraini's works is, however, just one of the configurations of them that she used in these novels—all of which could perhaps be called "campioni d'esistenza al femminile" (Nozzoli 69; "examples of women's lives"). Enrica, Vanna, and Teresa are therefore "campioni d'esistenza al femminile" because they are examples of the lives of women to whom the woman-writer Maraini gives voice and with whom she herself identifies in a personalized dimension of awareness and self-awareness—even though the three novels employ different modes of plot exposition.

Indeed, *L'età del malessere* follows a chronological division of the novel into parts, while the two subsequent works fit more clearly into the traditional genre definitions of the personal diary and autobiography. In contrast to them, Enrica's account can almost be considered a journalistic report. Her story is told in sections, which are not necessarily numbered, and it evokes several of Alberto Moravia's existentialist novels as models. From the very first page, the use of the report creates a sense of detachment between the "I" of the narrator and her experience, as though the story she is telling were not her own—and in doing so she effectively portrays a sense of alienation from self in women. *L'età del malessere* opens with the single phrase:

"Mi venne ad aprire il padre di Cesare" (9; "Cesare's father . . . opened the door for me"), where the contrast between the anonymous indirect object pronoun in the first person and the tight introduction of the other two male characters is immediately apparent. To find out the gender of this "mi," one must read through the following nine sentences and then identify it in the phrase "mi aveva già sentita arrivare" (9; "he had already heard me arrive"). Here the letter "a" at the end of the past participle "sentita" is recognized as grammatically feminine and singular and, consequently, so is the pronoun "mi" to which it refers. Still, the name of the narrator-protagonist "I" is not revealed to the reader until the second chapter, when she is called by name by another male character, Carlo. In the first two segments, the narrator does not identify herself, nor explain who she is, where she lives, or what she does. This narrating "I" is defined by other characters (Cesare's father, Cesare, Cesare's fiancée on the telephone, Enrica's mother, Enrica's father, Carlo, and the friends at the party) who are introduced in their order of appearance according to the unfolding of events.

In *Donna in guerra,* apart from the detailed exposition of the daily diary entries and the precise annotation of dates, the narrator's personal description of herself follows a pattern that is more or less analogous to that in *L'età del malessere*—but here the reader is immediately aware of the writer's gender from the title and the first page of the diary. Vanna presents herself doing household and cooking chores at the time of menstruation:

> Mi sono vestita. Ho pulito la casa. Ho messo a posto il baule. . . . Quando ho finito erano le dodici. Avevo ancora da preparare i peperoni ripieni. Dovevo pulire l'insalata. Mi facevano male le gambe. E avevo una fitta ai reni. . . . Mi sono addormentata. Ho sognato che una talpa scavava un tunnel nel mio ventre. Mi sono svegliata con una fitta, un dolore sordo e fondo. Qualcosa di caldo mi bagnava le cosce. Ho cacciato una mano sotto la gonna. L'ho ritirata macchiata di sangue. (3)

> I got dressed. I cleaned the house. I finished packing the trunk. . . . It was noon when I'd finished. I still had to cook the stuffed peppers and wash the lettuce. My legs hurt and I had a sharp pain in my lower back. . . . I fell asleep and dreamed a mole was digging a tunnel through my abdomen. I woke up with a deep, stabbing pain. Something warm was

Elisabetta Properzi Nelsen

> running down my thigh. I stuck my hand up under my skirt.
> I pulled it back stained with blood.

The diary, which begins on August 1, 1970, recounts various kinds of personal female trauma: (1) precipitated by events (Vanna's account of her vacation in Addis); (2) related to social class (Vanna, an elementary school teacher, is married to Giacinto, a mechanic); (3) psychological (Vanna makes us experience her feelings and her way of perceiving and relating to her partner and the other characters); and (4) physiological (from the very beginning, we know when Vanna is menstruating). I would say, moreover, that the physiological trauma Vanna suffers is the most significant new element in this novel: the existential story of the main character coincides with what she is undergoing physiologically during the course of her inner experiences and with the ordinary physical manifestations of the female body. It is in this sense that the diary of her vacation begins with a "rivolo di sangue benefico" (4; "a trickle of healthful blood"), which marks her potential sense of freedom and happiness.

As an autobiographical novel halfway between a book of memoirs (as suggested by its title) and a police report, *Memorie di una ladra* recounts the main character's personal history from past to present. She begins the story at her birth and continues until she has nothing left to recall, which is up to the present—a point in time where she describes herself as a chronically incarcerated thief. This sort of feminine "mie prigioni," while certainly less romantic and disenchanted than the *Risorgimento* novel, is interesting precisely because of the way it uncovers the past.[6] In the previous two novels, the present was the current time from which the protagonist's future would begin, but in *Memorie di una ladra,* Teresa's journey proceeds in reverse and constitutes a personal and political revision, respectively, of her past experiences and her social condition as a disenfranchised woman.

The language of the body is apparent even in the first pages, where Teresa recalls her own birth:

> Dicono che sono nata male, mezza asfissiata dal cordone ombelicale che mi si era arrotolato attorno al corpo come un serpente. Mia madre credeva che ero morta e mio padre stava per buttarmi nell'immondizia. (5)

> They say I was ill born, nearly asphyxiated by the umbilical cord wrapped around my body like a snake. My mother thought I was dead, and my father was going to throw me in the garbage.

Here the physical language has psychological and mythological overtones. For example, the umbilical cord functions as a biblical image that links women to the root of evil in an almost archetypal and primal way: "Dicono che sono nata male" ("They say I was ill born"). In other words, being "nata male" is an experience that not only describes the specific way in which Teresa was born but also constitutes a more general, negative symbolism that applies to the birth of every woman.

Elsewhere, language specifically pertaining to the female body appears in the sixth paragraph of Teresa's childhood recollections, where she recounts seeing her mother masturbating. This is a memory that she doesn't fully understand until she personally experiences the same act:

> Ho messo l'occhio al buco della chiave e ho visto mio padre che dormiva raggomitolato a bocca aperta e mia madre seduta tutta nuda sul letto che rideva e si toccava con le dita in mezzo alle gambe.
> Lì per lì ho pensato che giocava. E così ho continuato a pensare per molti anni. Poi però ho cominciato a farlo anch'io questo gioco e allora ho capito che non era per niente un gioco ma qualcosa di forte e di ubriacante. (6)
>
> I put my eye up to the keyhole and saw my father sleeping curled up with his mouth open and my mother sitting up naked on the bed laughing and touching herself with her fingers between her legs.
> At the time I thought she was playing, and I continued to think so for many years. But later on I, too, began to play this game and then I realized that it wasn't a game at all, but something powerful and intoxicating.

This is a description of intimate sexual behavior—all but unacceptable in literary work by women until the mid-twentieth century.[7] While doing so in terms that are far from graphic, Maraini did break a taboo by representing what had been traditionally unmentionable—in this case, the fulfillment of female sexual desire without a man. This can be explained if one surmises that she had already devised forms of expression that were symptomatic of what would later be defined as female writing.

"The Laugh of the Medusa," Hélène Cixous's 1975 essay, a true manifesto of the concept of *écriture féminine,* sparked the debate about the specific issue of woman's language.[8] If one's mind is aware of one's own gender, can one identify a characteristic pattern of knowledge informing women's creative expression? Cixous defines *écriture féminine,* ultimately, as a liberating act—and she says so emphatically, in a tone that is alternately polemical, combative, and exhortatory. According to this scholar, a woman must write about herself as well as about other women, and above all, must bring women back to writing—from which they have been driven away as violently as they have been from their own bodies: a woman has to put herself into the text at least as much as she participates in the world around her and becomes a part of history. The concept of *écriture féminine* is defined as "physical" writing, and, thus, the mastery of one's own body goes hand in hand with the mastery of one's body of prose or poetry:

> Write yourself. Your body must be heard. . . . TO WRITE. An act which will not only realize the decensored relation of woman to her sexuality, to her womanly being, giving her access; it will give her back her goods, her pleasure, her organs, her immense bodily territories which have been kept under seal. . . . (250)

It is remarkable how Maraini's early prose resembles the energy of these subsequent declarations by Cixous as well as the commitment to overcome the so-called neutrality of writing and the idea of woman as a "dark continent"—a place that cannot be explored, the realm of the Medusa and the Abyss, synonyms for death (Magli 167–68). Maraini notably anticipated others in proving that the "inside" of a woman can be released, exploded, and reinvented in her own language. This personal mode of expression has a subversive quality deriving from its novelty and distinctiveness. In the same way that literary writing establishes itself as radically altered and divergent—the "elsewhere" of language—a woman's use of language constitutes a different voice from male social, political and historical writing.

Écriture Féminine and Maraini's Early Narrative

With her early novels, Maraini took the function and practice of language in a different direction and produced a remarkably original use of it as a result. In bringing her own sexual body into the bodiless realm of forms, Maraini alludes not only to a prelinguistic sexuality (which would correspond to an organic concept of language), but also raises the issue of how language differentiates gender and plays a part in the formation of subjectivity (Fusini 17).

One of the events that leads to the conscious attainment of self by the main character is the act of abortion, a recurring theme in Maraini. The abortion episode is also intertwined with the protagonist's friendship with another female character in the novel, who plays a key role in her development. Both Enrica and Vanna experience an abortion, having made their own choice to terminate an unwanted pregnancy. In Enrica's case, the abortion occurs midway through the novel. This event marks the beginning of the second half of the story, when she decides to leave her father's house to go to live with, and work for, Countess Bardengo. For Vanna, the abortion takes place almost at the end of the book. It seals her decision to leave her husband and begin a new life. Following her friendship with the rebellious, morally ambiguous, and suicidal Suna, Vanna too finds the strength to leave Giacinto after meeting her eccentric colleague Rosa, a sad, older woman who has turned her apartment into a menagerie for household pets.

Both Vanna and Enrica obtain an abortion illegally.[9] Through their personal testimony, Maraini describes the medical procedure from an exclusively female point of view. She presents a situation of bodily suffering that cannot be "urlato" ("screamed out") because the operation is carried out clandestinely. In these terms, she effectively conveys the loneliness and physical pain of the experience, which is described as "acuto" ("acute"), "brutale" ("brutal"), and "selvaggio" ("savage"). It surges through the body like a "scossa elettrica" ("electric shock"). The protagonist also tries to give meaning to the sensation of "frugare" ("being poked and prodded") inside her woman's body in order to have it emptied after having been "aperta, squarciata e raschiata a lungo" ("opened, ripped, and scraped for a long time") (114–15).

These two experiences of "writing" abortion closely correspond to a concept elaborated by Cixous. She has postulated the presence of a dramatically autonomous "I" that seizes control as an "author," creator and authority on language—which then functions as an "inscription of the feminine" (Conley 14). It was an act of courage on Maraini's part to talk about a subject as sensitive and secret as a woman's decision to reject motherhood. It is as though the writer saw in the decision to have an abortion one of her protagonists' few opportunities for self-affirmation as "authors." Paradoxically, their "authorship" is born of their courage to admit explicitly their nonmotherhood and their decision to not create—in order to attain their wholeness as women. Conversely, in the novels of other Italian female writers, the relationship between mother and child has often functioned as a common thematic device of narration leading the mother/protagonist to a conscious awareness of both her own generative force and the new being that issues from it. But in these early novels by Maraini, the narrating I / female protagonist achieves self-affirmation, alone and radically free, outside of motherhood.[10] "L'estate è vicina pensai e presto comincerà per me una nuova vita . . ." (*L'età* 195; "Summer is just around the corner, I said to myself, and I'll start a new life . . ."; *Age* 203); "Gli ho detto che voglio stare sola. Gli ho chiuso il portone in faccia. . . . Ora sono sola e ho tutto da ricominciare" (*Donna in guerra* 269; "I told him I wanted to be left alone and I closed the door in his face. . . . Now I'm alone and I must start everything again from the beginning"; *Woman at War* 282).

Perhaps it is precisely in these uncomfortable endings of our protagonists that we can detect the birth "of the new type of intellectual" who is, above all, female, as would be foreseen by Kristeva only a few years after the publication of *Donna in guerra*. These early Marainian women, eternally exiled from *Sense* and the *Law* (in Kristeva's evocative terminology from *Hérétique de l'amour*), reclaim their right to the uniqueness of their voice, their subconscious, their desires, and their needs. Through "heretical" writing, wrested from the ever-recurring paternal discourse, they assert their own "I" in a new narrative identity.

Love

> Sentivo contro le mie caviglie i suoi piedi freddi. Mi strinse fino a farmi soffocare. Finì subito e si buttò dall'altra parte a dormire. (*L'età* 11)

> I felt his cold feet against my ankles. He held me so tight I nearly suffocated. It was quickly over, and he rolled onto the other side to go to sleep. (*Age* 9)

> Abbiamo mangiato il pesce arrostito sul carbone. Abbiamo fatto l'amore. In fretta, come al solito, senza darmi il tempo di arrivare in fondo. . . . Poi lui si è messo a dormire nella sua solita posizione contratta di difesa, le gambe e le braccia piegate sotto il mento. (*Donna in guerra* 11)

> We ate the fish and afterwards we made love. Quickly, as usual, without giving me time to come properly. . . . He falls asleep in his usual contracted position, his legs and arms bent under his chin. (*Woman at War* 11)

Despite their love for their partners, the protagonists Enrica and Vanna are in a subordinate position in their relationship with men. Enrica loves Cesare, but she knows that her relationship with him will not lead to marriage. The tone of their lovemaking conveys to the reader the girl's feeling of being drawn into an abusive and dead-end relationship. We find the same atmosphere in the relationship between Vanna and Giacinto. The author introduces us to them in a summer setting and presents what at first glance appears to be a happy couple on vacation; but Vanna's description of her sexual relationship with her husband replicates the same level of female dissatisfaction and male indifference underscored by Enrica. The woman seeks out and wants sex as the fulfillment of her feelings, but the boredom in the relationship, which is controlled by the man, is the consequence of the male partner's continual neglect of his female companion.

In *L'età* these types of love situations mirror the emotionally dysfunctional patterns that characterize the two partners' respective families. Cesare lives alone with his father, who is probably a voyeur attempting to cope with repressed sexual desire. Enrica's parents, in turn, live like two ghosts in the shadow of their former love, which neither can feel any longer. Her mother is haggard and neglected, and her father is preoccupied by his bird cages and his alcoholism. Vanna and Giacinto, on the other hand, give the appearance of being independent of their family backgrounds and a model nuclear couple, but their inability to communicate with one another increasingly wears away the traditional facade of their marriage.

Elisabetta Properzi Nelsen

From these portrayals of relationships, one deduces not only that the love they formerly contained has been totally exhausted, but that they also offer situations that are ripe in their potential for the exploitation of the woman. Indeed, Maraini's early fiction can be said to show that an amorous relationship for women forces them into a situation of emotional isolation. There is no expression of ecstasy, enthusiasm, exaltation, or the impulse to be happy. Rather, there is weariness, boredom, passivity, haste, silence, separation, and pain. The romantic dimension of love is deconstructed, and physical, emotional, and mental incomprehension are its manifestations.

The only one who seems to see clearly her own dire situation as a woman exploited by love is Teresa, the thief. From the beginning, Teresa is aware of the equation "woman = exploitation." This formula is particularly clear when she recalls her mother's life, which was marked by numerous pregnancies and endless catering to male needs. Consequently, it is no accident that both Enrica's and Teresa's mothers die prematurely because of the neglect of their health. In similar fashion, Teresa too will always seek protection in her encounters with various men: her husband Sisto and her lovers Nino Castagna and Ercoletto. In Teresa, we find an almost natural acceptance of society's violence against poor, disenfranchised women; and by creating her, Maraini boldly depicts a particularly provocative female character. The continual male violence to which she is subjected (she is committed to a mental institution for presumed mental illness, is abandoned by her husband, is lured into prostitution, and has her child taken away from her) makes her devise extreme defense mechanisms for her own survival, such as theft and fraud. Teresa, it appears, is drawn to love by curiosity and not by necessity. So it seems to be no coincidence that her last lover, Ercoletto, is also her "business associate" and fellow prisoner. According to this logic, her curiosity would also explain why she eventually learns to transform her need for love. But Teresa recasts her desire and, ostensibly, makes herself sexually independent with what she calls "sesso freddo" ("cold sex"). This is the term she uses to refer to her sexual fantasies, which are never expressed in any physical way. This kind of sublimation reveals itself in Teresa's creation of a vivid sexual imagination:

> Questo è il difetto che ho. Fisicamente sono un tipo freddo. Con l'uomo mi faccio pure la parte mia. Ma se l'uomo non c'è, me lo rinnovo nella fantasia, me lo rimiro al nudo, dentro la testa, lo bacio, lo carezzo, lo godo senza di lui, fra me e me. (*Memorie* 264)
>
> This is my flaw. Physically, I am a cold type. With a man, I'll do my part. But if there is no man, I make him up in my imagination, I gaze at him naked, inside my head, I kiss him, I caress him, I enjoy the man in his absence, all by myself.

Teresa modifies her need for love in this way. The man she loves becomes an inner image to be recalled and enjoyed (similar to a Petrarchan metaphor) who, "rimirata" ("gazed at") in the female mind, gives her pleasure without making her suffer. In this sense, the female is raised from her subordinate position by her ability to enjoy love in her mind all by herself—so that on the one hand we are tempted to interpret her solipsistic fantasies as an argument for sexual self-sufficiency. On the other hand, her imaginary erotic life can be seen as a "manifesto" that presents an indictment of male/female relations in patriarchal society.

A recurring motif in *L'età del malessere* and *Donna in guerra* is the woman's love for a younger man, who may be barely out of adolescence. In *L'età del malessere,* there is the scene between the decadent and romantic Countess Bardengo and Remo, and, in *Donna in guerra,* Vanna tells us about falling in love with Orio. Seemingly anomalous at first glance, these encounters are the realization of a secret desire related to the desire for motherhood and for that other form of self, the child. This is a unique relationship, controlled by the female character outside of any bourgeois paternalistic practice or use of the female body. Vanna associates Orio with another boy who is a student in her class, and with whom the schoolteacher feels an emotional involvement. The natural and spontaneous love encounter between Vanna and Orio is a result of their mutual sexual attraction. Vanna, the initiator, provokes it and becomes his teacher in love. In the dialogue between the two soon-to-be lovers and in the description of their lovemaking as experienced by Vanna, Maraini's language becomes free and uninhibited. It is as if the language of the woman overcomes the taboo put upon certain acts made unmentionable. Vanna becomes the expert at love who leads the boy Orio to knowledge of his own body and of hers without demeaning herself. For Vanna the encounter is a synonym for youth as opposed to the "old age" of her dull lovemaking routine with her husband:

> —Vuoi farlo con me?
> —Ma se poi tu non vuoi?
> —Te lo sto proponendo io.
> Ha chinato la testa imbarazzato. Era diventato rosso e si mordeva un labbro. Mi sono avvicinata. Gli ho preso la testa fra le mani. L'ho baciato sulla bocca. . . . Si muoveva con pazienza, lento, attento al mio ritmo. E io con lui. Lo stringevo, lo chiudevo fra le braccia con un amore struggente, violento. Ho avuto un orgasmo completo, estenuato. (*Donna in guerra* 102–03)

> "Would you like to do it with me?"
> "What if you don't want to?"
> "I'm suggesting it to you."
> He lowered his head, embarrassed. He blushed and bit his lips. I went up to him. I took his head between my hands. I kissed him on the mouth. . . . He moved slowly, adapting himself to my rhythm. I was doing the same. I clasped him tight in my arms in a violent torment of love. I had a total and uplifting orgasm. (*Woman at War* 104–05)[11]

The opposition between silence and language expresses all of the nuances of this difficult self-awareness gradually attained by the woman. Finally, however, silence is rejected and things are expressed in words in an increasingly confident voice. Taking into consideration Orio's embarrassment and Vanna's sense of daring and willingness to provoke her husband—as well as the shift to the adjective *struggente* ("consuming"; evoking the sublimity of the act) and the unusual use of the word *orgasmo* ("orgasm"; a lexeme that is conventionally not allowed to refer to female libido)—the entire passage resembles an incendiary manifesto that breaks the silence on female sexual desire.

Julia Kristeva provides us with the theoretical underpinnings of Maraini's trial narrative:

> What is it to love, for a woman? The same thing as to write.
> . . . A flash on the unnamable, a web of abstractions to be torn apart, that a body might at last venture out of its shelter, might dare the sense under the veil of words. WORD. FLESH. (31)

By deconstructing the literary theme of love and reinventing it in the affirmation of desire, Maraini releases the female character for the first time from worn-out patriarchal concepts of women in love and deliberately creates a disturbing and subversive figure.[12]

The Commitment to a Feminist Literature

Of additional importance is the fact that the sender and the receiver of Maraini's message are not one and the same, since Maraini's writing is not a kind of consolatory literature that she creates for herself alone. Her attainment of self and her commitment to creating a new type of literature are parallel—but she reveals the desperation and brutality of the everyday lives of her characters in order to reach an audience (specifically: female readers).

These early novels are narrations of individual experiences. However, the lives they recount are not separate from those of others. On the contrary: since the story of one individual woman exemplifies the experiences of many others, these life stories are told in order to bring them before the public. *Donna in guerra* becomes a group documentary precisely because it unfolds around the central nucleus of the relationship between an individual and a community of women. In *L'età del malessere,* this relationship is given form in Enrica's interaction with the other female characters—though they are limited to her mother, and later, to the Countess Bardengo (who assumes the role not only of putative mother, but also of sister in failed love). In *Donna in guerra,* on the other hand, it is the increase in the protagonist's political awareness that is especially striking, which we are able to observe as Vanna gradually matures through her contact with other women. First, Giottina and Tota (women from the lower classes of the island) step in and initiate her into a new type of magical and primal language. It is full of superstition, prejudice, gossip, and exciting anecdotes about sex and wealth.[13]

Later on, Vanna will be influenced by Suna, the beautiful and extremely sensual young girl who suffers from polio. Suna's inner conflict between her need for love and for an autonomous identity will provoke a full-blown crisis in Vanna and bring about a subsequent change in her. Suna will introduce her to a freer sexuality and awaken a political awareness in her of women's conditions.[14]

Finally, in *Memorie di una ladra,* Teresa, the thief, assumes the role of spokesperson for a chorus of unheard women who were abused in Italian slums, mental institutions, and prisons in the early seventies. She avoids any direct political statements—preferring to make tacitly understood references—but the remarks she does make are highly effective and are scattered here and there throughout the realistic narrative of her experiences. Teresa becomes the prototype of the hyper-real portrayal of exploited womanhood.

The three novels analyzed above follow the course of three different women's lives. While they focus on situations and problems of a narrating "I," the plots are constructed in such a way as to adhere to the complexity of women's issues.

As we know, many of the gains of the Italian feminist movement from the seventies have been lost as a result of the return of a certain conservatism over the past two decades. In *Liberazione della donna: Feminism in Italy,* Lucia Chiavola Birnbaum notes that the Italian feminist movement has perhaps been "co-opted" and hemmed in by familiar patriarchal conventions (204). Adele Cambria even goes so far as to conclude that defeat has already occurred, though mainly in the field of literature. She feels that recent writing by women is regressive and conciliatory, and that it has compromised too much with dominant literature (141). Symptomatic of a conservative backlash is the debate between feminism and postmodernism. The latter is a movement of ideas based on premises that have contributed to the gradual exclusion of women's issues. The postmodernists consider the feminist struggle to be over—as they do all political struggles. "The so-called end of 'history' is deemed to include the 'end of women's history' as well" (401).[15] We are witnessing a progressive lack of theoretical interest in the concept of "sexual difference," which has been fundamental to the discussions advanced by French feminists. More than anyone else, Luce Irigaray insisted unconditionally on this concept as the point of departure for creating a "new poetics" to reinterpret the entire relationship between subject and discourse, subject and reality, and between subject and cosmos (Whitford 10).

For her part, Maraini has also upheld the centrality of sexual difference to feminist thought and theory. In the introduction to *Donne in poesia,* she asserts that a separation does indeed exist in literature between masculine and feminine genders; although for her, words are just instruments and do not pertain to any one sex. Yet precisely because words are tools, they have been used to express a male—and not a female—point of view. In Maraini's opinion, women's literary production can successfully abandon accustomed identification with male values only through the agency of a female "solitary and isolated 'I'" who, at the same time, is also terrified of showing that she is different from men—in spite of being aware of and suffering for her diversity (*Donne in poesia* 29–34).

In conclusion, the first stage of Maraini's fiction is symptomatic of the profound changes brought about by feminist theory and literature during the vital formative years of the Italian women's movement. These early novels represent some of the most authentic examples of Italian feminist narrative and paved the way for many other writers whose voices had been previously unheard. They also left a legacy still present in Maraini's recent work: the uncovering and recapture of memory as well as the newfound calmness and self-assurance of her literary maturity, which are due in no small part to the courage she demonstrated in writing these first novels.

Notes

1. All translations are my own unless otherwise indicated.

2. The expression "anni di piombo" ("years of lead") was coined by Italian journalists to refer to the seventies, the famous decade marked by the use of force as a political weapon.

3. For a brief introduction to Italian feminism in the seventies, see Wood.

4. The whole "new wave" of French philosophers such as Jacques Derrida, Michel Foucault, and others (all male), together with the rejection of hierarchies implicit in the social protest movements that were born after 1968, may be seen as the precursors of feminist theory and of later developments such as postcolonial critical thought. All of these movements may be considered deconstructive, and thus they connect Maraini indirectly to what produced *écriture féminine.*

5. For an example of feminist autobiography based on the experience of psychoanalysis, see Cardinal.

Elisabetta Properzi Nelsen

6. I refer here to Silvio Pellico's 1832 book of memoirs *Le mie prigioni* (My prisons), about his ten years of incarceration for engaging in revolutionary activities during Italy's struggle for independence and unification.

7. This taboo did not weigh against male writers as long or as heavily as it did against women. Alberto Moravia's early novels about the Italian bourgeoisie are a case in point. Beginning with *Gli indifferenti* (1929), he published novels throughout his life in which characters define their search for identity in terms of sexual gratification and the pursuit of wealth. These themes are prominent enough to be of central importance to his novels' structure.

8. For an overview of the positions of Julia Kristeva, Hélène Cixous, Luce Irigaray, and Monique Wittig, see Jones.

9. Despite the fact that Maraini avoids the moral and political debate over the abortion issue, she intentionally underscores the fact that the procedure was illegal and that women who had abortions risked not only medical but possible legal consequences as well, since the act constituted a crime in Italy prior to the passage of the referendum on abortion in 1981. In both *L'età del malessere* and *Donna in guerra* the protagonists stress the clandestine atmosphere in which the two abortions take place. The secrecy involved in the operation lends it the significance of a full-scale criminal act (*L'età* 113–16; *Donna in guerra* 267). In *Donna in guerra,* another abortion story is told about Marta, the servant-lover of Oliver, Suna's teenage brother. In *Memorie di una ladra,* Teresa recalls being surrounded in prison by inmates who are thieves, murderers, and embezzlers, but also by women sentenced for abortion. These instances can also be compared to the account that the inmate Antonia gives of her abortion (296). It should be noted, moreover, that in her 1996 *Un clandestino a bordo* (*Stowaway on Board*), while seemingly reconsidering her views on abortion in the light of her own experiences, Maraini still supports the right to abortion in Italy. At the same time, however, she is concerned with the profound impact that abortion has on women. She concludes that abortion is ultimately a form of defeat, what she calls historical female impotence (24).

10. I am referring here to Elsa Morante's novels *Menzogna e sortilegio, L'isola di Arturo,* and *Aracoeli,* all three of which are built around a narrative recollection of a mother by her respective daughter or son as narrator, and, in an inverse process, to Lalla Romano's *Le parole tra noi leggere,* which revolves around the mother's memories of her relationship with her child. One could go back even further, to Neera (Anna Radius Zuccari) and her unforgettable *L'indomani.*

11. Since Benetti and Spottiswood translate the adjective *struggente* with the word *torment,* my remarks about this adjective in the following paragraph are more easily understood if they are read in relation to my own translation of the second sentence in the last paragraph of *Donna* *in guerra* quoted above. I translate it thus: "I clasped him tight in my arms with a consuming and violent love."

12. Some female characters often resolve the conflict of heterosexual love by choosing homosexuality. In *Donna in guerra,* Suna begins a lesbian affair with Mafalda after her relationship with Santino (she had also been attracted to Vanna). By confronting this aspect of love, which was still considered strange at the time (and was indeed divergent from what most Italians considered acceptable in sexual behavior), Maraini examines nontraditional love relationships that are experienced outside of the mainstream and censured or negated because of it. In the tradition of the Italian female novel, Suna can be considered the forerunner of characters who turn to lesbian love as an attempt at liberation from the traditional heterosexual relationship. On the theme of conflict in the love relationship between two women, see also Maraini's *Lettere a Marina* (1981; *Letters to Marina*).

13. This kind of language, new to Enrica, should also be compared to analogous instances on pages 5, 9–10, 12–13, 23–25, 45–50 and to the episode about the search for the tourist's body, which is emblematic in its use of a narrative fragment as a plot device. Here (74–81), Maraini uses language that resonates with magical and religious overtones because of her repetition of ritualized formulas and mysterious, incomprehensible incantations, and she achieves this in a narrative situation about the plundering of the dead woman's body.

14. One can compare this episode to the one in which Vanna, having returned to teaching, makes her student Maria Stella aware of rape as an act of male violence against women. With regard to this point, see also Tamburri.

15. I am referring to the section "Feminism" in *Postmodernism,* which includes two exhaustive articles: one by Morris (368–69) and the other by Lovibond (390–414).

Works Cited

Aleramo, Sibilla. *Una donna.* 1906. Milan: Feltrinelli, 1977.

Banti, Anna. *Artemisia.* 1947. Milan: Mondadori, 1974.

Birnbaum, Lucia Chiavola. *Liberazione della donna: Feminism in Italy.* Middletown, CT: Wesleyan UP, 1986.

Cambria, Adele. "Il neo-femminismo in letteratura: dove sono le amazzoni." *Firmato donna: una donna un secolo.* Ed. Sandra Petrignani. Rome: Il Ventaglio, 1986.

Cardinal, Marie. *Le parole per dirlo.* Trans. Natalie Banas. Milan: Bompiani, 1979.

Cixous, Hélène. *Entre l'écriture.* Paris: Des Femmes, 1986.

Cixous, Hélène. "The Laugh of the Medusa." *New French Feminisms.* Ed. Elaine Marks and Isabelle de Courtivron. Amherst: U of Massachusetts P, 1980. 245–64. Originally published in French in 1975.

———. *Three Steps on the Ladder of Writing.* Trans. Sarah Cornell and Susan Sellers. New York: Columbia UP, 1983.

Cixous, Hélène, and Catherine Clément. *The Newly Born Woman.* Trans. Betsy Wing. Minneapolis: U of Minnesota P, 1986.

Conley, Verena Andermatt. *Hélène Cixous: Writing the Feminine.* Lincoln: U of Nebraska P, 1991.

Docherty, Thomas, ed. *Postmodernism: A Reader.* New York: Columbia UP, 1993.

Frabotta, Biancamaria, ed. *Donne in poesia: antologia della poesia femminile in Italia dal dopoguerra a oggi.* 1976. Rome: Savelli, 1977.

Fusini, Nadia. "Sulle donne e il loro poetare." *Nuova DWF* 5 (Oct.–Dec. 1977): 5–21.

Ginzburg, Natalia. *É stato così.* Turin: Einaudi, 1947.

Irigaray, Luce. *Passions élémentaires.* Paris: Minuit, 1973.

Jones, Rosalind. "Writing the Body: Toward an Understanding of 'l'écriture féminine.'" *Feminist Studies* 7.2 (1981): 247–63.

Kristeva, Julia. "Hérétique de l'amour." *Tel Quel* 74 (1977): 17–38.

Lovibond, Sabina. "Feminism and Postmodernism." Docherty 390–414.

Magli, Ida. *La donna: un problema aperto.* Florence: Vallecchi, 1974.

Maraini, Dacia. *The Age of Malaise.* Trans. Frances Frenaye. New York: Grove, 1963.

———. *Un clandestino a bordo.* 1993. Milan: Rizzoli, 1996. Published in English as *Stowaway on Board.* Trans. Giovanna Bellesia and Victoria Offredi Poletto. West Lafayette, IN: Bordighera, 2000.

———. *Donna in guerra.* Turin: Einaudi, 1975. Published in English as *Woman at War.*

———. *L'età del malessere.* Turin: Einaudi, 1963. Published in English as *The Age of Malaise.*

———. Introduction. *Donne in poesia: antologia della poesia femminile in Italia dal dopoguerra a oggi.* 1976. Rome: Savelli, 1977.

———. *Lettere a Marina.* Milan: Bompiani, 1981. Published in English as *Letters to Marina.* London: Camden, 1987. Freedom, CA: Crossing, 1988.

———. *Memorie di una ladra*. Milan: Rizzoli, 1994. Published in English as *Memoirs of a Female Thief*. London: Abelard-Schuman, 1973.

———. *Woman at War*. Trans. Mara Benetti and Elspeth Spottiswood. New York: Italica, 1989.

Morante, Elsa. *Aracoeli*. Turin: Einaudi, 1957.

———. *L'isola di Arturo*. Turin: Einaudi, 1957.

———. *Menzogna e sortilegio*. Turin: Einaudi, 1948.

———. "Nove domande sul romanzo." *Nuovi Argomenti* 38–39 (1975): 17–38.

Morris, Meaghan. "Feminism, Reading, Postmodernism." Docherty 368–69.

Neera [Anna Radius Zuccari]. *L'indomani*. Palermo: Sallerio, 1981.

Nozzoli, Anna. "Sul romanzo femminista italiano degli anni settanta." *Nuova DWF* 5 (Oct.–Dec. 1977): 55–74.

Romano, Lalla. *Le parole tra noi leggere*. Turin: Einaudi, 1969.

Tamburri, Anthony. "Dacia Maraini's *Donna in guerra*." *Contemporary Women Writers in Italy*. Ed. Santo Aricò. Amherst: U of Massachusetts P, 1990. 139–51.

Whitford, Margaret, ed. *The Irigaray Reader*. Oxford: Blackwell, 1991.

Wood, Sharon. Introduction. *Italian Women Writing*. Ed. Wood. New York: Manchester UP, 1993. 1–25.

Part 3
Poetics and Practices of Liberation

Virginia Picchietti
Symbolic Mediation and Female Community
in Dacia Maraini's Fiction

Giovanna Bellesia
Variations on a Theme: Violence against
Women in the Writings of Dacia Maraini

Daniela Cavallaro
Dacia Maraini's "Barricade Theater"

Virginia Picchietti

Symbolic Mediation and Female Community in Dacia Maraini's Fiction

In her project for women's liberation, Dacia Maraini looks beyond the entrenched family structure to give primary space in women's lives to female friendships.[1] Historically, friendships between women have been culturally devalued and relegated to separate "female" spheres. But as Maraini shows in her works and as Italian feminists have long theorized, these bonds play a prominent and powerful role in effecting personal as well as social change. In the works examined here—the 1970 play *Il manifesto* (The manifesto), the 1975 novel *Donna in guerra* (*Woman at War*), and the 1981 novel *Lettere a Marina* (*Letters to Marina*)—the heroines embark on a journey of self-discovery facilitated and even made possible by friendships with other women. These friendships counter the heroines' conventional relationships—bonds in which the heroines must negotiate positions that deny them subjectivity. Female friendships situate the heroines in community with other women and ground their identities as women in feminine cultural legacies previously unknown to them.

The development of identity involves the negotiation of self in social relationships.[2] The works examined here investigate this process. They define and challenge conventional relational models, including relationships within the family, the first site of the negotiation between self and other. They also, however, focus on the possibilities these relationships offer to women, contemplating ways in which the bonds can be *redirected* to benefit the women themselves.

One result of this redirection is the focus on friendships between women. The works do not construct friendships as restrictive parallels of family relationships. Rather, they develop the friendships by redirecting family bonds, sometimes even successfully filtering out the power dynamics defining familial relationships, and endowing the friendships with the most promisingly beneficial aspects of relationships. Although many of Maraini's works, including those analyzed in this essay, criticize the family as limiting women's potential, they nevertheless recognize the potential such unions as the mother-daughter bond can have for women's identity. This union, reconceptualized as a process of symbolic mediation between two subjects, can make possible a new relationship beyond the realm of family ties, and can also be converted into a bond between women friends.[3] The result is an often fulfilling friendship, and, although it is not always tension free and does not consistently guarantee a successful union, it nonetheless has the potential of being one in which the heroine develops a sense of who she is.

Contemplating the possibilities these bonds offer to women, theorists such as Simone de Beauvoir, Rossana Rossanda, and Gabriella Paolucci all identify the relationship between the historical marginalization of women and the failure to acknowledge female friendships as legitimate bonds. For Beauvoir, women's friendships form complicitous bonds of common experiences, based not on discussions of ideas (the male domain), but on the "exchange [of] confidences and recipes" (604). For Rossanda, they can constitute the site for exploring previously hidden realities and, in defying codified relational structures, create a "rebellious identity" (140). Finally, according to Paolucci, these relationships become the most significant ones in feminism, for in bringing to light previously silenced experiences, they offer the possibility of rewriting traditional codifications of being. Together, these definitions construct a model of women's liberation useful to our exploration of Maraini's works.

Despite, however, the attention focused on female friendships in feminist theory, the assimilation of these bonds into women's lives often proves a difficult task to accomplish. Although these unions can produce affective bonds, their implementation for personal and political change transgresses social law by defying codified relational structures, as Rossanda notes. Therefore, in order to understand the potential of friendships in women's lives, Maraini explores the hidden spheres in which those relationships have developed. As a reflection of their historical realities, she portrays them primarily in the closed spaces in which, as Beauvoir notes, they are traditionally formed. Maraini builds models of female friendships by tapping into "underground" communities of women and distinguishing the bonds as symbols of difference. Together, her works reveal how the traditions of women's friendships (including Beauvoir's "recipes") comprise cultural legacies transmitted from woman to woman.

This model of sisterhood in which women's previously hidden realities are finally expressed is implemented through feminist practices of personal growth used widely in the 1970s and 1980s. Since the early 1970s, Italian feminists have in theory and in practice revised the definition of female friendships in women's lives. As a foundation of their projects for women's liberation, these relationships bring individuals of different backgrounds and ideologies together through bonds of complicity. The revision, succinctly outlined by the members of the Milan Women's Bookstore Collective, has been progressively advanced by such feminist practices as *autocoscienza* ("consciousness-raising"), popular in the 1970s, and *affidamento* ("entrustment"), mapped out in the 1980s, both of which emphasize dialogue, reflection, and inquiry.[4] By uniting women in an open dialogue about their lives, these practices situate women in a community, lift their achievements out of obscurity, and, through communal recognition and validation, encourage subjective expression.

In the practice of *affidamento,* one woman mirrors herself in another woman, who reflects back potentialities the first woman did not know she possessed (Paolucci 58). The Italian feminist concept of *rispecchiamento* ("mirroring"; Paolucci 58), does not imply a static reflection of one individual in another, but rather a gradual discovery of oneself through and made possible by the other. This fragmentary process promotes a greater understanding of the whole self. Emphasis is placed on differences between women, for they reveal the untapped in the reflected subjects.

The works examined in this essay reflect models of female friendships built on these practices of sisterhood. While friendships between women perform narrative functions in many of Maraini's works, especially since *Il manifesto,* the three works I have chosen to analyze are exemplary of the author's vision of the value of friendships in women's lives. Moreover, they map out Maraini's regeneration of certain familial bonds through friendship as essential components of a woman's journey to her self. Together, the works chart the different relational modes that constitute women's friendships and create models for their successful implementation in a feminist project for women's liberation.

In *Il manifesto,* friendships between the characters mirror the early practice of *autocoscienza* and anticipate the theory defining the practice of *affidamento* that evolved from it. As the play's protagonist, Anna, traverses the terrain of her sanctioned social and cultural experiences, and her "storia pellegrina" ("pilgrimage hi/story") leads her to pen her own *manifesto* of women's rights, the play itself becomes a virtual manifesto for social relations.[5] While in later works Maraini will negotiate new, broader relational spaces for her characters, which include restructured family bonds, in *Il manifesto* she focuses relational discourses on other women, "sisters" if you will.

Autocoscienza and *affidamento,* I would argue, constitute the play's primary focus and structural frame. Anna, who dies while serving time in prison for theft, is exhorted to tell her story by a chorus of four deceased women who divulge aspects of their own lives as well. The ensuing dialogues reveal obscured histories and in part fulfill the popular 1970s credo of *autocoscienza,* "the private is political." More importantly for Anna, these personal stories, whose enunciation lifts them out of obscurity, form a sort of female genealogy in which she can situate herself. These feminist practices, sites of the articulation of the self, set up a dichotomy between Anna's life without the support of meaningful female friendships and her own reconstruction of her personal history through interaction with these women. In life, Anna clashes with the tenets of femininity she is forced to uphold and assimilate. Without the support of friendships with other women who understand her struggle and can even guide her, she is restricted to living on society's fringes. Within the *autocoscienza* sessions of the play's frame, however, she can interpret her own life while inspiring the other women to do the same.

Anna, who embodies the female authoritative figure central to the relationship of *affidamento,* also motivates her prison companions to talk and think through their enforced situations as they entrust themselves to her. Thus, for example, when the prisoner Pia attempts to rigidly structure a meeting using bureaucratic jargon incomprehensible to the others, Anna interjects and solicits her companions' personal opinions on their treatment in prison. At work in a factory, she informs her coworkers about birth control and abortion, subjects on which they are ill-informed. In the first example, Anna struggles to create a collectivity by discussing issues in a language accessible to everyone. In the second case, the women around her actually entrust themselves to her for information that creates new choices and new ways to control their own lives. In both instances, interaction and Anna's guidance open the women up to rights, choices, and possibilities they did not know or were little aware they had.

Within the prison walls, Anna's friendships become clear acts of "rebellious identity," since, significantly, this setting represents a microcosm of the family. The prison symbolizes a hierarchical family structure in which its director is a paternal figure. By cultivating friendships through feminist practices and penning her *manifesto* in this institution, Anna's actions become as much a symbol of her rebellion against women's condition as a symbol of her challenge to the codification and enforcement of femininity in both penal and familial institutions. The rebellion against the hierarchical prison establishment becomes one against the repressive strictures that shape the family hierarchy it represents. Anna's actions and *manifesto* symbolically free women's lives from the oppressive institutions that define and mold their identities. It is significant within the play and within a project of women's liberation that these actions arise out of practices of *autocoscienza* and *entrustment*. Indeed, the *manifesto* Anna drafts is a product of these practices and outlines the facts of women's subordination, as it reflects and anticipates feminist issues and writings of the 1970s.[6]

The friendships developed in *Il manifesto* are also a focal point of the 1975 novel *Donna in guerra,* itself a virtual feminist manifesto. While the play centers on friendship's role in women's struggle against the institutionalization of their lives, the novel explores different arenas in which friendships develop and the range of possibilities they offer to women. The novel investigates friendships evolving in the public sphere as well as those developing in an "other" world. The first realm offers hope for political change, but can overpower women's struggle by privileging conventional gender roles. The second space, exclusively female, ideally allows women to play out their concerns, but can run the risk of not accomplishing tangible goals for the legal protection of women's rights.[7]

The novel's protagonist, Vannina, enters friendships with different women and chronicles their development and her own in her journal entries, which constitute the novel.[8] As wife and schoolteacher, she leads a self-effacing life in which she dutifully, even if unhappily, fulfills her roles. But the friendships she develops help her redimension the way she lives her life and allow her to nurture and fulfill a repressed part of her self. On vacation on the island of Addis, she meets the island laundress Giottina and her friend Tota. Through their friendship, Vannina ventures out of the Symbolic sphere and (back) into the pre-Oedipal sphere of the mother-daughter relationship. Although the friendship with the two women replays the tension the daughter feels toward the mother as she attempts to individuate herself, it nevertheless motivates Vannina's communion with other women, something lacking in her life until now. The protagonist also meets the Anglo-Turkish feminist Suna, and subsequently moves into the political arena in which Suna works. Here, she discovers the political neglect of women's concerns. Finally, with her colleague Rosa Colla at home in Rome, she enters a friendship of entrustment that uncovers issues of difference and motherhood with which she herself grapples. Through these relationships, Vannina is forced to confront problems whose resolution, or at least contemplation, sets the path for her liberation.

The protagonist's friendship with Tota and Giottina is in part one of entrustment. In the novel, Vannina's married life is primarily represented within the closed quarters of her vacation house, a fact, she later notes, that renders venturing out into the open disorienting. Under these circumstances, it is her husband, Giacinto, who brings the outside world in to her, acting as mediator. In the friendship with Tota and Giottina, however, the two women act as mediators for her. As such, they allow her to encounter a site similar to her first relationship with a woman—the mother-daughter bond. The site represented by the laundry shop in which Giottina works and Tota visits is a symbolic world of women's subjectivity and customs, silenced in the androcentricly defined Symbolic sphere represented by Vannina and Giacinto's household. Enveloped in steam and therefore secluded from the outside world, it physically resembles a cave, a prehistoric—and symbolically pre-Oedipal—dwelling.[9]

In this setting, Vannina assumes the role of symbolic daughter to the women, who deliberately take her under their wings. However, while the bond reinstates the pre-Oedipal female reference point in her life, Vannina relives both the positive and negative aspects of the mother-daughter bond. She is at once the willing daughter, ready to share in her mother's female "secrets," and the wary one who, having already acceded to the Symbolic sphere of paternal law, resists the warnings the mother issues to protect her. Indeed, at moments during the friendship, Vannina is at once attracted and repulsed by the affection the two women have for her.[10]

While she becomes a part of their sisterhood, and, in her development, recognizes the social and personal value of the women's friendship, Vannina's return to the mother-figure is by no means an effortless one. Psychoanalytically, the symbolic return to the mother is defined as a regression backward into a narcissistic mode of being, the self reflected in and mediated by another woman who is similar to oneself. Socially, it represents surrender to the maternal role, an entrapping gendered role involving effacement in and subservience to the family. But what Vannina does not yet understand is that the return to Tota and Giottina's sphere entails the reevaluation of the transformation that communication with another woman can bring to her life. It will take her friendships with social sisters Suna and Rosa Colla to ultimately awaken her to the possibilities of liberation. In the meantime, while these bonds provide the social extension into adulthood of the symbiotic bond of entrustment, Tota and Giottina initiate the heroine to her awakening, for they offer her foremost a recipe for communion with, to borrow a metaphor from Maraini's poem "Demetra ritrovata" (Demeter regained) the other side of the social sphere.

As the ambivalent daughter who attempts to free herself from the mother's influence, Vannina experiences a liberating relationship in her friendship with Suna. This bond underscores the role entrustment plays in raising a woman's consciousness about women's traditional roles. More specifically, it exposes Vannina to both the feminist discourses of the time and the importance of individual and collective—as opposed to party—action. Suna awakens Vannina to her rights in her relationship with Giacinto, and reveals the role friendship plays in opening women up to new possibilities of being. While the friendship with Tota and Giottina integrates Vannina into a female legacy, Suna introduces her to the project of women's liberation.

While Suna's feminist struggle represents the difficulties women face without a political arena in which to articulate their concerns, the discourse of women's rights she articulates greatly influences Vannina's life. Indeed, the friendship with Suna arms Vannina with the political awareness needed to effect personal change. Suna awakens Vannina to her rights, to the necessity of asserting control over her body and of expressing her own desires. While Vannina's journal entries reveal early on her unhappiness with her marriage, she remains complacent in her role as wife. When she entrusts herself to Suna, however, she begins to understand the ideological roots of that unhappiness. Indeed, Giacinto himself perceives Vannina's growing assertiveness and attempts to grapple with her changing role. Because he is unable to cope with her personal growth, he exerts physical power over her by raping and impregnating her and thus containing her within the maternal role she has rejected in this union. Suna's assertions about Vannina's marriage, and Vannina's assimilation of the tools needed to investigate her life, help her put the marriage into perspective according to her own repressed needs.

While the actual encounters between Vannina and Suna illustrate the advantages of friendship in Vannina's life, they also paint a rich portrait of the union that goes beyond a one-way trajectory. By operating in a political group that enforces traditional ideologies and conventional relational dynamics, Suna loses her ability to understand the plight of those women she so adamantly wants to help.[11] Vannina, on the other hand, successfully unites Suna's guidance with her own experiences, thus achieving an understanding of women's situations that can effect more profound change. It is through friendship with Vannina

Symbolic Mediation and Female Community

that Suna herself comes to appreciate her problematic situation. This understanding exposes Suna to weaknesses she cannot fathom rectifying. Unable to repossess herself from her marginalization, she commits suicide. However, after her death, her relationship with Vannina becomes a regenerative bond. Vannina, armed with her experiences in the friendships on Addis, can carry out a more enlightened plan of women's liberation outside the established arena in which Suna herself worked.

Vannina finally gains the strength necessary to effect change in her life through her friendship with her eccentric colleague Rosa Colla. This friendship represents the culmination of Vannina's friendships on Addis, of her awakening, of the daughter's development into maturity and self-assertion. The heroine entrusts herself to Rosa Colla through growing complicity, and is finally able to apply Suna's politicized views to her own life. Rosa's independent lifestyle offers positive proof that a woman can live happily on her own. Indeed, Vannina not only considers Rosa, whose eccentricities symbolize difference, an example of a woman's strength, but also gains a perspective on issues of motherhood through Rosa's own experiences with the maternal role.[12]

Rosa's ordeal with this gendered role confirms Vannina's fears of women's subordination to motherhood. While in several works, Maraini looks at the empowering potential of motherhood, here she considers the consequences of its institutionalization. Rosa became pregnant through her relationship with a young homeless man, whom she housed and fed. When he deserted her, she terminated her pregnancy. Upon returning and learning of the abortion, the man beat her, then left again. The man's reaction to Rosa is one of possession and dominance. Rosa's experiences and Vannina's own not only motivate Vannina's rejection of the institution of motherhood, but, in keeping with *affidamento,* also inform the assistance Rosa offers her. By entrusting herself to Rosa, she is able to make choices regarding her life that she otherwise would not have had the strength to make. Facing the same disempowering situation as Rosa, Vannina decides to abort and, through her informed decision, gains the strength to start her life anew.

The diverse friendships Vannina chronicles in her journal have all advanced her journey to self-discovery. Her friendship with

Tota and Giottina recasts her as daughter, allowing her to begin exploration of her self as a woman within a female community of difference. The bond with Suna politicizes Vannina, raising her consciousness not only of her immediate situation, but also of the possibilities for change that lay ahead. These friendships converge in the relationship with Rosa, a relationship of entrustment with someone considered unconventional and that situates Vannina in a female space of difference. The strength gained through these friendships prompts the heroine to leave the confines of her marriage and to challenge the archaic educational system she has complacently supported until now. In changing her life and in raising her students' consciousness to issues of gendered domination and repression, she indeed begins to build a paradigm for women's liberation.[13]

The semiautobiographical epistolary novel *Lettere a Marina* offers a more introspective look at the role friendship plays in reshaping a woman's life. In this novel, friendship helps the protagonist Bianca reconstruct her past and situate her in a self-affirming cultural legacy of womanhood. Bianca is an example of a woman who, functioning in the Symbolic realm, has lost touch with her past as a woman and, therefore, with her subjectivity. If, as psychoanalyst Silvia Vegetti Finzi asserts, subjectivity is a developmental process in which the individual creates his/her own hi/story (231–32), then recuperation of Bianca's past is a recuperation of her self.[14]

Bianca's journey out of the Symbolic and into the pre-Oedipal sphere in her friendship with her neighbor Basilia mirrors Anna's reconstruction of her past and Vannina's relationship with Tota and Giottina. However, unlike the journeys of the two previous heroines, Bianca's journey, which comes at a time when feminist theories of women's subjectivity were evolving, is self-initiated and self-propelled. Through relationships with other women, Bianca delves into her past in search of the prediscursive self repressed in the acquisition of social roles. Her search is made possible by an examination of past relationships with women, including her mother, her sister, and her lover Marina, as well as by chronicling her growing friendship with Basilia. The movement between past and present not only re-creates a past for Bianca, but also thrusts her into the future.

Through this journey that maps out the hidden geography of the self, Maraini examines diverse permutations of friendships: from the mother-daughter bond at the basis of Bianca and Marina's relationship to the relationship of *affidamento* and *rispecchiamento* between Bianca and Basilia, she investigates the significance of the different unions to Bianca's exploration of the self. The figure who ultimately propels Bianca forward into her past is Basilia. The bond of entrustment between Bianca and Basilia extends the pre-Oedipal relationship between mother (Basilia) and daughter (Bianca) into the present, and becomes central to Bianca's journey to self-knowledge.[15]

It is through the unfolding of the friendship tucked away in Bianca and Basilia's apartments that we witness the generative possibilities of the symbolic mother-daughter relationship. The relationship with Basilia unfolds in the pre-Oedipal site of women's customs and traditions, as does Vannina's with Tota and Giottina. But unlike Vannina's position, Bianca's does not vacillate between acceptance and rejection. Rather, it is based on a reconstructive complicity of reciprocal growth.

As symbolic mother to Bianca, Basilia personifies the complexities of motherhood at the same time that she reinforces the maternal role in the heroine's life. She is at once the member of the family who is most exploited, the basic and powerful purveyor of life, and the transmitter of women's past, represented by the stories she tells. As mother within her family, Basilia embodies those self-effacing traits of the traditional maternal discourse Maraini dismantles in other works. When Bianca meets her, the thirty-six-year-old Basilia is unquestioningly dedicated to her role as wife and mother. This dedication manifests itself physically through her body, which prematurely ages and decays as it becomes fodder for her two young sons. The self-effacement demanded by the role also causes Basilia to lack a sense of self separate from her family and the roles she fulfills within that sphere. Even in Bianca's apartment, where Basilia does not function in the capacity of wife and mother, she does not lose her posture of self-effacement. Basilia's inner self is unleashed and her subjectivity allowed to develop through her friendship with Bianca, however. She is longingly called upon to reveal herself, to transmit her knowledge to the searching daughter. In this configuration, she can articulate her self and cherished traditions passed down by generations of female ancestors.[16]

In continuing reciprocity, this puts Bianca, the *tabula rasa* represented by her very name, in touch with a female ancestral identity—the past she lacks at the beginning of the novel. While at first Bianca perceives only the painful aspects of Basilia's life, as the relationship progresses, she recognizes the richness of her friend's character. By entrusting herself to Basilia, the heroine comes to understand the value to women of comprehending the mother, thus heeding Irigaray's plea to "ne pas retuer [la] mère" (*Le corps* 28; "not murder the mother again"). As the protagonist slowly grows to know Basilia, she, though still recognizing her exploitation within the family, celebrates her physical and emotional strength as procreator.

Through Basilia, Bianca is able to glimpse the ancient roots of a maternal discourse based on women's subjectivity and power. Hearing her neighbor sing a song "come avrebbe fatto sua madre contadina" (*Lettere* 120; "as her farmer mother would have done"), the protagonist appreciates the value of possessing and being in touch with a female past. The neighbor's link to the past and her articulation of stories steeped in ancient beliefs result in a subjective expression through which she speaks, as Luciana Percovich notes with regard to women's self-expression, "not only of herself but from her self" ("non solo di sè ma a partire da sè"; Percovich 55). But while Basilia tells stories "from her self" ("a partire da sè"), Bianca is still writing letters that speak "of herself" ("di sè"). She has not yet tapped into her connection with her past. While, as she herself notes, the *autocoscienza* sessions with her friends at home allowed her to "dire di me" (*Lettere* 40; "tell of myself"), it is the more profound, more involved relationship she has with Basilia— that of *affidamento*—that allows her creativity to be unleashed and energized at the end of the novel. Exposing Bianca to women's oral traditions through her stories, and symbolically (re)-creating her through a technique—*kneading* her shoulders—transmitted from grandmother to mother to daughter, Basilia helps Bianca replant her roots in a symbolic community of women.

But the friendship does not constitute a one-way process of development from Basilia to Bianca. In this union, Basilia has not simply and predictably slipped into the maternal role. On the contrary, she also symbolically figures as Bianca's daughter, completing the *rispecchiamento* of sharing knowledge and experiences. As daughter, Basilia grows through the bond, which helps her develop a sense of self outside her family. Bianca detects the change deep in Basilia's eyes, where she sees vestiges of the Furies' power and understands the strength of Basilia's character and this woman's struggle for survival.

By novel's end, Basilia has the confidence and courage to invite Bianca out for dinner. By expressing her desire for pleasure, and by leaving the home to fulfill it, she is finally able to achieve wholeness—to be "interamente se stessa" (*Lettere* 120; "entirely herself"). On the women's final evening together, they share a dance symbolizing their mutual confirmation and newfound inner strengths. The relationship between the two women proves beneficial because they have allowed each other to bring their strengths to it. While Basilia helps Bianca recover her past, Bianca helps Basilia recover the power within her. Thus, while Bianca will set off in the morning to rediscover her roots in Sicily, Basilia has just begun to find her inner power, "[ride] come una donna che si sente bella e sicura" (202; "she laughs like a woman who feels beautiful and secure").

Along with the relationships examined in *Il manifesto* and in *Donna in guerra,* Bianca and Basilia's relationship shows how essential friendships between women are to women's liberation and to their journey to self-discovery and authenticity. These friendships reverse patterns of socialization. Their purpose is not to ensure women's adherence to conventional gender roles or their successful integration into a heterosexual union— friendship's historical function as a literary trope. Rather, in Maraini's works they take shape as moments of *autocoscienza, affidamento,* and *rispecchiamento,* and, at times, offer alternatives to restrictive family relationships by drawing from and re-creating some of their more beneficial qualities. This relational paradigm clearly evolves in the works examined here, from the abolishment of family *in Il manifesto,* to its redirection in *Donna in guerra* and *Lettere a Marina.* Tellingly, it continues to figure prominently in Maraini's works. The 1993 short story "Cinque donne d'acqua dolce" (Five sweetwater women), for example, features *autocoscienza* sessions between five women friends and focuses on both their complicity to bond together and the subsequent reconstructions of their pasts. Friendships between Maraini's heroines in this and other works become propitious sites for experiencing bonds of community with other women and exploring issues of womanhood, difference, and the self.

Notes

1. I use the term *liberation* to recall the historical context of the women's movement in which the works I examine took shape. More importantly, however, I extend its definition to include the notion that developing women's subjectivity and freeing their relational possibilities liberate them from restrictive historical paradigms of being.

2. For a discussion of this process, see, for example, Chodorow.

3. *Symbolic mediation,* as defined by the members of the Milan Women's Bookstore Collective in *Sexual Difference,* constitutes real or symbolic relationships between women. The maternal bond is recognized as the first site of mediation between the daughter and the world. In her development, however, the daughter must repress communion with the primary female figure in her life to accede to the symbolic social order the father represents. Feminists define the return to the mother, and the development of bonds with other women, as essential to the development of women's subjectivity, for these offer a female reference point as guidance in women's lives. See, for example, Boccia, Braidotti, and Raymond.

4. *Autocoscienza* is a collective practice of consciousness-raising that involves understanding oneself through dialogue with other women (Bono and Kemp, *Italian Feminist Thought* 8). *Affidamento,* historically practiced but not theorized until the 1980s, is an extension of *autocoscienza,* and involves one woman entrusting herself to another, who becomes a symbolic point of reference for her development (de Lauretis 9).

5. All translations are mine unless otherwise indicated.

6. Anna's *Manifesto* is a distillation of several feminist manifestos of the period. Manifestos by such groups as Demau and Rivolta Femminile, and writings such as Carla Lonzi's *Sputiamo su Hegel* (1970) advocate the dismantling of existing social and cultural structures and the restructuring of relationships. Interestingly, Anna's manifesto also anticipates the feminist group Anabasi's 1972 *Donna è bello* ("Woman is beautiful"), which sees the potential of *autocoscienza* to reveal the fact that the imposed, traditional model of femininity is a social and political problem, not a personal one. Anna's own manifesto casts such issues as sexuality, work, and the family as social, political, and cultural dilemmas. Likewise, in a phrase that opens and sets the tone of her manifesto as it anticipates the phrase "Donna è bello," it recasts womanhood as a "beautiful" mode of being liberated from such negative characteristics as subordination: "Non c'è niente di vergognoso ad essere donna. Anzi è bello" (*Lettere* 272; "There is nothing embarrassing about being a woman. Actually, it is beautiful"). For manifestos by Demau and Rivolta, see Bono and Kemp, *Italian Feminist Thought*.

7. The exclusively female practice of *autocoscienza* proved extremely successful as a foundation for relationships in which women could express and explore their concerns. However, it proved too personal and too limiting in the political struggle for rights. As a result, women extended their efforts into the political arena. Participation in both areas became known as *doppia militanza* ("double militancy"), successful in establishing legal enforcement and protection of women's rights.

8. For analyses of *Donna in guerra* as bildungsroman see Lazzaro-Weis and Tamburri.

9. Despite their position within the novel, Tota and Giottina are not frozen in time, stuck in the pre-Oedipal. Although the relationship proves a site of development primarily for Vannina as the novel's protagonist, it becomes the stage on which Tota and Giottina express their own thoughts and differences. Highlighting similarities and differences adds greater depth and color to the tapestry of women's lives, and reveals to Vannina the way friendship can indeed encourage self-expression.

10. Tota and Giottina's imposing sentiments and emotions can be read as the traditional attitude attributed to the "overbearing" maternal figure. Luce Irigaray chronicles the daughter's struggle against this overwhelming aspect of the bond, noting how it represents her struggle not only for identity but also for a redimensioning of this coveted relationship. The two Addis women represent the mother who, as Irigaray notes, must go back "under the ground" as the daughter desperately grasps for her social identity. When Vannina thinks about returning to the cavelike shop, she symbolically feels a loss of the adult social identity she has cultivated, experiencing what the French theorist describes as the "opening to the mother": "threats of contamination . . . madness, death" (*Sexes* 15). Vannina's own attitude reveals this struggle: "Mi sentivo mancare l'aria. Quegli abbracci fangosi mi scaldavano il ventre. Non volevo essere travolta. Ho fatto per liberarmi. Ma ero . . . vincolata" (*Donna in guerra* 143; "I couldn't breathe. Those muddy hugs warmed my belly. I didn't want to be caught up in them. I tried to free myself. But I was trapped . . .").

11. Suna's work in the political arena is not successful. Waging her campaign for women's rights in this traditional site forces her to subordinate her concerns to those of the party. Her lack of a supportive practice such as *autocoscienza* makes it difficult for her to resolve both basic problems of love and belonging and of political struggle, and the result is crippling marginalization.

Virginia Picchietti

12. For an analysis of motherhood in *Donna in guerra,* see Pickering-Iazzi.

13. Vannina's role as schoolteacher reveals how personal development can ultimately effect social and cultural change. She decides to give a lesson in sex education excluded from the school curriculum and to demystify the socialized roles of male dominance and female submission already assimilated by her male and female eight-year-old students, whom she catches simulating a rape scene.

14. In a letter to Marina, Bianca asserts she is "una donna senza storia nata ogni giorno dalla pancia buia del tempo" (*Lettere* 5; "a woman without hi/story born every day from the dark womb of time").

15. Pauline Dagnino offers a sensitive critique of Bianca's journey, identifying it as a search for that part of her self not represented in culture but found in the pre-Oedipal relationship with the mother. For Dagnino, it is the relationship with her lover Marina that fuels Bianca's journey and makes its success possible. While Marina does indeed play a primary role in Bianca's mnemonic re-creation of her past, she remains, in the economy of the novel, in the past—someone with whom Bianca must come to terms to move on. In my own reading of Bianca's relationships, I see Basilia as the ultimate catalyst for the final stages of the part of the journey represented in the novel. It is the bond with Basilia that contains fundamental elements of the contemporary feminist discourse on female friendship.

16. Tellingly, when Basilia narrates stories to Bianca, she also "kneads" her shoulders, a symbol that as symbolic mother she "re-creates" the daughter's physical placement within the present. Here, Basilia is once again linked to the mothers before her, "[i]mpasta diligentemente muovendo le dita come avrebbe fatto sua madre sua nonna" (*Lettere* 170; "[s]he diligently kneads, moving her fingers like her mother and grandmother would have done"). As daughter, Bianca relies on her for spiritual nourishment.

Works Cited

Beauvoir, Simone de. *The Second Sex.* Trans. H. M. Parshley. New York: Vintage, 1952.

Boccia, Maria Luisa. "L'identità nella relazione." *I quaderni dell'associazione culturale Livia Laverani Donini* 3.6 (May 1990): 15–25.

Bono, Paola, and Sandra Kemp, eds. *Italian Feminist Thought: A Reader.* London: Blackwell, 1991.

Braidotti, Rosi. *Nomadic Subjects: Embodiment and Sexual Difference in Contemporary Feminist Theory.* New York: Columbia UP, 1994.

Chodorow, Nancy. *The Reproduction of Mothering: Psychoanalysis and the Sociology of Gender.* Berkeley: U of California P, 1978.

Dagnino, Pauline. "Fra madre e marito: The Mother/Daughter Relationship in Dacia Maraini's *Lettere a Marina*." *Visions and Revisions: Women in Italian Culture*. Ed. M. Cicioni and N. Prunster. Providence: Berg, 1993. 183–97.

de Lauretis, Teresa. "The Practice of Sexual Difference and Feminist Thought in Italy: An Introductory Essay." Milan Women's Bookstore Collective 1–21.

Finzi, Silvia Vegetti. "Alla ricerca di una soggettività femminile." *La ricerca delle donne: studi femministi in Italia*. Ed. Maria Cristina Marcuzzo and Anna Rossi-Doria. Turin: Rosenberg and Sellier, 1987. 228–48.

Irigaray, Luce. *Le corps-à-corps avec la mère*. Montreal: Les Éditions de la pleine lune, 1981.

———. *Sexes and Genealogies*. Trans. Gillian C. Gill. New York: Columbia UP, 1993.

Lazzaro-Weis, Carol. *From Margins to Mainstream: Feminism and the Fictional Modes in Italian Women's Writing, 1968–1990*. Philadelphia: U of Pennsylvania P, 1993.

Lonzi, Carla. *Sputiamo su Hegel: la donna clitoridea e la donna vaginale e altri scritti*. Milan: Rivolta Femminile, 1974.

Maraini, Dacia. "Cinque donne d'acqua dolce." *Il pozzo segreto*. Ed. Maria Rosa Cutrufelli, Rosaria Guacci, and Marisa Rusconi. Florence: Giunti, 1993. 145–52.

———. "Demetra ritrovata." *Mangiami pure*. Turin: Einaudi, 1978. Published in English as *Devour Me Too*. Montreal: Guernica, c1987.

———. *Donna in guerra*. Turin: Einaudi, 1975. Published in English as *Woman at War*. 1981. New York: Italica, 1988.

———. *Lettere a Marina*. Milan: Bompiani, 1981. Published in English as *Letters to Marina*. London: Camden, 1987. Freedom, CA: Crossing, 1988.

———. *Il manifesto*. In *Il ricatto a teatro e altre commedie*. Turin: Einaudi, 1970. 187–279.

Milan Women's Bookstore Collective. *Sexual Difference: A Theory of Social-Symbolic Practice*. Trans. Teresa de Lauretis and Patricia Cicogna. Introductory essay by de Lauretis. Bloomington: Indiana UP, 1990.

Paolucci, Gabriella. "Amiche: figure dell'amicizia femminile e femminismo." *Memoria* 32.2 (1991): 56–66.

Percovich, Luciana. "Relazione." *L'etica necessaria: eredità materna e passione politica*. Milan: Melusine, 1993. 55–65.

Pickering-Iazzi, Robin. "Designing Mothers: Images of Motherhood in Novels by Aleramo, Morante, Maraini, and Fallaci." *Annali d'Italianistica* 7 (1989): 325–40.

Raymond, Janice. *A Passion for Friends: Toward a Philosophy of Female Affection*. Boston: Beacon, 1986.

Rossanda, Rossana. *Anche per me: donna, persona, memoria dal 1973 al 1986*. Milan: Feltrinelli, 1987.

Tamburri, Anthony. "Dacia Maraini's *Donna in Guerra:* Victory or Defeat?" *Contemporary Women Writers in Italian: A Modern Renaissance*. Ed. Santo L. Arico. Amherst: U of Massachusetts P, 1990. 139–51.

Giovanna Bellesia

Variations on a Theme
Violence against Women in the
Writings of Dacia Maraini

Dacia Maraini has been socially very active in the fight for new laws to protect women as well as for a reduction of violence and pornography in the media. All her books explicitly denounce the constant abuse of women and the violent crimes committed against them. This essay investigates how Maraini's mode of presenting these issues has changed through the years, how it has mirrored the development of Italian society and found ways to reach an increasingly wider audience. It is important to bear in mind that Maraini's approach has also been influenced by her own process of growth over the last decades and her witnessing the many failed attempts to modify a legal system that further violates women who report a crime.

The new Italian law against sexual violence was first debated in Parliament in 1979. It was not the product of enlightened politicians who had finally realized that rape could not continue to be prosecuted simply as a crime against morality. It was introduced in Parliament through the efforts of many Italian women who, after drafting the text of the law, collected 300,000 signatures (far more then the 50,000 needed) to have a "Popular Initiative Law" enter Parliament. After a struggle of over fifteen years, all parties finally agreed that rape, like other forms of personal assault, is a violent crime against a person and should not be dismissed as an issue dealing only with honor and morality. This delay reveals a lack of understanding of the power relations between genders, endemic to all patriarchal societies. Even better laws and an increased awareness of sexual harassment have had little effect on the continued abuse of women. As the new millennium approaches, violence against women seems to be escalating in Italy and elsewhere. In order to stop this devastating trend, people must become aware of the underlying causes of the problem. Socially committed writers can help their readers understand the true motives of this enduring cycle of violence.

Dacia Maraini's contribution in this field is evident in her novel *Voci* (1994; *Voices*), in which a gripping search for the killer of a young woman is used as the literary framework for the presentation of a series of data about the brutal murders of little girls and women of all ages and social backgrounds. The narrative voice is that of Michela Canova, a radio journalist who is asked to prepare a series on the unsolved murders of women. We are told that 65 percent of women's killers are never apprehended and that one of the main reasons for this failure is that most murders of women happen within the family structure, with people often accusing each other and creating a tangled mass of evidence.

Domestic abuse, although usually not resulting in physical death, is not a new theme in Maraini's books. In the seventies it was widely portrayed in her work of poetry and prose. Clear cases of assault, beating, and even conjugal rape were described, along with the daily abuse suffered by unaware, seemingly content women who spent their lives burdened with household chores, selflessly attending to every need of their ungrateful husbands and children. Vannina, the protagonist of Maraini's 1975 novel *Donna in guerra* (*Woman at War*), embodies this sad condition. Giacinto, her husband, is not described as a brutal, uncaring man, yet as a product of sexist upbringing, he is utterly unaware that he is hurting and abusing his wife. As the novel opens, Vannina seems content with her life. Gradually, however, through the agency of significant events and characters, it becomes clear to her, and to us readers, that she is not satisfied with her marriage. Giacinto and Vannina's sexual life is totally one sided. One third of the way through the book, Vannina remarks that Giacinto, when he makes love, only thinks of himself and does not care about her. He simply uses her; her participation and consent are irrelevant. At the end of the book, when Giacinto decides that having a child would turn Vannina back into the crushed and contented woman he married, his disregard is indisputable. In order to regain control over her, he impregnates her while she is asleep. It never occurs to him that his act was an actual rape. Vannina leaves him

Variations on a Theme: Violence against Women

and decides to have an abortion, yet another form of mental and physical violence she has to go through because of her husband's behavior. As Maraini recently stated in her "Lettera sull'aborto" (1996; Letter on abortion), abortion, while it may represent a victory over social rules and moral/religious constraints, also exemplifies women's lack of control over their own bodies (24).[1] The paradox of Vannina's abortion is that it signifies her freedom from her husband and from social laws and opinions, but it remains an expression of her lack of power and comes at the cost of great pain and suffering. In her seminal feminist work *Sputiamo su Hegel* of 1974, Italian philosopher Carla Lonzi reflected on this when she wrote that a woman does not become unwillingly pregnant because she has expressed herself sexually, but rather because she is "sexually colonized," conditioned to conform to men's idea of pleasure, which always implies penetration and coitus. Lonzi sees in the unwanted pregnancy the result of a form of violence perpetrated by male culture against woman. She points out that by denying women the freedom of abortion, men transform their abuse into women's guilt (*Sputiamo* 70–71).

Another type of domestic abuse present in *Donna in guerra* is suggested through the description of Vannina's daily chores. All housework, of course, falls on her shoulders. Vannina simply lists her activities, trusting her rebellious message to the monotonous tone of her words:

> Ho riempito di acqua calda la vasca. Ci ho versato dentro il detersivo in polvere. Intanto ho messo il sugo sul fuoco. Avevo anche da pulire per terra, da cambiare le lenzuola, da sgrassare la cucina . . . (229)

> I filled up the bathtub with hot water. I poured the detergent in. Meanwhile I started cooking the pasta sauce. I also had to scrub the floors, change the sheets, wipe the kitchen surfaces . . .[2]

It is particularly interesting to notice how Maraini also manages to point out that the traditional attitude toward women's work and behavior is fully shared by the new breed of young leftist men. Let us not forget that this is a book from the seventies when men in Italy were supposedly becoming more sensitive to women's issues. As Vittorio and Faele—two of Giacinto's leftist friends—discuss class oppression with him, Vannina can only get bits and pieces of their enlightening conversation, as she is too busy serving them: "Io andavo e venivo dalla cucina portando i piatti puliti, versando il vino, preparando il caffé, seguendo a pezzi e bocconi i loro discorsi" (106; "I kept running in and out of the kitchen bringing clean dishes, pouring the wine, making the coffee, following only bits and pieces of their conversation"). When Vittorio eventually marries, he rejects the liberated and strong Mafalda in favor of a beautiful rich virgin who is perfectly happy in her subservient role and eagerly fills the traditional wife's role he demands.

In *Donna in guerra* there are other overt cases of severe domestic abuse. One of the worst is that suffered by Orio's mother. She seems to exemplify the many Southern Italian women of her generation who found themselves married to ignorant, backward men, and were trapped into raising sons who perpetuated their fathers' violent and disparaging behavior toward women. She is clearly afraid of her family and when she tries to object to her sons' boasting of having raped a young British tourist (guilty of swimming alone and topless), she is immediately frightened into silence by her husband, who is the source of their sons' warped values. Her relationship with her husband is such that when he dies, Vannina notices a hint of joyful relief in her eyes as his coffin is lowered into the grave. She is unfortunately still surrounded by her sons, whom Vannina describes as "threatening angels" (55).

In homosocial societies, women are not allowed to think on their own. As J. G. Peristiany notes, in *Mediterranean Family Structures,* the head of the family (the father) is despotic and has real power of control over his wife and children. Sons are second to the father in authority and influence and, once widowed, the mother is economically and socially dependent on them for survival. She is thus forced to go along with their beliefs.

Family violence takes a different slant in *La lunga vita di Marianna Ucrìa,* written in the eighties. This historical novel is a fictional re-creation of the life of one of Maraini's own ancestors, a noblewoman who lived in Sicily in the first half of the eighteenth century. Marianna has lost the ability to hear and speak and, as the book opens, is being taken by her beloved father to witness the gruesome execution of a young boy.

Variations on a Theme: Violence against Women

Later in the book, Marianna and the reader find out the reason for her father's odd behavior. He was hoping to shock her into speaking again, as he was aware that Marianna had lost her voice because of a brutally traumatic experience. As a little girl of five, she had been raped by the same uncle her parents had her marry at the age of thirteen. This revelation comes toward the end of the book, after we have learned to almost like this husband/uncle.

We as readers are left feeling confused and ambivalent toward him and Marianna's parents. We find ourselves forced to re-evaluate our assessment of the situation; grasping for an explanation, we try to look beyond the text. We then realize that Maraini is reminding us that not all rapists are strangers who attack women in the dark. Statistics prove that most are known to their victims and often related to them. She is also denouncing the silent complicity of all the family members involved. They failed to protect Marianna, and they betrayed her twice, first by not punishing her aggressor and then by shamelessly marrying her off to him. This brings to mind the infamous Italian law ("Codice Rocco") that used to allow rapists to go scot-free as long as they were willing to marry their victims, thus restoring the honor of the victims' families.

As Lonzi argues, honor in patriarchal society is the repressive codification of women's virginity, chastity, and fidelity: the "virtues" used to build and sustain the family (*Sputiamo* 12). In his study of the anthropology of honor in Mediterranean societies, Julian Pitt-Rivers defines honor as the value of a person in his own eyes as well as in the eyes of his social environment. He points out that "[m]en think themselves responsible for the behaviour of their women because this is where the essence of *their* moral honour resides." Pitt-Rivers also remarks that the most serious insult to a man is that against his female kin, not himself (*The Fate of Shechem* 79; italics in the original). Thus a violent act against woman is seen as an attack on the family and not the individual. Marriage can erase the threat to the family's honor, and take away the shame of rape in the eyes of the community. The abuse of the individual is ignored, since woman is not perceived as having an independent identity, with rights of her own that have been violated.

The problem of incest and child abuse is clearly addressed in the books Maraini wrote in the nineties, *Bagheria* (1994) and the already mentioned *Voci*. *Bagheria* is an autobiographical account in which Maraini is not so much talking *about* herself as *to* herself. It is a search for origins, a coming to terms with a part of life she had repressed and loathed. She recounts her own personal experiences with child molestation, a first attempt at the hands of an American sailor. She was eleven and returning to Italy with her family from a concentration camp in Japan, where she had spent the first part of her young life. The sailor, after taking her to his cabin, showed her a picture of his daughter and proceeded to touch her inappropriately. She remarks on the paradoxical aspects of fatherly love, tender and lascivious, delicate and imperious. In the same text she talks about a man, in the town of Bagheria, who had fathered a child with his daughter and about another who had sexually molested all of his three young daughters, making one pregnant and forcing her to have an abortion. Maraini's comments are very perceptive on the psychosocial formation of such men. She remarks that the Church and common moral values forbid these incestuous relationships, but that these kind of men are pushed by primordial forces profoundly embedded in them, having nothing to do with sexual desire. They consider their daughters their own flesh and blood, their property. Their way of thinking predates the established codes of behavior and actually finds commonly accepted biblical counterparts (e.g., Noah and his sons, Lot and his daughters).[3] Maraini is certainly not excusing these men. Rather, instead of limiting herself to denouncing their abuse, she is now providing her readers with a study on the origin of this behavior. She can then demonstrate how widespread and damaging it is.

Jane Gallop, in *The Daughter's Seduction,* reads the relationship between Freud, Lacan, and Irigaray—psychoanalysis and feminism—in terms of the seductive relationship between father and daughter. She explores the power relation with the father as the model for the many complex relations that are the basis of patriarchal society. Maraini seems in agreement with this theory, and often remarked on her own relationship with her father. In her novel *Dolce per sé* (Sweet by nature), she writes that the first signs traced by the father in the tender heart of his daughter resurface at every turn of her adult life. In the same text, talking about her passion for Mozart's *Don Juan,* she defines her father as the first charming, lovable Don Juan that captured her imagination. She suffered because of his tumultuous love life, but she was at the same time proud of it, as his conquests proved his attractiveness (*Dolce* 181). In an interview with Anna Maria Mori, she states that as a child she had been in love with her father because he represented something exotic, different; he was escape, adventure, travel, what she wished for herself (*Nel segno della madre* 129).

A complex analysis of an incestuous father-daughter relationship is found in *Voci*. At the end of the novel we find out that Angela, the young murder victim, was killed by her stepfather, who had sexually and mentally abused both Angela and her sister Ludovica from a very young age. Each girl coped with this traumatic experience in her own way. Ludovica sought refuge in a life of lies and mental illness, and still lived in an abusive relationship. Angela, on the other hand, had learned to use seduction as her primary way of communicating and surviving. The readers realize that she, not unlike Marianna Ucrìa, has lost her real voice and has resorted to the only effective language she knows, that of her body.[4] In her most recent book of essays, *Un clandestino a bordo* (*Stowaway on Board*), Maraini discusses the implications of the double way of communicating that women learn almost instinctively from a very early age. She stresses women's fascination with that linguistic code that is centered on their bodies, that seems to have a voice of its own and is easily acknowledged and understood. She remarks that long years of servitude have taught women that the language of the body works better in silence as its voicelessness guarantees its power (66). In *Dolce per sé* Maraini comments on the fact that thought and spoken language were historically not part of women's education and were regarded, even by women, as less credible ways of expressing themselves. She remarks that if women today do not resort any longer to "body language," such as fainting, it is because they have found other possibilities of resistance (*Dolce* 28).

Angela's use of her body proved to be her downfall. As Rosetta Di Pace-Jordan remarks in her review of *Voci,* the stepfather kills Angela "because her seductive behavior toward others represented an act of emancipation on her part and his loss of control over her" (Review 341–42). This is a very accurate description of the stepfather's own perception of the situation. Maraini's ability to explore complex issues is exemplified here. We can find a reason for the murder, but not for the abuse that preceded it. Maraini writes in *Un clandestino a bordo:* "Lo stupro è certamente un oggetto misterioso nella storia dei sessi. Si può raccontarlo ma non spiegarlo" (86; "Rape is certainly a mysterious element in the history of the sexes. You can talk about how it happened but you cannot explain it"; 63). We know a lot about the stepfather. We know how he feels and how he can justify his behavior in his mind. Behind Maraini's ability to penetrate his psychology lies an explanation of how this could possibly have happened and an even more haunting reminder that it will happen again. We as readers realize that unless the ancient patriarchal beliefs that produced and justified this kind of aberrant behavior are extirpated, women's condition will never change. Notwithstanding her stepfather's perception of the situation, Angela remains to the end a victim, certainly not an emancipated woman, but rather the type of woman that, according to Maraini, opens the door to welcome her assassin.

In the long fight to stop violence against women, Dacia Maraini's outcry of the seventies has, in the eighties, found an outlet in her search for its roots. The nineties seem to be for her a time of further reflection on the causes of this phenomenon. This is also the time when Maraini seems to come to the realization that violence against women keeps getting worse, and that the only way to stop it is to eradicate the patriarchal mentality that produces it, what she calls the "culture of the fathers" (*Lettera* 18). The widespread use of rape as a weapon during the war that tore the former Yugoslavia apart is a brutal reminder for all of us of the fact that rape has much more to do with power, humiliation, and submission than with sexual desire.

This was already evident in the issue of male prostitution in *Donna in guerra.* In Addis, the island where Vannina is spending her vacation, many of the young men sell their bodies to the older foreign women who wish to buy their services. Orio's brothers are not among them but one, Toto, is propositioned by a German tourist. After agreeing on a price for his performance, he signals to his three brothers, who follow him to her house, where all take turns holding her down and raping her. Toto, his brothers, and his father all feel this violence to be absolutely justified. They see it as a way to re-create the "right"

Variations on a Theme: Violence against Women

balance of power. As Vittorio, the leftist friend of Vannina, will later put it, prostitution is much worse for men because "una donna è abituata a una certa passività, è la sua natura, ma un uomo deve salvare il suo orgoglio e come fa?" (*Donna* 118; "a woman is used to a certain degree of passivity, it's part of her nature, but a man, a man must watch out for his pride, how can he do it?"). The German tourist had humiliated Toto by thinking she could buy him. He saw rape as the way to settle the score. Sexual desire had hardly anything to do with what happened.

That men see sexual dominance as the only definitive way to assert power is also clearly borne out by the case of Marianna Ucrìa's son-in-law Giulio. He brings one of his mistresses home and even puts her in his wife's bed. Marianna at first cannot understand his reasons, but after talking to her daughter, the situation becomes clear. Giulio is not doing it out of lust or perversion. His wife has started to read the books of some forbidden French writers. She is beginning to think on her own and to demand more freedom. Putting his mistress in his wife's bed was his indirect, brutal way of reiterating that he was the one in control. Marianna understands the motivating factors and tells her daughter that she has to gain her husband's respect to resolve her predicament. What actually solves it, though, is women's solidarity. Giulio had underestimated his women. Forced into proximity, the mistress and the wife end by becoming friends. The mistress leaves, and the wife becomes interested in another, more understanding man.

When sexual desire does play a role in sexual violence, it still goes along with a desire to possess and dominate the other. When Maraini describes the mentality of the most backward Sicilian men from Bagheria, she remarks that a woman's will is absolutely irrelevant to them since they see women as a passive object of prey. According to such mentality, a body with a uterus must only hide and deny itself. Any consent to be in the company of a man is an implied surrender to the man's desire. This is exemplified in *Marianna Ucrìa* in the character of Ciccio Panella, one of Marianna's sharecroppers, who "le donne se le acchiappa quando vuole iddu" (174; "grabs women whenever he likes"). Two hundred years later, his mentality is well and thriving in the town of Bagheria.

This mode of thought is fostered early in a child's life. At the end of *Donna in guerra,* Vannina witnesses her pupils mimicking a gang rape of a girl, as a game. She confronts them and declares that rape is an act of violence. She then interprets the other girls' passive watching as conditioned acceptance of the boys' right to violate. She also tells the little "victim" that she had been picked precisely for being small, defenseless, and female (256–58).

Maraini often remarked on women's double victimization, first as the object of crime, then as hostages of the male mentality that produced it. In the book of poems *Donne mie* (Women of mine), she clearly refers to mothers as having "una mano di donna che . . . insegna le regole dell'uomo" (6; "a woman's hand that teaches men's rules"), denouncing women's lack of support for each other. As in *Marianna Ucrìa,* women's solidarity could be a strong weapon, but it is often absent when needed. When Vannina and her friend Suna in *Donna in guerra* are carrying out their investigation on the underpaid, exploited women who make gloves in the Neapolitan sweat shops, they realize that their poverty and abysmal situation go hand in hand with total ignorance of their rights and their unconditional espousal of male values. As Vannina and Suna try to make the women aware that they are being exploited, the women turn against them. Even their threats are based on their husbands' sexual prowess: "se arriva mio marito la incula dritto, dritto. . . . Il mio ti butta sul letto e ti infila un coso così dentro la carne tua per disonore" (183; "if my husband arrives he will stick it straight up her ass. . . . Mine would throw you on the bed and stick something this big inside of you to shame you"). Suna, the voice of reason and liberation, replies:

> Se vuoi picchiarmi perché non lo fai tu? mi metti subito sotto, sei forte e grossa, io sono sciancata. Ma no, la tua difesa, come la tua sopravvivenza, come il tuo onore lo metti in mano a tuo marito, che e il tuo padrone dopo quello dei guanti, il padrone peggiore perché ti possiede anima e corpo e tu manco lo sai. (183)
>
> If you want to beat me up, why don't you do it yourself? You could overpower me right away, you're big and strong and I am crippled. But no, you hand it over to your husband, your defense, your survival, your honor, everything.

Variations on a Theme: Violence against Women

> He is your second boss after the one you make gloves for, the worst boss because he owns you completely, flesh and spirit, and you don't even know it.

Twenty years later, in *Voci,* Maraini is not so overt in her condemnation of women's attitudes but makes an even more poignant case when she demonstrates that Angela's mother could have prevented her daughters' sexual abuse but instead she simply shut her eyes and her heart for fear of losing her husband. Talking about her stepfather's sexual abuse, Angela's sister Ludovica explains that:

> Era come se mia madre mi avesse fatto capire che quello era un sacrificio necessario per tenerlo in famiglia, per mantenere la sua protezione, la sua benevolenza. Era un sacrificio non detto, e segreto ai suoi stessi occhi, oscuro come la più oscura delle notti . . . non ci dovevano essere parole fra di noi, ma un consenso cieco e completo, la resa dei nostri corpi alla sua ingiustificata ingordigia paterna. (262)

> It was as if my mother had made me understand that it was a sacrifice necessary to keep him in the family, to maintain his protection, his benevolence. It was an unspoken sacrifice that was occult and secret in her eyes too, obscure like the most obscure night . . . no words were to be used among us, but a blind and complete consensus, the capitulation of our bodies to his unjustified paternal greed.

Dacia Maraini is keenly aware of the importance of women's solidarity. In her writings she has not only tried to condemn the "culture of the fathers," but also tried to awaken and incite women to improve their situation and fight abuse. Many of her characters find their salvation through the help and protection of other women. Women's solidarity works, even against the will of men. Good examples are Vannina and Suna in *Donna in guerra;* Marianna and Fila in *Marianna Ucrìa;* Adele Sofia and Michela Canova in *Voci.* The supportive and positive relationships between these women are fictional instances of the practice of *affidamento,* "entrustment," advocated by the feminist group Diotima, through which women mentors help younger, inexperienced, less powerful women find their own voice.[5]

In her life Dacia Maraini has always counted on women's help to address major social issues. A recent example of this is her being one of the founding members of Controparola, a group of women writers and journalists who are fighting the exploitation and degradation of women's bodies in the media. In a recent interview with Paola Gaglianone, *Il piacere di scrivere: conversazione con Dacia Maraini* (1995), Maraini points out that women writers do not share a particular style but rather a common point of view, a common historical subjectivity passed down through the generations of women who lived before them. She concludes by stating that a woman writer will concentrate her attention on certain aspects of reality that are different from those of men (12–13). Such an aspect is violence committed against women. Although she has addressed this issue in different ways through the years, Maraini has maintained a strongly politicized female perspective on the matter. The crimes are seen from the victim's point of view. There is no doubt that *these women are victims* and that their behavior did in no way justify violence. In books and movies, violence against women is so often portrayed from men's point of view. The implicit condemnation of their acts is not enough when we, as readers and viewers, are asked to witness the men's excitement and a glamorous view of their destructive behavior. The issue of violence against women cannot be seen in terms of good and bad, black and white. There are no monsters, just regular men, who have been taught that this kind of behavior is natural and sanctioned by society. By making her readers understand the complex factors that trigger the cycle of violence against women, Dacia Maraini is certainly leaving her mark as a socially committed writer.

Notes

1. "Lettera sull'aborto" was first published in *Nuovi argomenti* 1–2 (Jan. 1996): 18–25, and subsequently reprinted in *Un clandestino a bordo* (9–34). The English translation, *Stowaway on Board,* by Giovanna Bellesia and Victoria Offredi Poletto, has just appeared.

2. All translations, unless otherwise indicated, are mine. For *Donna in guerra* they are often partly based on the published translation, *Woman at War.*

3. For an interesting study of incest in the Bible, see Edmund Leach, *Genesis as Myth and Other Essays,* and Leach and D. Alan Aycock, *Structuralist Interpretations of Biblical Myth.*

4. It is interesting to notice that in *Voci* (which literally means voices), the one voice we never really hear is precisely that of Angela. In the first pages of the book, Michela Canova, the radio journalist, thinks that two messages she finds on her answering machine might be from Angela, but we never know what she meant to say, as her few initial words are interrupted as abruptly as was her life.

5. On the philosophy and practices of the Diotima group, see Virginia Picchietti, "Symbolic Mediation and Female Community in Dacia Maraini's Fiction" in this volume; Teresa de Lauretis, "The Practice of Sexual Difference and Feminist Thought in Italy: An Introductory Essay," in *Sexual Difference: A Theory of Social-Symbolic Practice;* and Giovanna Miceli-Jeffries, "Caring and Nurturing in Italian Women's Theory and Fiction." in *Feminine Feminists* 102–03.

Works Cited

de Lauretis, Teresa. "The Practice of Sexual Difference and Feminist Thought in Italy: An Introductory Essay." *Sexual Difference: A Theory of Social-Symbolic Practice.* By the Milan Women's Bookstore Collective. Trans. Patricia Cicogna and de Lauretis. Bloomington: Indiana UP, 1990.

Di Pace-Jordan, Rosetta. Review of *Voci. World Literature Today* 69.2 (Spring 1995): 341–42.

Gallop, Jane. *The Daughter's Seduction.* Ithaca: Cornell UP, 1982.

Leach, Edmund. *Genesis as Myth and Other Essays.* London: Jonathan Cape, 1969.

Leach, Edmund, and D. Alan Aycock. *Structuralist Interpretations of Biblical Myth.* Cambridge: Cambridge UP, 1983.

Lonzi, Carla. *Sputiamo su Hegel: la donna clitoridea e la donna vaginale.* Milan: Rivolta Femminile, 1974.

Maraini, Dacia. *Bagheria.* Milan: Rizzoli, 1994. Published in English as *Bagheria.* London: Peter Owen, 1995; distributed by Dufour.

———. *Un clandestino a bordo.* 1993. Milan: Rizzoli, 1996. Published in English as *Stowaway on Board.*

———. *Dolce per sé.* Milan: Rizzoli, 1997.

———. *Donna in guerra.* Turin: Einaudi, 1975. Published in English as *Woman at War.*

———. *Donne mie.* Turin: Einaudi, 1974.

———. *La lunga vita di Marianna Ucrìa.* Milan: Rizzoli, 1990. Published in English as *The Silent Duchess.* London: Peter Owen, 1992. New York: Feminist, 1998.

Maraini, Dacia. *Stowaway on Board.* Trans. Giovanna Bellesia and Victoria Offredi Poletto. West Lafayette, IN: Bordighera, 2000.

———. *Voci.* Milan: Rizzoli, 1994. Published in English as *Voices.* London and New York: Serpent's Tail, 1997.

———. *Woman at War.* Trans. Mara Benetti and Elspeth Spottiswood. New York: Italica, 1988.

Maraini, Dacia, and Anna Maria Mori. *Nel segno della madre.* Milan: Frassinelli, 1992.

Maraini, Dacia, and, Paola Gaglianone. *Il piacere di scrivere*: *conversazione con Dacia Maraini.* Rome: Òmicron, 1995.

Miceli-Jeffries, Giovanna, ed. *Feminine Feminists.* Minneapolis: U of Minnesota P, 1994.

Peristiany, J. G., ed. *Mediterranean Family Structures.* Cambridge: Cambridge UP, 1976.

Pitt-Rivers, Julian. *The Fate of Shechem or the Politics of Sex.* Cambridge: Cambridge UP, 1977.

Daniela Cavallaro

Dacia Maraini's "Barricade Theater"

The decade of the 1970s was a period of intense struggle and remarkable success for the Italian women's movement. As Lucia Chiavola Birnbaum recalls, it achieved such changes as the divorce law (established in 1970 and confirmed in 1974), protective legislation for working mothers, equal family rights, equal pay, equal treatment of male and female workers, and the legalization of abortion (established in 1978, and confirmed by a popular referendum in 1981) (89–90).

Women's theater during those years, from the first all-woman company La Maddalena, established in Rome in 1973, to other smaller experimental groups that performed their plays in the streets, garages, and political festivals, expressed these same social and political concerns. "That was the 'white-hot' time of feminism," recalls Dacia Maraini. "We started out with a theatre that broke with the past, attacked, set up barricades.... We wanted to spread ideas that very few people held and very few people agreed with" (qtd. in Bassnett 455). Theater was the privileged means of expression for the feminist movement of the 1970s. It was considered the best way to elicit reflection on the social situation and on women's condition. When writing for theater, Maraini declared in 1974, "I always start with content and stay close to reality, since I believe that theater, more than any other art form, is imbued with ideology" (*Fare teatro* [Making theater] 8).[1] Thus it was the period when Maraini wrote what she later defined as her "ideological texts": "I used the allegorical, almost religious theater above all in the ideological texts, where I wanted to make a polemical statement, to oppose the female condition—treating abortion in *La donna perfetta,* and discrimination against women in *Manifesto:* these are ideological texts" (qtd. in Anderlini 159).

Daniela Cavallaro

I have chosen *Il manifesto* (1969; The manifesto), and *La donna perfetta* (1974; The perfect woman) in order to present what appear to me exemplary expressions of the feminist and political issues of the time. In addition to their ideological value, however, I will highlight how Maraini's mixture of prose and poetic elements, and her refined use of biblical and fairy-tale images and references, go well beyond the immediate political purpose of the plays. Through the analysis of these examples of Maraini's early dramatic production, I hope the reader might gain some appreciation of this kind of "barricade theater," performed in Italy between the late sixties and the early seventies, which opened the way to today's women's theater.

Il manifesto, completed in November 1969 and staged as *Manifesto dal carcere* (The prison manifesto) in March 1971, originated from a survey of the conditions of women's jails that Maraini did for *Paese sera*.[2] *Il manifesto* stages the exemplary story of the upbringing and maturation of a young woman, Anna Micolla, her rebellion against authority and the system, her consequent violent death, and a promise that her suffering was not in vain.

Scenes in prose from the life and death of Anna are alternately framed by sections in verse in which already deceased women ask Anna to tell her story, comment on it, and in which they recall their own experiences.[3] Thus the text is divided into two styles: one realistic, aggressive, at times violent; the other poetic, more reflexive, almost sacral. Maraini, in fact, has admitted that she often mixes two different styles in her writing: on the one hand, an "attachment to reality, a mainly illuministic, rational and realistic vision; on the other hand, a temptation, a strong feeling of something which cannot be explained rationally which in my works is embodied in death" (Montini 102). The presence onstage of life and death, prose and verse, "document and lyricism" (Tian), gives this play a tone that goes well beyond that of pure testimony. In fact, the play's language, plot (story of the birth, life, teaching, suffering, death, and "resurrection" of Anna Micolla), and scene division (thirteen framed by fourteen interventions by the dead women)[4] bring to light the religious connotations of this work.[5] *Il manifesto* can be compared to the "Way of the Cross," a series of "14 chosen representations of the suffering of Christ on His way to Calvary. Each station or stop," the *New Catholic Encyclopedia* tells us, "is a halting place at which the soul of the onlooker is moved to sorrowful contemplation" (14: 832). Each scene or station of *Il manifesto,* therefore, becomes a halting place at which the audience is presented with a different stage in Anna's presumed way to death—and expected final resurrection. The purpose of participating in the traditional Lenten celebration of the Way of the Cross is also resonant here. The "onlooker," who witnesses the suffering of Christ, experiences a process of purification that leads to rebirth, resurrection, Easter. In the case of Maraini's *Manifesto,* it is the theatrical audience who, through identification with the protagonist's suffering, should be led to "new life."

Anna's salvific destiny is not at first apparent in the episodes of her life that the audience witnesses: her childhood rebellion against authority—her father and the nuns at boarding school; her short-lived career as prostitute and thief; her first experience in jail, followed by a failed attempt to settle down in a "normal" life; her underpaid work in a factory and her final incarceration. Anna's rebellious attitude is sterile; she lacks the capacity to successfully fight against the different stages of oppression that she experiences—in her own life and in the lives of friends, coworkers, and other inmates. It is only at the end of her life that Anna becomes aware of her strength and is finally able to articulate her thoughts. The "good news" preached by Anna takes the form of a manifesto written in jail the night before a planned revolt. Once again drawing on and subverting a religious pattern, Maraini has her Anna dictate eleven "commandments," in which she explains that women should not be ashamed of being women, that they should work, be independent, have a life outside that of their husbands and children, and claim the right to a sexual life. The last commandment demands that women acquire freedom by themselves, and not wait for others to give it to them. The following day, the attempted revolt results in the death of many of the prisoners. Anna is restrained in a straitjacket in a criminal asylum and suffocated to death with a wet towel by four nurses. They will call her death a suicide.

Throughout the entire play, the dead women who have elicited Anna's story talk about their own oppression based on their "difference": abortions resulting in death, sexual experiences punished with violent death. These memories form a desolate image of women's predicament. Anna's life would appear, therefore, to be but one more exemplary story to illustrate women's oppression. Nevertheless, in the very last part of the work, after her death has been played out, Anna refuses to simply join this group of the dead. When the women tell her to quiet down, and suggest that nothing of her life will be left, and that the world will go on as always, Anna disagrees. She declares that, though her body has been defeated, her manifesto is still alive. It will wake women up; it will serve to change the world and make it better.

The play ends with the protagonist coming on front stage, while the dead women retreat. Anna repeats the final message of her manifesto, inviting all women to acquire freedom with their own hands:

> siate orgogliose, imprudenti, feroci, sicure.
> Prendete con forza e violenza la libertà
> che volete e non aspettate mai, non aspettate
> che qualcuno vi compatisca e vi protegga. (281)

> be proud, imprudent, wild, and confident.
> With strength and violence seize the freedom
> you want, and never wait, never wait
> for somebody to pity and protect you.

The play's finale thus makes explicit reference to the Communist *Manifesto,* which, projecting a better future, calls on proletarians throughout the world to join forces and violently end their oppression. At the same time, the final scene draws once again on the analogy Anna-Christ, by promising a resurrection and a salvation that will be not only individual, but for all women. Furthermore, as Jesus did with reference to the kingdom of God, so too Anna stresses that her future kingdom is not something of which to dream, but something that can exist in the "here and now." Women must strive to obtain it.

La donna perfetta, staged in October 1974 by the Maddalena theater group, might be considered a "double" for *Il manifesto.*[6] If, in the latter, Anna Micolla died for her lack of respect for authority, if she was condemned for her aggressivity, because she did not conform to the expectations of society, then how must a woman behave? And if a woman were to behave as society asked, what would her life be like? In Nina Battaglia, the protagonist of *La donna perfetta,* Maraini constructs the opposite of Anna: Nina is a woman who loves and obeys her man, and who sacrifices herself. In the end, however, her destiny will not be different from that of Anna.

In relation to structure as well, the two plays present many similarities. In *La donna perfetta,* Maraini refuses any naturalism; in her stage directions she indicates that "it will be necessary to eliminate any kind of verism.... Acting must be as demonstrative and detached as possible, in order to stress the didactic character of the text."[7] She adds that the rhythm of the play should be that of a popular ballad. She creates this ambiance by framing the love story of Nina and Elvio with the presentation of a "dicitrice," a female storyteller, who introduces and comments on the scenes of the story. Once again, as in *Il manifesto,* the frame makes use of poetic language, while the scenes are in prose style. The audience is explicitly invited to participate emotionally in and reflect on the development of the play. In fact, at the beginning, the storyteller poses to the public a fundamental question: was Nina's behavior finally dictated by "coraggio leonino" ("a lion's courage") or "supina viltà" (6; "passive cowardice")?

Nina's tale is quite simple: as a young woman of sixteen, she has a love affair with Elvio, a twenty-year-old student. He is very pleased with her, since she is the "perfect woman": "Dolce, pudica, sottomessa, sensibile" (10; "Sweet, modest, submissive, tender"). Her submission to his desires includes eating or not eating certain foods, smoking, having certain friends, telling him where she goes, and trusting him for birth control. When she becomes pregnant, he promises to give her money to pay for an abortion, but then suddenly disappears. He claims she has been unfaithful, and that the child is not his.

Parallel to this love story between Nina and Elvio, we are presented with the relationship between Gigi, a friend of Elvio's, and Christa, a young German woman who had been Elvio's girlfriend before Nina. Christa is everything Nina is not. Elvio describes her as "dura, sboccata, violenta, prepotente . . . una piccola troia invertita" (15; "hard, vulgar, violent, aggressive . . . a little invert whore"). Christa is the only one who offers support and help to Nina, giving her money to pay for the abortion. But the doctor butchers her and she is left to bleed to death, while Christa seeks medical help in vain.

As Maraini pointed out in her stage directions, this is an openly didactic text. It denounces legislation that does not allow women to have safe abortions and leaves them in the hands of butchers (not by chance, the doctor who performs the abortion is called "Professor Macelloni"), often causing their death. This is a criticism of the medical profession, as represented not only by the doctor who performs the abortion, but also by the one who diagnoses Nina's pregnancy and will do nothing to help her. Many other themes come into play: the weakness of the older generation of women, represented by Nina's mother, who is so frightened of what her husband will say and what the neighbors will think that she refuses to take Nina to a hospital; the exploitation of Nina the worker by her female boss who underpays her, refuses to give her a monetary advance, and, when she faints on the job, continues to attend to a client rather than help the young woman.

Above all, however, *La donna perfetta* satirizes men's expectations of women. Nina, the "perfect woman," is so submissive, so nice, so understanding, and so ready to obey all of Elvio's wishes, that even when he disappears she does not criticize him; she refuses to believe that he is acting cowardly. Indeed, Nina only wishes to have the chance to explain that she has always been faithful.

Male characters are stereotypes as well. Elvio, like his friend Gigi, is the embodiment of selfishness, superficiality, callousness, paternalistic attitudes, and the exploitation of women. Long before his abandonment of Nina, the audience sees how he manipulates the innocent protagonist to his own advantage. After the two make love, Elvio reproaches Nina for being too compliant; although he enjoys their lovemaking, he feels she yielded too easily to him. Elvio's attitude toward Christa also reveals his selfish character: he leaves the German woman because she is not ready enough to satisfy his needs. Thus, Elvio generously "gives" Christa as a gift to his friend Gigi.

In *La donna perfetta,* Maraini uses two contrasting fairy-tale motifs:[8] the guilty woman who is justly punished at the end, and the innocent woman who will ultimately be exonerated from guilt. Nina's story, in a traditional reading, would be a parable of punished vice, as in the type of "edifying" stories the nuns of the boarding school used to tell Anna Micolla and her schoolmates in *Il manifesto*.[9] Nina is guilty of sinful behavior (fornication) and murder (abortion). Consequently Nina's death represents just punishment for her sins. In the celebration at the end of the play, in fact, the doctor, followed in a chorus by Elvio, Nina's mother, and Nina's boss, explains that "l'aborto è un attentato alla vita e deve essere punito con la morte" (47; "abortion is an attack on life and must be punished with death"); he further proclaims the sanctity of motherhood for the good of the Italian people. Nina's death is the price paid in order to preserve the sacredness of life.

The storyteller, on the other hand, invites the audience to lament Nina's sad death, subverting the traditional interpretation of the story, and presenting instead another fairy-tale pattern: that in which the protagonist is an innocent woman, unjustly accused, made to undergo suffering and endless trials. Nina's death, the storyteller concludes, is the result of the guilt of everyone around her; Nina herself is innocent. Thus Maraini suggests a different ending for Nina's story. As in *Il manifesto,* the death of the protagonist is not an acceptance of defeat: the storyteller, in fact, foresees a time in which all women who have died because of abortions will rise from their tombs to teach the living about the centuries of female submission. Again, the play's finale is a vision of utopia, a cry for all women, dead and alive, to join forces and throw off their oppression:

> Verrà un giorno che le morte
> si uniranno alle vive in una
> guerra rabbiosa che ridarà
> onore alle donne . . . (48)

> the day will come when the dead women
> will join the living in a
> furious war which will return
> honor to women . . .

Although Nina, like Anna of *Il manifesto,* dies, the audience is invited to fight so that her death will not be accepted, justified, and repeated. Her death, therefore, will have a purpose, to save other women from the same destiny. Unlike Anna, Nina does not appear to be a Christlike figure, a model to follow,

Daniela Cavallaro

since she does not have a gospel to teach to all women and she will not be the one to start the fight against oppression. Indeed, she represents an antitype, a role not to be imitated. However, Nina's suffering and death do have their biblical reference in the destiny of the suffering servant in Isaiah, chapter 53. Like the protagonist of this biblical text, Nina went to her death "like a lamb led to the slaughter" (Isa. 53.7), and her acceptance of unjust suffering will lead to other women's salvation. The spectators of Maraini's *La donna perfetta* then function as do the witnesses of the afflictions of Isaiah's servant. They too understood the proportions and the consequences of the servant's sacrifice only after his death. The audience of Nina's parable finally comes to realize that it will be by the wounds of women like Nina that we will be healed.

Anna, Nina: different facets of women's oppression. Anna is exploited, confined, locked up, and finally erased by a society that does not accept rebellious women. Nina does not even realize that there is something wrong in the way her lover, her doctor, her family, her boss treat her; she will die trying to prove her innocence, while everyone around her is guilty of causing her death.

The two plays paint a sad portrait of women's condition in society, of their awareness (or lack of awareness) of oppression, and of the possibility to enact change. Anna, the protagonist of *Il manifesto,* goes through a process of maturation during the unfolding of the play. Her attempt at rebellion, however, meets with death. Nina, the perfect woman, dies completely unaware of having been killed by a society that later will hypocritically cry over her death. In other words, the plays do not appear to convey confidence and a sense of victory, but rather the opposite. What is Maraini's theater trying to tell us?

The playwright herself addressed this at the time. "Is there any chance for theatre to act in order to change society? Or must theater be but the passive reflection of a certain social situation?" Maraini wondered (qtd. in Sumeli Weinberg, *Invito* 132). Although these plays present but a dismal account of women's condition, still there is also a definite call to action. One notes that though the female characters are not presented as role models, the audience is invited to reflect on their stories of oppression, to realize that social change is necessary, and to accept Maraini's resistance. Through poetic, tragic, prose-style, or declamatory frames, through references to the tragic destiny of women in fairy tales, or to the messianic future prophesied by the protagonists, Maraini's plays exude a desire for change. If in the "Way of the Cross" the audience must be moved to compassion, the audience of Maraini's "ideological texts" must be moved to action.

Nevertheless, aside from noting a passive reflection of women's oppression and the call to action, one must wonder if Maraini was already admitting defeat in the women's movement and its attempt to create a better reality. In an interview of 1987, reflecting back on those early years, Maraini appears to imply just that. After summarizing her experience with political theater, she went on to conclude: "My last phase is one that has to deal with defeat, not my defeat, but the world's. It is the defeat of some ideological certainties by reality. . . . We had a great dream in the Sixties; to change the world and, maybe, to change it quickly and easily. We found out that it was impossible" (qtd. in Sumeli Weinberg, "Interview" 68).

Thus Maraini's plays do express a sort of defeat, but one, it appears, that leads to maturity. It would probably be very hard to stage *Il manifesto* or *La donna perfetta* in the nineties. The feminist movement has become much more sophisticated, and many of the battles proposed in these plays have already been fought and won. As the playwright explains, when feminism had gained a certain ground, "you couldn't do barricade theatre any more . . . . From the political shows of the first . . . years of questioning we moved on to more sophisticated, more 'thought-out' performances that expressed our contradictions as well as our certainties" (qtd. in Bassnett 455). Thus it would be too late for this kind of "barricade theater" to instill a revolutionary fervor in the audience; but it would also be unjust to view these plays exclusively as "time pieces." Rather, through the stories of Anna and Nina, Dacia Maraini puts onstage the history of women's oppression that mixes reality and allegory, condemning the present, and giving hope for the future. Moreover, her plays already indicate a transition from these more didactic and aggressive early attempts to articulate a feminist art, to the much more refined development of women's theater that we find in Italy today.

Daniela Cavallaro

Notes

1. Unless otherwise indicated, all translations are mine.

2. *Manifesto dal carcere* was staged at the Teatro Centocelle under the direction of Maraini. The cast included Rosabianca Scerrino, Viviana Toniolo, Carla Tatò, and Luigi Mezzanotte.

3. This mixture of life and death is due, Maraini explained in an interview to Ileana Montini, to the influence of Japanese theater, with which she became familiar during the years spent in Japan (Montini 101).

4. The scenes in the play are not numbered. If the interventions of the dead women divide the scenes, as I have suggested, then they number thirteen. However, if one counts the scenes according to the interruptions of darkness and light, the number rises to seventeen.

5. Grazia Sumeli Weinberg also has noted that the structure of *Il manifesto* shows the influence of plays like *Pilgrim's Progress* (*Invito* 142).

6. *La donna perfetta* premiered at the Venice Biennale. The cast included Ornella Grassi (Nina), Luca dal Fabbro (Elvio), Claudio De Angelis (Gigi) and Silvia Poggioli (Christa). Claudia Ricatti and Yuki Maraini played the storyteller. Dacia Maraini directed the staging, with Annabella Cerliani. For further information about the premiere staging, see *La donna perfetta* 2.

7. The stage directions are published as an introduction to the text of *La donna perfetta,* without page numbers.

8. Maraini also uses fairy-tale phrases, as when, for example, the storyteller summarizes Nina's suffering: "Sette paia di scarpe ha consumato / sette fiaschi di lagrime ha versato . . ." (37; "Seven pairs of shoes she has worn out, seven flasks of tears she has cried . . .").

9. In particular, a nun tells the story of a young woman who, having yielded to a handsome young man's rather charming talk, found herself pregnant. But the man was already married and there was no remedy for the situation. The Lord then, the nun explains, punished the young woman. Run over by a streetcar, she remained without use of her legs for the rest of her life (*Il manifesto* 205).

Works Cited

Anderlini, Serena. "Prolegomena for a Feminist Dramaturgy of the Feminine: An Interview with Dacia Maraini." *diacritics* 21.2–3 (1991): 148–60.

Bassnett, Susan E. "Towards a Theory of Women's Theatre." *Semiotics of Drama and Theatre: New Perspectives in the Theory of Drama and Theatre.* Ed. Herta Schmid and Aloysius Van Kesteren. Amsterdam and Philadelphia: Benjamins, 1984. 445–66.

Birnbaum, Lucia Chiavola. *Liberazione della donna: Feminism in Italy.* Middletown, CT: Wesleyan UP, 1986.

Maraini, Dacia. *La donna perfetta.* 1974. In *Il cuore di una vergine.* Turin: Einaudi, 1975.

———. *Fare teatro.* Milan: Bompiani, 1974.

———. *Il manifesto.* In *Il ricatto a teatro e altre commedie.* Turin: Einaudi, 1970.

Montini, Ileana. *Parlare con Dacia Maraini.* Verona: Bertani, 1977.

Sumeli Weinberg, Grazia. "An Interview with Dacia Maraini." *Tydskrif vir letterkunde* 27 (1989): 64–72.

———. *Invito alla lettura di Dacia Maraini.* Pretoria: U of South Africa, 1993.

Tian, Rienzo. "Dal carcere con rabbia." Review of *Manifesto dal carcere. Il Messaggero* 19 Mar. 1971.

"Way of the Cross." *New Catholic Encyclopedia.* 17 vols. New York: McGraw, 1967–79.

Part 4
Historiographies

Giancarlo Lombardi
A memoria: Charting a Cultural Map for
Women's Transition from *Preistoria* to *Storia*

Maria Ornella Marotti
La lunga vita di Marianna Ucrìa: A Feminist
Revisiting of the Eighteenth Century

Paola Carù
Vocal Marginality: Dacia Maraini's Veronica
Franco

Giancarlo Lombardi

A memoria
Charting a Cultural Map for Women's Transition from *Preistoria* to *Storia*

> 8 dicembre. "Sai da quanti anni siamo sposati?" "Da otto. Perché?" "Siamo sposati da otto anni." "Da quanto?" "Da otto anni." "Sono molti." "Troppi?" "No. Sono giusti." "Che vuol dire giusti?" "Sono quelli che sono. Né troppi né pochi." "Siamo sposati da quasi sei anni." "Sono sei anni che siamo sposati?" "Quasi." "Sono molti." "Troppi?" "No. Sono giusti." "Cosa vuol dire giusti?" "Che vanno bene così." "Fra un mese saranno dieci." "Dieci cosa?" "Dieci anni che siamo sposati."
>
> Dacia Maraini
A memoria

> December 8. "Do you know how long we've been married?" "Eight years. Why?" "We've been married for eight years." "For how long?" "Eight years." "That's a lot." "Too long?" "No. It's a fair amount of time." "What does fair mean?" "That it's just what it is. Not too much, not too little." "We've been married for almost six years." "Have we been married for six years?" "Almost." "That's a lot." "Too long?" "No. It's a fair amount of time." "What does fair mean?" "That it's fine as it is." "In a month, it will be ten." "Ten what?" "Ten years that we've been married."

The stichomythic lines exchanged by Maria and Pietro at the inception of Dacia Maraini's *A memoria* (1967; By heart) immediately introduce the reader into a fictional world ruled by contradiction, alienation and, most of all, forgetfulness.[1] Maria, who soon thereafter comes to be identified as the diarist, is a woman who suffers from an uncommon form of mental disease: dysmnesia, the lack of social memory.[2] As a consequence, she seems to have lost self-consciousness, not being able to link the past with the present, or to make any form of rational connection. Deprived of the knowledge that lies at the basis of cultural, intellectual, or affective life, Maria appears as a robotic creature exclusively driven by instincts. In her journal she coldly transcribes conversations without even bothering to specify the interlocutors, or she mechanically registers her daily activities, always described from the outside, and usually in a contradictory fashion. Such bizarre diary entries are also punctuated by the interspersion of a series of letters she receives from Giacomo, her husband's colleague who, while disguising himself as Pietro's best friend and admirer, desperately attempts to seduce her. In the five months covered by the journal, the reader witnesses a series of events that culminate in the death of both protagonists, preceded by Pietro's long agony caused by cancer of the bowels. While her husband is still alive and suffering, Maria goes from one adulterous encounter to another, always playing the role of the temptress with young men that she picks up during her aimless wandering in the streets of Rome. Soon after her husband's untimely demise, however, Maria suddenly withdraws from the world, as if deprived of her only reason for existing: her former restlessness is replaced, in the last few entries of her diary, by the impossibility of leaving what becomes, in a short amount of time, her deathbed. A handful of characters revolves around the singular *ménage* established by Maria and Pietro. Giacomo plays the third cusp in an impossible triangle, voicing lustful craving for Maria while betraying latent homosexual desire for Pietro. On the borders of this triangle lie three uncommon families: three mothers uncannily characterized by a voracious hunger; two greedy siblings, Pietro's brother Davide and Giacomo's sister, "la piattola," the leech. There are no fathers, since both Maria's and Giacomo's fathers are dead while Pietro's hardly ever makes his presence felt.

What immediately strikes the reader upon the completion of the novel is the rigid differentiation between male and female characters: prisoners of their bodies, women are all instincts and voracity, from Maria's uncontrollable sexual drives to the intimately related ferocious desire for food of the three mothers. On the other hand, intellectual speculation appears to fall entirely in the male domain: both of them high-school teachers, Pietro and Giacomo are the only characters who seem to be endowed with the ability to think. Such a contrast is established at the beginning of the novel, with Pietro's reiterated claim that he can remember everything of his past: "Io invece ricordo tutto" (20; "I, however, remember everything") in response to Maria's often repeated "Non ricordo niente" (20; "I don't remember anything").

Maria's mental condition assumes symbolic overtones, especially when her behavior is analyzed in light of statements made by Maraini in her *diacritics* interview. Asked by Serena Anderlini if the present time could be considered one of transition for women, Maraini said that "it's a change from *preistoria,* prehistory, to *storia,* history. . . . *Preistoria* is characterized by lack of consciousness: letting yourself live, living by instinct, or even by reason, but a reason fairly well closed up in that particular moment. Conversely, the characteristic of *storia* is reflecting on yourself at the moment you're living, while you look at yourself live. This is *storia,* a continuity of memory. *Preistoria* is, precisely, outside of *storia*. The day is sufficient unto itself; it has no memory. Women are entering *storia* in our era" (qtd. in Anderlini 159).

Written in 1967, *A memoria* portrays women's *preistoria:* it was penned, in fact, before the official advent of feminism in Italy. Indeed, while writing in her diary, Maria, the woman with *no memory,* does not reflect on her actions, merely transcribing them as if they were deeds accomplished by somebody else. In order to show the degree of her disassociation in the most effective way, Maraini adopts the technique *du regard,* the peculiar trait of the French *nouveau roman*. Maria's daily actions are described with extreme precision by an I/eye that is only concerned with the external mechanics of her actions, an I/eye that hardly ever contemplates the possibility of enriching its text with any sort of psychological nuance. In an effort to render reality in the most meticulous fashion, the description often turns on itself, accruing and changing some of the details.

Giancarlo Lombardi

While the descriptive journal entries certainly bring to mind the *nouveau roman* as practiced by Alain Robbe-Grillet, the passages exclusively devoted to conversations employ stylistic devices borrowed from the *nouveau roman* as practiced by Natalie Sarraute. Indeed, different types of dialogues are interwoven in these scenes, *conversation* and *sous-conversation,* typical elements of the Sarrautian novel, come to be juxtaposed. No information is provided about the identity of the interlocutors who, at times, remain anonymous throughout the entire passage. No room is allotted to the inscription of their impressions, they have no depth, they are all surface.

Among the many novels written by Maraini, *A memoria* is certainly the only one that has been consistently avoided by the critics because of its utmost obscurity. Impossible even to summarize, this work seems to reject critical exegesis. No explanation of the events is ever provided. The entire novel seems to be wrapped into a veil of mystery, in a veil of silence that bespeaks the deep sense of despair that subtly pervades it. The harshly realistic quality of Maraini's writing is intimately related to an avant-gardist project that attempts to depict reality in its incomprehensibility, in its disorder, in its innate contradiction:

> Paradoxically, it was, above all, the avant-garde that proposed new forms of naturalism. . . . Today's naturalism . . . uncritically mimics a reality that has become incomprehensible. A senseless world that produces in its observers those effects of malaise, of loss, of delirium that are considered essential for the modern artist.
>
> But we're still talking about naturalism. About abstaining from moral and political judgment. The writer, in brief, declines to intervene upon narrative matter, declines to offer a subjective angle on things. He limits himself to giving back the disorder, as is. His work consists in miming, through verbal and syntactic irregularity, the irregularity of the real. ("Riflessioni" xxiv)[3]

The presence of Robbe-Grillet and Sarraute is powerfully evoked in these haunting statements, along with that of another master of Western modernism, Samuel Beckett. *Waiting for Godot, Endgame,* and many other of his works patently resist interpretation. "No concessions are made to the comfort of readers, in terms both of form and of the conventional consolation of fiction," writes Marguerite Alexander (54); what the readers face is thus a most unusual confrontation with a work of art that stems from profound existential despair. Maria and Pietro's stichomythic exchanges, vivid reminders of Estragon's endless conversations, are both dramatic and comic at the same time, and constantly repeat themselves without ever achieving proper closure: instead of reaching a climactic stage, these conversations only spiral down into silence, in the same way that both Pietro and Maria eventually fall into an aphasic state that precedes their death. Such failure of communication is powerfully evoked by Maraini and Beckett through a similar device: the characters never actually listen to one another. Like Didi and Gogo, Maria and Pietro seem to be uttering monologues instead of participating in a dialogue, and the fragmentary nature of their discourse is only one instance of the fragmentary quality of the entire narrative, composed of short entries grouped in three different sections. Indeed, fragmentation appears as the stylistic and thematic characteristic of the section containing Giacomo's letters, striking for their uncanny punctuation, which elliptically breaks down sentences into meaningless syntagmas:

> È qui il nodo. Il cuore proliferante e bruciato. Io sento il fumo a un miglio. Perché il saperti. Così e così. Tu sai. Lo vuole. Vuole che tu. Insomma vorrebbe che anch'io . . . (*A memoria* 65–66)

> The knot is here. The burning and proliferating heart. I can feel smoke at a mile's distance. Because to know you. So and so. You know. He wants it. He wants you to. Basically he would expect me as well . . .

As a matter of fact, division and fragmentation at the formal and stylistic levels serve to reconfirm the internal rift experienced by the female protagonist, who could be considered an ideal example of the Laingian divided self.[4]

Like many Beckettian characters, Pietro and Maria live at the margins of society. A failed existentialist, Pietro rejects his materialistic family to the extent that he does not allow it to assist him in his long agony, while Maria, a wild nymphomaniac, appears to be able to communicate only through her body.

Giancarlo Lombardi

When, at the end of the novel, Maria's mother decides to send her to a psychiatrist, Maria refuses to be treated, avoiding societal normalization of her behavior. In several instances Maraini voiced her opinion about women's madness, defining it as an act of resistance against the strain imposed on them by a paternalistic society:

> Madness is not adjusting to the world. Women find themselves, objectively, in a non-adjusted condition, because this is not a world made to a woman's measurements. It's made to a man's measurements. So many women don't fit in it, and the damage that this does to some women is so severe that some go crazy. Some do not hold. You could say that it is actually the most sensitive who go crazy, the ones who feel the most strongly this violence that is being done to their psyches, to women's psychological integrity, by the male world, which is very powerful. My play *Clytemnestra* is the story of female madness, as rejection, incongruence, non-relationship with the male world. Also, if you look deep enough, you can find this theme of madness in other texts of mine. (Qtd. in Anderlini 150)

Through the estranged perspective of the madwoman, Maraini thus launches into an attack against societal values, and the opacity of her work only reinforces such a political stance. Leo Bersani defines opacity in Beckett as the necessary element that turns artistic products into *acts of resistance*, because "they refuse to serve the complacency of a culture that expects art to reinforce its moral and epistemological authority. We could even speak . . . of an art at war with culture" (8). In refusing to adjust to the world, both Beckett's and Maraini's characters establish their subversive role and bear out the subversion already enacted through stylistic techniques proper to the avant-garde.

Formally subversive, Maraini's novel places equal subversive potential in its female protagonist as threat to patriarchal society. Maria's sexual aggressiveness is a potent sign of the danger she incarnates as a deviant member of a society that has built its foundation on the objectification and submission of women. In Catholic Italy, religion has always played a fundamental role in subjecting women to a condition of inferiority, especially through its strenuous reinforcement of sexual taboos: for this reason sexual promiscuity appears as the most transgressive act that a woman can possibly perform in such a society. Maria's revolutionary misdeeds take on an even stronger symbolic relevance because of her first name, which binds her to the image of the Madonna. Furthermore, the fact that the novel's first entry falls on December 8, the day Italians celebrate the Immaculate Conception, only enhances the role of such a connection. In the introduction to her interview *Parlare con Dacia,* Ileana Montini discusses at length the role of the Virgin Mary within the Catholic and the feminist contexts:

> Mary is an ambiguous figure, on one hand she represents *wisdom* and on the other she represents women's dutiful submission as symbolized in the fideistic acceptance of the mystery of incarnation. To disobedient Eve is counterposed obedient Mary. The order unsettled by Eve is reestablished by Mary. . . . Mary's *place* in the Church depends on divine maternity. What characterizes her is her willing and total "consecration" of herself as God's *Handmaid.* . . . She is the image of the true woman, whose relationship with God must pass through the mediation of Man. (94–95; emphasis in the original)

Instead of being an *obedient* Mary, Maraini's protagonist definitely comes closer to the image of the disobedient Eve. Always, in the description of her adulterous encounters with several young men, Maria is depicted as the agent of a castrating threat. Because of their youth, the *ragazzi* she seduces all share an uncommon sexual vitality, as well as an extreme frailty, which usually becomes evident once they undress. The Achilles' heel of the heterosexual macho is symbolically unveiled as these men shed their clothes, revealing their own fallibility, inevitably defined by the inadequacy of their genital apparatus: a penis that cannot aspire to the role of the Lacanian phallus because it cannot match its symbolic "size." The shrinking male member betrays the presence of fear at a moment when it should least appear: under the castrating eyes of Maria the temptress:

> "Mentre mi spoglio, tu voltati dall'altro lato." "Perché?" "Adesso vado nel bagno, tu non ti voltare." . . . "Siediti sul letto. Vuoi una sigaretta?" "Ti dispiace se chiudiamo gli scuri.

Giancarlo Lombardi

> Io alla luce, mi sento impacciato." . . . "Vieni vicino. È buio, non vedo niente." "Quando fa così, è tutto rovinato." "Chi fa così?" "Lui, il verme." "Chi?" "Non mi toccare. Mi sento tutto rattrappito e indolenzito." (*A memoria* 52–53)

> "Turn on the other side, while I undress." "Why?" "Now I'll go to the bathroom, don't turn your back." . . . "Sit on the bed. Do you want a cigarette?" "Do you mind if I shut the blinds? I feel awkward when there's light in the room." . . . "Come closer. It's dark, I can't see anything." "When he does that, it all goes to pot." "Who does that?" "He does, the worm." "Who?" "Don't touch me. I feel all shriveled and in pain."

Freud maintained, in his analysis of a tale of male disempowerment in "Das Unheimliche," that the female gaze can act as the purveyor of castration, and a scene excerpted from Maraini's novel appears to prove the same point. In the only passage in which she describes herself, Maria faces her image in the mirror as she is about to open the door of a shop:

> La mia figura mi viene incontro dalla vetrina . . . la piccola faccia dai tratti duri, fortemente marcati, si muove sul collo magro come una testa di uccello rapace . . . alla maniera di un uccello affamato. (*A memoria* 116)

> My image comes toward me from the shopwindow . . . the small face with hard features moves on the neck that is as thin as the head of a rapacious bird . . . as if it were a starving bird.

With features resembling those of a preying animal, an "uccello rapace," Maria is portrayed as a menacing presence, threatening because of her animal lack of awareness of those societal norms that she defies as if in compliance with the primitive, prehistorical law of the survival of the fittest. The young prey on which she feasts are already marked by previous encounters with the enemy, they have scars on their bodies to prove it, scars that speak their vulnerability as well as their ability to overcome the adversary:

> Il ragazzo adesso è nudo. Si china sul lenzuolo, la testa affondata nel cuscino, le ginocchia piegate. . . . Adesso viene

verso di me. Una cicatrice rossa gli attraversa la coscia destra . . . in mezzo al petto gonfio brilla una medaglia d'oro con l'effige della Madonna. (156)

Now the boy is naked. He bends on the bedsheet, his head buried in the pillow, the knees bent . . . now he comes toward me. A red scar runs across his right thigh . . . a golden medal with the effigy of the Madonna shines in the middle of his swollen chest.

Even though the fetal posture of this body betrays the young man's innocence, revealing his initial unwillingness to participate in the sacrificial coitus, the presence of the red scar on his thigh acts as a memento of his past encounters. Furthermore, the effigy of the Virgin on the medal plate definitely comes across as a polysemic signifier: as a religious token, it is both a reminder of his youth and naiveté, and a talisman on which the *framed* image of Mary acts as the symbol of the phallocratic disempowerment of women. However, because of the uncanny equation between Maria and the Madonna, the previous symbolism could be reversed, thus making the talisman come to signify its opposite, representing a mark of the young man's idolatrous submission to the novel's Maria, the quintessential man-eating witch.

But as the unfolding of her sexual escapades progresses, Maria slowly sheds her aggressiveness, assuming a position of inferiority. Her process of self-destruction, already initiated through sexual promiscuity, reaches its climax during her encounter with a young bartender, an opportunistic *ragazzo di strada* ("hustler") whose assertiveness dethrones Maria from her active role of seducer. Refusing to eat the apples that Maria is offering him, he proclaims his superiority over atavistic temptations: "'Cosa hai da mangiare?' . . . 'Ci sono le mele.' 'Che me ne faccio delle mele?'" (199–200; "What do you have to eat?" . . . "There are some apples." "What would I do with apples?"). Asking her to surrender her precious ring, "'È bello questo anello, allora me lo regali?'" (201; "This ring is beautiful, will you give it to me, then?"), he eventually leaves the scene as the phallocratic conqueror, an epic hero who, upon killing the mythical dragon, returns home with a symbolic prize. In another relevant scene, Maria suddenly turns into Mary Magdalene, washing the hair of a poor teenager that she has accidentally met. The path that led her from the virtual freedom experienced in the days of her wild promiscuity to the eventual framing in the role of the redeemed prostitute can be safely identified as a slow operation of normalization performed on her by society. One more step needs to be taken, however, before she can be acknowledged as a full-fledged societal member, and it is the normalizing step *par excellence:* psychotherapy, which would enable her to overcome her diversity and thus bring about rehabilitation. Her refusal to give in, to surrender her wild side, appears as an ominous indication of her will to self-destruct. Until her husband died, Maria seemed to be allowed any sort of infringement against the behavioral rules established by the community, but once she is alone, either she conforms or she perishes. Abandoned to a destiny that she appears to choose, she retreats from the world and slowly drifts into a solitary death, which she experiences in the same unconscious fashion with which she has lived all her life: "Scrivo la data. Sei giugno. Apro il quaderno, scrivo la data sei giugno. Sei giu . . ." (223; "I write today's date. June six. I open the notebook, I write today's date June six. Sixth of ju . . ."). What makes this entry even more symbolic is that its last two words, in their truncated state, actually acquire a different meaning: not only does "Sei giu" represent a failed attempt to write "sei giugno," but it also means, through a most significant Lacanian slippage, "You are down," where "down" should be interpreted as a synonym of "depressed." Could despair be inscribed in a text in a stronger fashion?

While Maria, in her lack of self-awareness, paradoxically stands up against a phallocratic society that demands her submission, all the other female characters in the novel seem to have voluntarily chosen to remain in the shadows. Abiding by the Catholic *dictatum* that requires them to depend on their men, they manifest their repressed instinctual subversiveness through their compulsive hunger. Like the fallen goddesses whose matriarchal reign preexisted the advent of patriarchy, they still request sacrificial offerings from their male companions, offerings of food that are ritually served in order to appease them. In the following scene, Pietro is depicted as bringing pastry to Maria's

A Cultural Map for Women

mother. As usual, the passage contains several contradictory versions of the same scene, and in each of its versions Maria's mother eats a differently shaped type of pastry:

> 12 dicembre. Pietro ha posato il pacco sulla tavola. . . . Ha posato il vassoio davanti a mia madre. . . . Pietro le ha indicato una sirena di marzapane. Mia madre ha addentato la coda della sirena, dipinta di azzurro e di argento. . . . Pietro . . . ha posato il vassoio davanti a lei, sulla tovaglia . . . ha indicato una pasta intrisa di liquore. Mia madre ha allungato le dita. La pasta trasudava umore colloso. Mia madre l'ha portata alle labbra, stringendola fra il pollice e l'indice. Un rivolo di liquore rossiccio le è scivolato sul mento. . . . Pietro . . . è rientrato reggendo un vassoio di cartone dove erano allineate una decina di paste. . . . Pietro ha allungato il braccio verso un corno di pasta sfoglia da cui straboccava una crema densa e gialla, molto grassa. Con due dita si è aperto un varco fra le labbra di mia madre. Le ha spinto il corno fra i denti. . . . Pietro le ha indicato una pasta quasi nera, rinchiusa in un involucro di caramello bruciato. Mia madre l'ha stretta fra due dita. Nel fare questo gesto la crosta trasparente si è spaccata, due lame di zucchero cotto, dal bordo filettato di giallo si sono sollevate verso il suo mento. Pietro ha allungato un braccio; con il pollice ha spinto due lame brune nella bocca di mia madre. (29–30)

> 12 December. Pietro put the pack on the table. . . . he puts the tray in front of my mother. . . . Pietro points her to a marzipan mermaid. My mother snatches the mermaid's tail, painted in blue and silver. . . . Pietro puts the tray in front of her, on the tablecloth . . . he points to a pastry full of liquor. My mother stretches her fingers. The pastry exuded a gluey humor. My mother took it to her lips, holding it tight between her index and thumb. A little red stream of liquor drips on her chin. . . . Pietro comes back holding a tray containing a row of about ten pastries. . . . Pietro stretches his arm toward a pastry horn from which spills a dense and yellow cream, very greasy. With two fingers, he makes room for the pastry between my mother's lips. He pushes the horn down her throat. . . . Pietro points her to a blackish pastry, enclosed in a wrapping of caramel. My mother holds it with two fingers. While doing this, the transparent crust breaks in two, two blades of cooked sugar, with a yellow border, move up toward her chin. Pietro stretches his arm; with the

thumb he pushes the two dark blades into my mother's mouth.

The first pastry is in the shape of a mermaid, which can be read as a symbol of female threat. When Maria's mother bites off the tail, she replicates the voluntary mutilation that Hans Christian Andersen's mermaid underwent in order to be with her male companion, performing a sacrificial act of female self-disempowerment. Both the second and the third pastry seem to be offered through a staging that vaguely resembles a ritual offering of the male phallus: while in its first version the woman takes it by herself and the liquid that drips from it has the color of blood, in the other version the man shoves it in her mouth and its liquid, "una crema densa e gialla, molto grassa" ("a dense and yellow cream, very greasy"), has a different color and consistency. What seems to be portrayed, in the first case, is an act of male castration, followed by the ingestion of the member, as if to signify female empowerment through incorporation of the sign of power. In the second stance, instead, it is the woman who is subjected to a symbolic rape through the virtual staging of oral sex, an act through which she acts as the disempowered provider of pleasure. The blackness of the last pastry, and the sugar blades that compose its shape, certainly render it another bleak symbol that ominously repeats women's dark condition: when Pietro pushes the two blades down into his mother-in-law's mouth, he definitely performs another violating gesture. The highly charged symbolism of the food offering is differently portrayed, however, with the other female characters: both Pietro's and Giacomo's mothers are seen as voracious women who do not hesitate to steal food from their children's plates. Pietro's mother selfishly feasts on chicken while her son is dying at the hospital: "'Non ti mangiare tutto il pollo, mamma.' 'Credevo che l'aveste già preso'" (144; "'Don't eat all the chicken, mother.' 'I thought you had already taken it'"). Giacomo remembers his own mother as a ghostly, animal-like creature who thrives on meat:

> Mia madre, pover'anima. È viva dico. Non credere. Né si cura di me. D'altronde. Pover'anima. Che mangiatrice. Non fai in tempo a riempirle il piatto. È ghiotta di carne. Te lo giuro. Si mangia mezzo chilo di carne al giorno. (47)

A Cultural Map for Women

> My mother, poor soul. She's alive I mean. Don't think. And she doesn't care about me. But of course. Poor soul. What an eater. You barely have time to fill her plate. She craves meat. I swear it to you. She eats a pound of meat each day.

Her presence is so menacing, so castrating that her son cannot stand to look at her:

> Mia madre mi guarda. Non ti piace? dice. Dalla a me. Lo so. Non posso alzare gli occhi. Perché incontrarla mi è. Mi disgusta. Insomma. Alzo forse alla fine. I piedi forse. Le mani. Ma gli occhi no. Beh, lei si è già ripulita il piatto suo. E vedo una forchetta che vola. Rapidissima. Dove vai forchetta del cavolo? Ha agguantato un brandello di carne. Il mio piatto vuoto. Anche il suo. Perché io non la vedo. Ma so che mastica. Che ferocità! E il suo pallore, la sua calvizia, quasi senza denti. Mi capisci. (47)

> My mother stares at me. Don't you like it? she says. Give it to me. I know. I can't raise my eyes. Because meeting her eyes is. It disgusts me. Anyway. In the end I raise. Maybe my feet. My hands. But not my eyes. Well, she has already cleaned her plate. And I see a fork flying. Incredibly quick. Where are you going, you damn fork? It snatches a chunk of meat. My empty plate. Hers too. Because I don't see her. But I know she's chewing. What ferocity! And her pallor, her baldness, almost toothless. You see what I mean.

The chunk of meat, "the brandello di carne" that she is portrayed holding, actually seems to have been snatched off his own flesh. Colorless, hairless, and toothless, she is evil incarnate while personifying lack and deprivation at the same time.

Characterized by their hunger or by their restlessness, by their promiscuity or by their ruthlessness, the women of *A memoria* all share a profound segregation from the world of thought, all being imprisoned in their confining bodies. All actions and no thought, they make perfect characters for a bleak fairy tale, a mythic fable on the war of the sexes in pre-feminist Italy.

Indeed a magic aura surrounds Maraini's novel: the naturalistic streak of many a description does not clash with the rich symbolism that pervades a language that still remains, notwithstanding its many connotations, strikingly simple. The endless repetition of sentences and entire paragraphs entices and hypnotizes the reader, who is presented with a vision of the world as seen through Maria's alienated eyes. This is further reinforced by the presence, at the very heart of the novel, of an intriguing rewriting of Pedro Calderón de la Barca's *La vida es sueño,* a play that comments on the restraining power of societal values while destabilizing the boundaries between reality and dream. In a long passage where the lines uttered by Calderón's performers can hardly be discerned from the comments made by the characters of Maraini's novel, a significant interweaving of the two texts occurs. The characters of the play, Sigismondo and Rosaura, are portrayed in terms that would easily define Pietro and Maria. While the man is introduced as a failed thinker, the woman is depicted as an active presence, a threatening figure: armed with a sword that connotes her aggressiveness, she is alone. Both bent for revenge against phallocracy, Rosaura and Maria are alone in their quests, since their men seem to be either absent or too weak to help them. In both cases, revenge is pledged in obscure, haunting, dreamlike fashion. Maria's erratic prose and her hypnotic convolutions are powerfully reinforced by Maraini's paraphrase of the final line of Calderón's play: "Il più gran bene è niente; perché la vita è sogno e i sogni sono sogni" (131; "The highest virtue is nothing; because life is a dream and dreams are dreams"). These lines are meant to challenge the reader of *A memoria* with a statement that inevitably questions the fictional status of reality and fiction. If life is just a dream then what is the difference between fiction and reality? And how does Maraini's desperate portrayal of the women's *prehistoric* condition comment on reality? And how does Maria's lack of awareness, her going through life as if she were in a dream, change its meaning in the light of such new perspective? These are only some of the questions present in the mind of the reader at the end of this book, a book that, like all true avant-garde novels, disturbs its audience, unsettling its beliefs and instilling what Alexander called, in reference to Beckett's work, "the shock of recognition" (61). As the chart of Maraini's intellectual landscape gets drawn, as the intricate web of literary voices of protest and resistance finally unveils, what becomes evident, in its bleakness, is the absence of any Italian source of influence: Robbe-Grillet, Sarraute, Beckett, Sartre, all spoke, in revolutionary fashion, of an existential *malaise* that keenly applies to the tormented condition of Italian women before feminism, but none of them was Italian, and none was ever really concerned with the feminist cause. And Calderón's voice, so different from that of the avant-garde, yet so powerful in its rich texture, is another cultural reference that excludes Italy. No inspiration, the author seems to be implying, could ever be derived from the same intelligentsia that contributed so powerfully to the laying of the foundations of phallogocentric constriction, erecting the bars of those symbolic prisons women never chose to inhabit.

Notes

1. Unless otherwise indicated, all translations are mine.
2. In his introduction to the first and only edition of *A memoria,* Renato Barilli states: "While Maria possesses an 'autistic' memory, that is a memory 'which does not respond to logic, temporal, or rational links . . . the memory of the unconscious where everything is the equivalent of itself' (*A memoria* 206) . . . she has completely lost the 'social' memory, on which the rational and correct employment of our acts depends, acts falling within the framework of collective goals and values" (7).
3. This translation is from "Reflections on the Logical and Illogical Bodies of My Sexual Compatriots," at pages 34–35 in this volume, a revision and translation of Maraini's "Riflessioni."
4. In *The Divided Self,* Laing attempts to understand schizophrenia in its different manifestations. The figure of the schizophrenic, as outsider to himself/herself and to society, is particularly central to Laing's investigation, and quite relevant to my own analysis of Maraini's novel.

Works Cited

Alexander, Marguerite. *Flights from Realism: Themes and Strategies in Postmodernist British and American Fiction.* London: Edward Arnold, 1990.

Anderlini, Serena. "Prolegomena for a Feminist Dramaturgy of the Feminine: An Interview with Dacia Maraini." *diacritics* 21.2–3 (1991): 148–60.

Bersani, Leo. *Arts of Impoverishment: Beckett Rothko Resnais.* Cambridge: Harvard UP, 1993.

Freud, Sigmund. "The 'Uncanny.'" 1919. *Standard Edition of the Complete Psychological Works of Sigmund Freud.* Trans. and ed. James Strachey. Vol. 17. London and New York: Norton, 1966. 219–52.

Laing, R. D. *The Divided Self: An Existential Study in Sanity and Madness.* London: Tavistock, 1959.

Maraini, Dacia. *A memoria.* Introd. Renato Barilli. Milan: Bompiani, 1967.

———. "Riflessioni sui corpi logici e illogici delle mie compagne di sesso." Introd. to Maraini's *La bionda, la bruna e l'asino: con gli occhi di oggi sugli anni settanta e ottanta.* Milan: Rizzoli, 1987. V–xxx. "Riflessioni" has been revised and published in English in this volume as "Reflections on the Logical and Illogical Bodies of My Sexual Compatriots," 21–38.

Montini, Ileana. *Parlare con Dacia.* Verona: Bertani, 1977.

Maria Ornella Marotti

La lunga vita di Marianna Ucrìa
A Feminist Revisiting of the
Eighteenth Century

In his introduction to *Tropics of Discourse* (1978), Hayden White writes: "When we make sense of such problematical topics as human nature, culture, society, and history . . . our discourse always tends to slip away from our data towards the structures of consciousness with which we are trying to grasp them" (1). In her 1990 novel, Dacia Maraini purposely slips away from data to embrace a method of interpretation based on the imaginative reconstruction of consciousness. *La lunga vita di Marianna Ucrìa* (*The Silent Duchess*) can indeed be read as an attempt to create a cultural and social history of the Sicilian eighteenth century from the perspective of a female consciousness who is, at the same time, central and marginal, inside and outside language.

Because of the way in which she deals with every institution of the Sicilian society of the time, Maraini's project is reminiscent of Michel Foucault. Like Foucault, Maraini unmasks the game of power embedded in institutions. Her scope is all-encompassing. The tenuous plot of the novel leads the reader from the aristocratic palace to the prison and the gallows, from the country mansion to the peasants' huts, from the wedding party to the convent, from the kitchen to the fashion tailor's atelier, and so on. Her project is informed by an awareness of not only the game and strategies of power at work in Sicilian society, but also the resistance opposed by the objects of that power. In this respect, Maraini's perspective seems to be equally under the influence of the practice of cultural history and reminds one especially of Michel de Certeau's and Carlo Ginzburg's works. In the Sicilian society that Maraini describes, the arrogance of power is countered by the ability to survive expressed by both the plebeian characters and the aristocratic protagonist.

Maria Ornella Marotti

Like several contemporary historical novels, *La lunga vita di Marianna Ucrìa* tries to fill the void left by historical narration by encompassing the lives of people who are not historically representative. Although Maraini's re-reading of eighteenth-century Sicilian history does not stray from factual evidence recorded by official historical records, it is based on a subjective point of view that validates individual experience. Notes to Marianna, written in a spoken language filled with Sicilian idioms, comment on the turbulent events of those decades, while the protagonist's observations of everyday reality and her own notes—her only verbal vehicle of communication—create a web of relations and social customs.

For the reader of Maraini, it is clear that her reconstruction of the Sicilian eighteenth century is not solely dictated by an archeological interest for its own sake. Her political commitment to the cause of feminism in Italy dates back over thirty years and this is so well known to any student of Italian culture that it seems legitimate to ask: Why the eighteenth century? Which aspects of that century serve Maraini's feminist theory? And why does she choose the duchess Marianna Ucrìa as protagonist and center of consciousness of her semihistorical novel?

Throughout the novel, Maraini makes it clear for the reader that the choice of the time setting of the novel is part of a conscious discourse on the cultural period. Marianna Ucrìa sees herself as the product of her century and often contrasts her way of reasoning with that of her husband, thirty years her senior.

> Per molti nobili della sua età, vissuti e maturati nel secolo passato, i pensieri sistematici hanno qualcosa di ignobile, di volgare. Il confronto con altre intelligenze, altre idee, è considerato per principio una resa. I plebei pensano come gruppo o come folla; un nobile è solo e di questa solitudine è costituita la sua gloria e il suo ardimento. Marianna sa che lui non la considera sua pari per quanto la rispetti come moglie. Per lui la moglie è una bambina di un secolo nuovo, incomprensibile, con qualcosa di triviale nella sua ansia per i mutamenti, per fare, il costruire. (53)

> For many of the noblemen of his age, who grew up and lived in the previous century, logical thought has something ignoble, even vulgar about it. To confront other minds, other

> ideas, is considered in principle an act of perfidy. The common people, with their crowd mentality, behave like flocks of sheep; only the nobleman stands alone, and out of this aloofness come his glory and his daring. Marianna knows he does not think of her as an equal, although he respects her as a wife. For him, his wife is the child of a new century, incomprehensible, with something trivial in her passion for change, for action, for building. (49)[1]

Throughout the novel, the character of the aristocratic Pietro, Marianna's uncle and husband, accurately reflects some of the predominant traits of the Sicilian aristocracy, as described by Denis Mack Smith in his *History of Sicily*. Pietro's resistance to scholarly knowledge as well as his deep class consciousness are the common signs of an aristocratic class that kept Sicily in a state of feudal subjugation and cultural and economic backwardness at a time of social change and economic growth almost everywhere else (2: 271–304).[2] "Not only was nearly everyone in Sicily illiterate, but higher education concentrated on theology and law, and both these disciplines were geared to an obsequious respect towards tradition and authority," writes Mack Smith. He also adds: "Among cultured aristocrats, interest rarely stretched beyond antiquarianism, numismatics and archaeology" (2: 301). One should also note that the couple's differences take on the connotation of a dialogic relation between two eras, two philosophical views of existence, and two cultural moments. The eighteenth century represents for Maraini a moment of rupture, the emerging of new philosophical attitudes that bring about historical change. What interests her, in particular, is that it is a moment of incipient feminization of the culture, the emergence of the other. However, this emergence is not without resistance and conflict. The traces from the previous century impinge upon the newness, and reaction against the threats to the status quo is always at work.

If one then understands Maraini's view of the eighteenth century as a moment of rupture and emergence of the feminine, the choice of Marianna Ucrìa as female center of consciousness of the novel is also justified. Despite her aristocratic position in society, Marianna represents those who are erased by official history, those who are never the subject and only occasionally the object of history. However, through imagination,

Maria Ornella Marotti

and only through imagination, the writer can reconstruct the history of those whose traces have been erased from history. Thanks to Maraini's handling of her story, and despite her marginalized position as woman and deaf-mute, Marianna Ucrìa acquires the status of critical subject.

In *La lunga vita di Marianna Ucrìa,* Maraini rewrites the literary plot of the European eighteenth-century novel from the unusual perspective of a female point of view, as JoAnn Cannon argues (136). Unlike other rape heroines of eighteenth-century novels, Marianna does not succumb, but instead resists and survives, despite her handicap, and becomes at the end the protagonist of an almost picaresque plot. This subversion of the conventions of literary genre is accompanied by a re-reading of the cultural history of the time, which even though not substantially different in the handling of historical data from other more official reconstructions of Sicilian history, differs radically in mode of narration. Even though similarities between historical and fictional narration have been pointed out, especially by White (82–85), differences still exist. The pretense of objectivity, one of the conventions of official historical narration, is here replaced by a subjective and feminine critical consciousness, narrating both history and personal stories with the same highly idiomatic language. The eighteenth century is thus revisited from the perspective of a cultural history that stems from personal life. Not only does Maraini rewrite the prevailing literary plot from a feminine point of view but she also reformulates the historical narration of the eighteenth century.

Marianna's aristocratic status grants her a vantage point from which to observe the mores of society. Because of her rank, she is connected with the upper classes; however, since her physical limitations make her more dependent on her servants, she keeps in particularly close contact with the lives of the lower classes. Even more than her social status, what makes her an ideal consciousness for the kind of novel Maraini intended to write is her inability to hear or speak. By blocking the auditory and oral communicative fields, her different sensory perception heightens visual, tactile, and olfactory sensations. The narrative center of consciousness stems from the body and indeed from the character's female gender. Moreover, in order to decode the complex situations of her environment, Marianna

Marianna Ucrìa: A Feminist Revisiting

develops a particularly keen awareness of the language of the body—facial expressions, gestures, and postures. In order to compensate for her handicap, she finds different ways of understanding and communicating. She is often shown to be endowed with ultrasensory perceptions that allow her to be aware of the other characters' thoughts and feelings. This leads her to develop a particularly inquisitive mind and a deconstructive attitude toward her class and time.

During a 1990 lecture at the Italian Cultural Institute in San Francisco, Dacia Maraini traced her literary foremothers back to Renaissance writer Isabella di Morra.[3] The writer's concern with creating a literary "gynealogy," a somewhat ideal matrilineage, suggests to me one more observation on the importance of the character of Marianna Ucrìa. Even though, unlike Morra, Marianna is not a recognizable literary figure to whom Maraini could look back for her artistic origin, she represents a foremother whose existence contributes to the reconstruction of a female symbolic order. But, like Morra, Marianna is a victim of patriarchal violence, and, like Morra, she is able to inscribe her voice despite limitations and family pressures. As Maraini tells us in *Bagheria,* Marianna Ucrìa was a distant relation whose existence became known to her through an old portrait, during a visit to the ancestral home in Bagheria.[4] Despite scant information about her, Maraini felt an emotional link that allowed her to re-create Marianna imaginatively. Her position of difference epitomizes women's essential difference: women's silence, exclusion, and marginalization, which places them at the same time inside and outside society, history, and culture. Moreover, Marianna's only communicative links with her environment are gesture and writing. Both these means of communication create a text inside the text that establishes the character as creator of language and, therefore, again, as a potential literary foremother for the author herself.[5]

Having mentioned the role that the protagonist plays in Maraini's feminist theory, I need to return to the novel itself and its historical/cultural background, and to the interlacing of the eighteenth century and the fictional plot. *La lunga vita di Marianna Ucrìa* is the story of the discovery by the protagonist of her own desire. This discovery, and the reclaiming of her own body that follows it, is prepared by a series of other discoveries concerning the cultural, philosophical, and historical contexts of her time and place. Marianna's gradual unveiling of her own femaleness has a definite place within the context of the eighteenth-century philosophy that, at least in some of its most significant trends, placed a great importance on bodily sensations. Conversely, her research in the philosophical thought of her time gains a deeper meaning because of her own personal quest.

A rape victim at age five, Marianna has lost both her hearing and her power of speech as a consequence of the trauma she had undergone and the injunction to be silent given to her by her father. Given away in marriage at age thirteen to the man who raped her, who is also her maternal uncle, she leads for the most part the life of an aristocratic Sicilian of her time. She bears five children, has a palace built and decorated by the Calabrian painter Intermassimi in the fishing village of Bagheria,[6] participates in the rituals of her society—festivals and public executions. She reads Hume and educates herself with whatever manuscripts she can find in her antiquated library. After her husband's death, she takes part in the management of some of her rural and feudal properties. Eventually, at age forty-five, she allows herself to have an affair with a young, charming servant. In the last episode of the novel, she leaves Sicily and her wealth behind and travels, with only the company of a semi-deranged servant, to continental Italy, in voluntary exile.

Beneath the surface of a conventional life, another life unfolds. It is the life of a consciousness locked in a body that has been silenced, bartered, and disowned. In the Sicily of the time, an early marriage at age thirteen or even twelve was quite a common practice for the daughter of an aristocratic family; the other choice was the convent. Marianna is given to the man who raped her because she is damaged property that might as well be returned to the one who damaged it. Raped again by her husband, she runs away only to be returned to her owner after having been severely reprimanded by her mother for the immorality and sinfulness of her rebellion. The system works to serve patriarchy. The mother instructs the daughter so that the rule will not be broken. The initial rape is hidden, buried, and forgotten; Marianna's father keeps it as his own secret. An incestuous marriage (to her uncle/rapist) is meant to cover up the crime forever.

Marianna Ucrìa: A Feminist Revisiting

It is obvious that sexual politics are determined not only by gender but also by class. Crimes go unpunished only if the perpetrators are aristocrats. The novel opens, in fact, with the public execution of an adolescent murderer. During the event, Marianna's father plays the mixed role of confessor and assistant to the plebeian criminal.[7] Hoping that fear will restore Marianna's voice and hearing, he has brought the child along to witness the execution. It is as if the father hoped that the plebeian's execution could erase the effects of the aristocrat's crime.

The transference of responsibility from the aristocrat to the pauper occurs in almost every aspect of social life, in every institution, from the prison to the insane asylum. Every threat to power posed by the poor, the rebellious, the heretic, and the woman is handled through incarceration, torture, and execution. During the eighteenth century, the Inquisition is still alive and well in Sicily, and the power of the Church is intertwined with that of the feudal aristocracy. Despite her class privileges, the aristocratic woman is the object of the system of power. Her body does not belong to her. Through Marianna's victimization, Maraini creates a case that epitomizes the female condition.

By contrast with Marianna's disowned body, her husband's body represents the aristocrat's perpetual body, the personification of body politics. At his death he is embalmed, according to an old practice, to be preserved and forever displayed in the convent of the Cappuccini in Palermo. Deprived of his individuality, his corpse will become an almost unrecognizable body, among other bodies, impersonal and rigid, the symbol of a power that transcends individuals and extends its tentacles from the past, impinging on the present, forever hindering change.

> Sopra gli scaffali di legno laccato giacevano altri morti: donne eleganti nei loro vestiti di festa, le braccia incrociate sul petto, le cuffie dagli orli ingialliti, le labbra stirate sui denti. Alcune stavano lì allungate da qualche settimana e mandavano un odore acuto di acidi. Altre erano lì da cinquant'anni, un secolo e avevano perso ogni odore. Una usanza barbara, si diceva Marianna cercando di ricordare le parole del signor Hume sulla morte; ma la sua testa era vuota. Meglio essere bruciati e gettati nel Gange come fanno gli indiani, piuttosto che starsene in questi sotterranei, ancora una volta tutti insieme fra parenti e amici dai grandi nomi, la pelle che si sbriciola come carta. (148)

Maria Ornella Marotti

> On top of the polished shelves lay other corpses: elegant ladies dressed in their best clothes, their arms crossed on their breasts, their bonnets yellowing at the edges, their lips stretched over their teeth. Some had been lying there for only a few weeks and emitted a strong acid smell. Others had been there for fifty or a hundred years, and had become quite odorless. A barbarous custom, Marianna told herself, and tried to remember what Mr. Hume had said about death; but her mind was blank. It would be better to be burned and thrown in the Ganges like the Indians rather than remain immured in these underground passages, gathered together with all one's relations and friends with exalted names and skin crumbling like paper. (134)

Nonetheless, some change occurs despite relapses and obstacles. It is not generated by Sicilian society, which during the eighteenth century is undergoing a phase of deep and irreversible decline after many foreign invasions and changes in dynastic power. It is filtered, instead, through cultural products from continental Italy, through books coming from abroad, fashion, and new societal attitudes. For the most part, change seems to remain on a superficial level. It does not alter the economic structure, which remains essentially feudal. Even popular uprisings appear like a distant memory of the past, unlikely to repeat themselves in the present.[8] However, evolution is generated inside the character's consciousness, through personal experience, contemplation of the lives that unfold around her, and especially reading.

Hume's philosophy plays an important role in summing up Marianna's process of self-discovery and in giving direction and permission to her sexual liberation. In basing ethics inside personal consciousness and feelings, in stressing the importance of pleasure in evaluating virtue, and in emphasizing the role of imagination as a tool of discovery, Hume validates Marianna's own introspective experience. Furthermore, the British philosopher's statements about the necessary subordination of reason to passion (echoed elsewhere in the book by a quote from Pascal: "Le cœur a des raisons que la raison ne connaît pas" ("The heart has reasons that reason does not know"), gives the character permission to explore her own sensuality. Quite interestingly, Hume maintains, in his *Treatise on Human Nature,* that what we consider to be "nature" is nothing other than an inscription

Marianna Ucrìa: A Feminist Revisiting

of long-established customs and social forces. Female nature should then be viewed within this context. Among the pages of a diary in which Hume's ideas have been transcribed—a further filter between the original text and the Sicilian reader—Marianna finds a portrait of the British philosopher.

> Lo apre e fra le pagine trova un disegno colorato: un uomo sui trent'anni con un turbante di velluto a righe che copre le tempie. Una faccia larga, soddisfatta, gli occhi che guardano verso il basso come a dire che tutto il sapere viene dalla terra sui cui poggiamo i piedi. (105)
>
> She opens it and among the pages discovers a colored picture: a man of about thirty years with a striped velvet turban that comes down over his forehead. A broad, complacent face, his eyes looking downwards as if to assert that all knowledge comes from the earth on which we rest our feet. (96)

Through Marianna's observations on Hume's earthy appearance, Maraini alludes to the need to return to the origin of life—a theme that is dear to Italian feminism.[9] Maraini's own narrative style, realistic and imaginative at the same time, is a praise to earthiness.

The protagonist's own journey of self-discovery brings her back to her body and to the rape trauma that has silenced her. During a feverish delirium, in a state of semiconsciousness she vaguely remembers her trauma and realizes that her rape went beyond sexual abuse; it amounted indeed to the silencing of woman by patriarchy.

> Ma chi è quest'uomo che le sta addosso e ha un odore sgradevole, estraneo? qualcuno che si è travestito da qualcun altro. Il signor marito? il signor padre? lui sì sarebbe capace di trasformarsi per gioco. In quel momento una idea la attraversa da capo a piedi come una saetta; per la prima volta nella sua vita capisce con limpidezza adamantina, che è lui suo padre, il responsabile della sua mutilazione. Per amore o per distrazione non saprebbe dire; ma è lui che le ha tagliato la lingua ed è lui che le ha riempito le orecchie di piombo fuso perché non sentisse nessun suono e girasse perpetuamente su se stessa nei regni del silenzio e dell'apprensione. (192–93)

> But who is this man on top of her and who has a strange disagreeable smell? Somebody in disguise? Uncle husband? Her father the Duke? He would be quite capable of putting on a disguise, just for fun. At that moment a revelation transfixes her from head to foot, like an arrow; for the first time in her life she comprehends with a diamond clarity that it was him, her father, who was the one responsible for her disablement. From love or from carelessness she can't say. But it is he who cut her tongue and it is he who filled up her ears with molten lead so that she can hear no sound and circles perpetually in the kingdoms of silence and fear. (172)

Marianna's recognition of the inherent significance of the trauma that she underwent as a child illustrates indeed a tenet of Maraini's feminist theory.[10] The Italian writer is constantly aware in her works of power relations, which she sees much in the way that Foucault does, as "a chain or a system . . . as the strategies in which they take effect, whose general design or institutional crystallization is embodied in the state apparatus, in the formulation of the law, in the various social hegemonies" (Foucault 92–93). For this reason, throughout the narrative both Marianna's father and even her uncle husband/rapist are never demonized; they are always shown in their human side, in their vulnerability, and even with their pleasant qualities. Their role inside the system is, nonetheless, that of patriarch and as such they oppress, silence, and even rape. Moreover, because of her focus on power relations, Maraini's portrait of Sicilian aristocracy is ultimately more humorous and lighthearted than Mack Smith's damning description of that class and time.

Class and ethnicity also play an important role in power relations, and their importance is stressed throughout the novel, through representation of the different layers of society and of regional customs. Institutions incarcerate, separate, punish, and isolate those who might threaten the established power relations; aristocratic wealth is based on the feudal system; heretics are burned alive by the Inquisition; women are kept in a state of subjection and ignorance; and a spendthrift aristocracy lives on debts and wastes wealth that it does not own any more. This is Sicily during the eighteenth century. Traveling from Palermo to Bagheria, Marianna has often seen bandits' heads stuck on poles to admonish the population: "Teste asciugate

Marianna Ucrìa: A Feminist Revisiting

dal sole, mangiate dalle mosche, accompagnate spesso da pezzi di braccia e di gambe dal sangue nero, incollato alla pelle" (54; "Heads dried by the sun, infested by flies, often with chunks of arms and legs with blackened blood sticking to the skin"; 50). If we compare the portrait that Maraini paints of the island with the image that we receive from eighteenth-century authors describing other parts of Europe, we realize that the writer has chosen to deal with a particularly marginalized society, living centuries behind the time, apparently static. "Qui regna l'ingiustizia più assennata. Tanto assennata da risultare ai più come 'naturale'" (258; "Here reigns the most judicious injustice. So judicious and so deep-seated as to be regarded as 'natural'"; 228), a character observes. During a visit to one of her feudal properties, Marianna encounters this injustice when she descends into the subterranean prison in which a peasant is incarcerated for not having been able to pay fees arbitrarily imposed on him by the feudal tax assessor. According to the Sicilian law of the time, the Sicilian barons had the rights of kings in their lands, and they owned their subjects. Because they neglected their large rural properties, the barons passed on their power to their overseers, who often managed to accumulate considerable wealth at the expense of the impoverished peasants and the barons themselves. Using the parish priest as an intermediary, Marianna interrogates the imprisoned peasant. Her questions show her to be unaware of a situation that must have been familiar to the male members of her family. She has the man freed and she also pays his debts. While her act of compassion does not subvert entrenched power relations, it shows her marginal position in the system.

In concluding our discussion, we may wonder again on Maraini's choice of time and place in her feminist novel. It may help us to further clarify this point to look at a recent interview given by Maraini. In discussing the phenomenon of the neofascist "nazi skins" (skinheads), she states: "It is the terrible, subconscious fear of the feminine, of new women's eroticism . . . of the feminization of society. I intend by this the acceptance of difference, a new way of understanding the issue of race, the rejection of war. In other words, the introduction of elements that so far were considered as losing ones. Feminine as synonym of weak, meek and losing." Elsewhere in the same interview, she also states that gender roles in *La lunga vita di Marianna Ucrìa* were "much clearer and neater [than today]. Today these roles have been exploded as code, even though they still exist as cultural habits. In fact, I would say that there has been a reinforcing of roles due to fear. Fear creates an almost pathological attachment [to roles]" ("Intervista" 95).

Looking at what the writer says about our time, and comparing with what she narrates about the past, helps us understand her interest in eighteenth-century Sicily. Quoting Gian Battista Vico's thought, a character of the novel argues: "ogni uomo e ogni epoca sono costantemente minacciati da una barbarie recondita e incombente" (258; "every human being and every epoch is constantly being threatened by an imminent hidden barbarity"; 227). As already stated, in her discourse on the past, despite the cultural accuracy of her minute descriptions, Maraini is not solely inspired by an antiquarian interest. In talking about the past, she has the present in mind. In the eighteenth century, she sees the beginning of that process of feminization of society that is more clearly emerging in our time. But she also sees a legacy from the past hindering the path to human liberation. Then, as now, fear of the feminine—in her definition as different and marginal—prompts regressive reactions.

The choice of Sicily is equally meaningful. In selecting a place that was at the margins of the European culture of the time, Maraini can better observe the influence of the past, the legacy of the era of the Inquisition and of the feudal system. This allows her to better develop a discourse on the interplay between subsequent centuries. Furthermore, by linking in her story the characters of Marianna Ucrìa and her husband to two different centuries, she endows the two eras with gender features: the seventeenth century is male, while the eighteenth century is female. Through the story of Marianna Ucrìa, Maraini thus creates not only a symbol of female endurance but also a gendered historical narration.

Notes

1. For the English text, I have used *The Silent Duchess*. Hereafter, all page numbers referring to this novel will be indicated in the text. All other translations, unless otherwise indicated, are mine.

2. Denis Mack Smith reports that Sicilian aristocracy was often illiterate and during the eighteenth century, to remedy this, a special school for aristocrats was created (2: 302). In his work, the British historian also documents the existence of a totally feudal agricultural system in Sicily, due to the power of the regional aristocracy that would not allow any change in power relations.

3. Isabella di Morra (1520–46) was the daughter of a Neapolitan nobleman. Accused of having betrayed the Spanish rulers, he was compelled to flee to France, leaving behind Isabella, who was kept prisoner in the Lucanian castle of Favale by her brothers. There she was killed by them after her letters to a neighboring Spaniard were discovered. Her poems were published posthumously in Venice and were rediscovered by Benedetto Croce after centuries of oblivion.

4. In *Bagheria* (161–68) Maraini narrates of her visit to villa Valguarnera, the mansion of her ancestors that had also been described in exalted terms by her aunt Felicità in a 1949 book. The description of the portrait of Marianna Ucrìa was also contained in that book. Viewing the portrait acted as source of inspiration for Maraini.

5. JoAnn Cannon argues that "Marianna, with her portable writing desk attached firmly at her waist, personifies the epistolary heroine par excellence" (142). Cannon also points out that epistolary novels with female protagonists were for the most part written by male writers. This genre represents, therefore, "men's appropriation and publication of the feminine epistolary texts." Far from representing "the entrance of the female voice into the predominantly male literary tradition," this genre "has paradoxically acted to silence the female voice" (142). Cannon, therefore, reads the novel as an anti-epistolary novel.

6. Mack Smith reports that over two hundred luxurious villas were begun in the countryside outside Palermo during the eighteenth century. However, a large number were never completed (2: 289).

7. Again, according to Mack Smith's account, some Sicilian aristocrats belonged to congregations that performed the charitable role of assistants to plebeians condemned to death (2: 285). One must also note that while a large number of death penalties by strangulation were publicly performed in Sicily during the eighteenth century, almost no aristocrats convicted of murder were executed. In any case, the contemplated method of execution for aristocrats was not strangulation but the more efficient guillotine (2: 296).

8. Mack Smith recounts the 1647 revolt in Palermo led by La Pilosa, "an escaped convict and murderer who seems to have linked the underworld of Palermo with that of the surrounding villages" (1: 213). Defeated and handed over to the authorities by the artisan guilds of Palermo, La Pilosa was tortured and put to death in a horrible way. Maraini has Marianna's grandmother Giuseppa write her granddaughter a series of notes in Sicilian telling her the story of the various popular uprisings of the previous century that she has personally witnessed (110–16).

9. See in particular, Luisa Muraro's insistence on this theme in *L'ordine simbolico della madre*.

10. Both Gabriella Brooke and Giuseppina Santagostino read Marianna's silencing in mythological terms, as the literary manifestation of the myth of Philomela. Moreover, Santagostino relates the mythological subtext of the novel to Cavarero's re-reading of myth (415).

Works Cited

Brooke, Gabriella. "Sicilian Philomela: Marianna Ucrìa and the Muted Women of Her Time." *Italian Culture* 13 (1996): 222.

Cannon, JoAnn. "Rewriting the Female Destiny: Dacia Maraini's *La lunga vita di Marianna Ucrìa*." *Symposium* 49.2 (Summer 1995): 136–45.

Cavarero, Adriana. *Nonostante Platone*. Rome: Riuniti, 1990.

De Certeau, Michel. *The Practice of Everyday Life*. Berkeley: U of California P, 1984.

Foucault, Michel. *The History of Sexuality*. Vol. 1. Trans. Robert Harley. New York: Random, 1990.

Ginzburg, Carlo. *I benandanti: stregoneria e culti agrari tra cinquecento e seicento*. Turin: Einaudi, 1966.

Mack Smith, Denis. *A History of Sicily*. Vol. 1: *Medieval Sicily 800–1713*. Vol. 2: *Modern Sicily after 1713*. New York: Viking, 1968.

Maraini, Dacia. *Bagheria*. Milan: Rizzoli, 1993. Published in English as *Bagheria*. London: Peter Owen, 1995; distributed by Dufour.

———. "Intervista." *Panorama* 20 Sept. 1992.

———. *La lunga vita di Marianna Ucrìa*. Milan: Rizzoli, 1990. Published in English as *The Silent Duchess*.

———. *The Silent Duchess*. Trans. Dick Kitto and Elspeth Spottiswood. Kingston, ON: Quarry, 1992.

Muraro, Luisa. *L'ordine simbolico della madre*. Rome: Riuniti, 1991.

Santagostino, Giuseppina. "*La lunga vita di Marianna Ucrìa*: tessere la memoria sotto lo sguardo delle chimere." *Italica* 73.3 (Autumn 1996): 410–28.

White, Hayden. *Tropics of Discourse*. Baltimore: Johns Hopkins UP, 1978.

Paola Carù

Vocal Marginality
Dacia Maraini's Veronica Franco

In *Veronica, meretrice e scrittora* (1992; Veronica, prostitute and female writer), Dacia Maraini presents her readers with her fictional interpretation of the Venetian poet and courtesan Veronica Franco (1546–91). Maraini does not intend to give us a depiction of Franco that is "true" to history, but rather "Un viaggio immaginario in alcuni luoghi della storia e della letteratura attraverso le suggestioni di una biografia reale" (*Veronica* 10; "an imaginary journey through literature and history that is based on the suggestions of a real biography").[1]

With the figure of Veronica Franco, Maraini's play explores places traditionally forbidden to the female: writing and prostitution. Both conditions determined for women a state of estrangement during Renaissance society, as well as in later periods. Yet, this "estrangement" brings Veronica Franco the paradoxical advantage of being, simultaneously, both on the margin and at the core of the patriarchal society in which she lives. A category of women who share with prostitutes the same marginalized yet relevant social position is that of cloistered women. They are the other marginalized group of women allowed, under certain conditions, to have access to reading and writing.[2] It is a nun that Maraini's Veronica Franco meets in her fictional stay at the *lazzaretto,* the quarantine station, during the plague, and it is with her that she sets off on her journey after having survived the epidemic. By choosing to feature the relationship between a mature Renaissance courtesan and a young nun, Maraini investigates the potentials offered to her female characters by the liminal spaces in their society. Both women ultimately refuse to live confined to a single "territory" and opt for a strategy of survival that consists in wandering across social "borders."

Paola Carù

In this study, I will analyze the way in which Maraini combines these two figures of marginality, the writer-courtesan and the nun, and I will examine how Franco is presented as a borderline figure, one attempting to translate and appropriate for herself the language of the patriarchal order.

Veronica, meretrice e scrittora is not meant to be an investigation of the "historical" Veronica Franco, yet Maraini's presentation does justice to the complexities of Franco's life and work as a "honest courtesan" in sixteenth-century Venice. Born in 1546, Franco was introduced to the courtesan profession by her mother, herself a courtesan. Franco was renowned for her literary production (*Terze rime*, 1575) and confident of her erudition and her ability to entertain relationships with members of cultural circles, in particular Domenico Venier's prestigious literary academy. Franco's artistic level and her active networking reached a high point with the "visit" of the future king Henry III of France, who was celebrated in Venice.

Besides being a refined and renowned courtesan, Franco occupies also a relevant position within a group of Italian women who became well-regarded as poets in the Renaissance: Vittoria Colonna, Chiara Matraini, Gaspara Stampa, and Tullia d'Aragona, who also was a courtesan. They wrote in the fashion of Petrarchism, the preeminent style in the sixteenth century. Franco stands out as an innovative poet with respect to this tradition, to the point that some critics (Natalia Costa-Zalessow and Margaret Rosenthal among them) define her as an anti-Petrarchan poet. Among the poetical features in Franco's works is the use of the *terza rima*, a metrical pattern that was used for love poetry in the fifteenth century (by Ariosto, for example) but that was not common for the same genre in the sixteenth century. The *terza rima* allowed Franco more freedom of expression than was permitted by the Petrarchan model (Wend 42). Furthermore, Franco's literary production is richer in content than that of many contemporaries, in that she writes explicitly erotic poems; thus, she covers a wider range of topics than does Petrarchism. Franco writes unambiguously about her profession, never denying its role in her life or its connection with her cultural activities.

Franco used her literary activity for social advancement. She presented herself as a public figure and addressed her male audience on an equal footing. She was one of the few Renaissance women who had the courage to oppose a long-standing (male) tradition that systematically silenced female writing by declaring it dangerous to women's "virtue." The logic of this prohibition assumed that a woman, by letting her written works circulate, would expose herself to public scrutiny, and therefore to men's desire. Franco stands out against this attitude: she claims the right to write, to write explicitly about her status as courtesan, and to promote her own public image through her erudition and rhetoric. This process, however, led Franco to embody a complex role, since she was forced to operate within the conditions dictated by a patriarchal society. As Ann Rosalind Jones argues, Franco's "desire to rise socially, to be defined through and benefit from ties with powerful men," brought her to a contradictory rhetoric: it is a transgressive rhetoric, as she rejects "injunctions to chastity and silence" and speaks "to and for women in ways that shift the man-woman focus of love poetry to new concerns and positions." On the other hand, it is also "a rhetoric shaped and contained by the constant presence of men as the ultimate critics" (304).

The figure of Veronica Franco, furthermore, must be considered within the specific context of the city of Venice. Franco as the writing "honest courtesan" exemplifies the tensions that existed in the Venetian social body. The republic of Venice exploited the attraction offered by its renowned courtesans, who were the object of curious interest for many learned tourists. The idealized image of the courtesan's profession invariably stood, for the foreign observer, "as a cultural code or cipher through which Venice, the secular city, publicized itself in the sixteenth century." The Venetian *cortigiane oneste* were an "eloquent proof of the republic's progressive social policies" (Rosenthal 3). Yet, in their daily work, Venetian courtesans had to fight to obtain patronage and to defend themselves against the assaults of envious male courtiers, who considered the courtesans to be their enemies in the competition for upward mobility.

In such an environment Franco "challenges and rewrites the textual stereotype of the venal, greedy, and deceitful courtesan" (Rosenthal 7), while, at the same time, she strives to negotiate her position in a society dominated by men. Thus, Franco's

Paola Carù

writing reveals the complex tangles of sociocultural layers in the republic of Venice—an exemplary center of Renaissance culture. It is the combination of transgressions and contradictions that interests Maraini; and it is her curiosity about the oxymoron of the "honest courtesan" that she explores in her play about Veronica Franco.

Veronica, meretrice e scrittora is divided into two acts. Act 1 opens on a scene during the plague, at the quarantine station, where Veronica is lying among the dying. She is being, rather carelessly and hastily, taken care of by a young nun, Anzola. Anzola wonders how long Veronica is going to last because she is eager to take Veronica's jewels and fine shoes, but Veronica has no intention of dying. On the contrary, she attempts to capture Anzola's attention and nurtures the peculiar friendship by telling about her past life. Act 1 proceeds with a series of flashbacks that depict Veronica's life in Venice and her relationship with her clients, her lovers, and the members of her household: Gaspara, her wet nurse; Paolo, her husband; and Vannitelli, her son's preceptor. The scenes from the past alternate with those at the *lazzaretto* in such a way that the episodes that represent Veronica's interaction with her nurse nun intertwine with the enactment of Veronica's recollections of her previous life. Act 2 opens at the quarantine station and closes on Veronica's recovery and her decision to go away with the nun Anzola.

The act of setting the beginning and the (open) ending of the story at the *lazzaretto* stresses the importance of the logic of circularity that highlights Veronica's relationship to words, both the written and the spoken. Veronica needs first to talk merely in order to feel alive. Later she must narrate in order to conquer Anzola's interest and to be nursed by her. The relationship between the two women gradually loses its imbalance and becomes friendship.

The symbolic value of the plague is exemplified in the initial relationship between the courtesan and the nun: the epidemic both heightens and erases differences between people of dissimilar social origins. The pestilence is a motif Maraini uses to emphasize Veronica's attachment to life and her ability to survive, to find alternative solutions in critical moments.

Vocal Marginality: Maraini's Veronica Franco

In reality, Veronica Franco never suffered from the plague, even though in 1575 Venice was devastated by it. Maraini's intention is not linked to a historically truthful rendition of facts; rather, her play aims at being "an imaginary journey" through history and literature.

Maraini writes in her introduction to the play that the main feature of Veronica's life is a paradox: as writer, Veronica belongs to the cultural "inside" of her society, while at the same time, as prostitute, she is identified with its "outside," for she is a social outcast. Recognized as an official courtesan and as a poet, Maraini's Franco attempts to keep a balance between the two worlds that she inhabits.[3] In at least one of the two, she plays a role that is strictly codified by the economy of patriarchal society. Her house becomes the space in which both "alterities" often coexist conflictually. What Maraini is interested in showing is how Veronica Franco acts out a *rovesciamento*, a "displacement": Veronica tries to create a space where she transgresses the laws of social economy that regulate the selling of her body and allows herself to fall in love with some of the men that visit her regularly.

But Veronica's house is not only the place where she works with her body, it is also the arena of her feelings, and, most importantly, the workshop for her writing, another significant realm of transgression. In her poems, indeed, Veronica writes openly of the bed where she receives her clients, without masking its reality under moral pretenses. Selling one's body implies a mute consent to a double behavior: "mute" and "double" not because it is a morally unacceptable activity, but because it obliges Veronica to silence the voice of her desire. By stating her right to love and be loved, she contradicts her presumed acquiescent role as an object of desire; in the process of actively seeking the bodies she loves, she is a desiring subject. By appropriating for herself the right to passion, Veronica the courtesan interrupts the chain of male expectancy and enacts a role reversal.

Veronica claims her desire, but she is also aware of the economic and social laws ruling her society. She wisely makes a show of respecting them when her position is endangered, for example, during her trial at the Tribunal of the Inquisition when

Paola Carù

she answers the inquisitor's questions in an ironical yet ingratiating way. In her relationships with the three Venier noblemen, Domenico, Maffio, and Marco (Domenico and Marco are her lovers), Veronica experiences disappointment in the amorous game; she must remind herself of the limited scope of freedom for a woman of her status in relation to love offered in exchange for money and the rules regulating the social structure in which she lives. In a patriarchal world, Veronica's body is considered common property. Such condition is exemplified in the episode in which Veronica is been "graciously" offered to the king of France by Marco Venier, her preferred lover. Veronica wants to know in exchange for which favors from the king she is being offered and whether Marco feels any jealousy in organizing this transaction. He answers negatively to her questions by saying, "Io vi amo Veronica ma non pretendo di essere il solo . . . Vi amo come amo Venezia e voglio che anche altri la godano" (30; "I love you Veronica, but I don't claim to be the only one . . . I love you as I like Venice, and I want others to enjoy her too").

Veronica's body is assimilated to the body of Venice. It is a public body, belonging to all who can "roam" her/it. Confined to a closed space (the house), accessible only to those who can pay to have it, Veronica's body is a territory "mapped" by the "expropriation" of male desire.

The body of Veronica does not belong to itself: it is repeatedly "dismembered" or valued specifically in its sectioned body parts (Veronica's feet, her face, her breast, her voice). Fragmented or fetishized, it is not "whole." It signifies the arena where male pleasure is explicitly associated with desire for control and competition. This is illustrated in the scene where Marco Venier rebukes Veronica, while reminding her how he likes her to dress for their preludes to lovemaking (55), or in the episode immediately following, in which Maffio and Domenico argue about poetry and about who should be Veronica's lover.

Correlated to the city of Venice, Veronica's body attains metonymical value. Its dispossession is paralleled in the text by the pervasive presence of the plague that "invades" Venice. Such comparison is implicitly marked when Domenico apologizes to Veronica for being partly responsible for her renown as a prostitute.[4] He tells Veronica: "quel trionfo vi inchiodava . . .

alle mura molli della città" (68; "that fame nailed you down ... to the soft city walls"). In a preceding episode this connection is reinforced by the personification of Venice: while nursing the fever-struck Veronica at the *lazzaretto,* Anzola remarks that the canal water of Venice is "malata" ("ill") and "dà calore, come avesse la febbre" (26; "it gives off heat, as if it had a fever"). The courtesan's body is likened to the body of the city both as a public space and as an invaded space.

Yet, notwithstanding her own dispossession, Veronica can expand the restricted boundaries of her condition through poetry. Writing is for her a strategy to make herself a highly priced courtesan as well as a freer woman: through writing she is temporarily at the same intellectual level as the poets who patronize her house. Within the limits of the social structures that control her life, Franco is able to create a space for herself in her own house and succeeds in being vocal, despite the marginalized position she holds in society. Writing becomes a way to dislocate herself from the structures that marginalize her and, consequently, to reterritorialize a space of her own where she is the center of expression. In this territory she can overcome the logic of the silent concession of her body. Writing accomplishes the same function as the journey she undertakes at the end of the play.

As a prostitute, Veronica is subject to social restrictions such as lack of freedom of movement. In fact, because prostitutes are forbidden to show themselves in church, she cannot even go to mass on Sundays. Thus she works and lives inside her house. In Maraini's play, the *lazzaretto* is an enclosure equivalent to Veronica's house—equally secluded and possibly deadly. It is again through words that Veronica can help herself out of it: not only do they sustain her courage, but her stories attract Anzola's interest, becoming the means through which she will survive the plague. Suddenly, because of her talent in storytelling, Veronica appears to Anzola to be a special patient among many, not only because she is the potential source of precious objects to be looted (her shoes, in particular), but especially because she reveals to Anzola previously unknown and fascinating realities. The singular friendship that develops between the courtesan and the nun is achieved specifically through Veronica's ability to tell stories, and Anzola's need to hear them:

Paola Carù

> *Anzola:* E ora, ecco . . . raccontéme.
> *Veronica:* Che cosa?
> *Anzola:* De vu . . . Me piason tanto le storie. (55)
>
> *Anzola:* And now, there . . . tell me.
> *Veronica:* What?
> *Anzola:* About yourself . . . I like stories so much.

Veronica acts like a Scheherazade who pays for salvation with her narrative power. But the one who can let her die or save her and who, in the meantime, is enchanted by her stories is no powerful king. She is a young, ignorant, and curious nun, and, through an unlikely circumstance, she is given the gift of a vicarious experience that she could never have attained in her cloistered life. Conversely, Veronica manages to save her own life and to find a companion with whom she can set off on a journey. In this female relationship, Maraini outlines an issue that interests her greatly: solidarity among women despite their differences—social, cultural, and temperamental. Bonding among women in general, and particularly between the protagonists and their servants, wet nurses, and lady companions, is a constant feature in Maraini's work.[5]

Veronica and Anzola belong to two opposite realms and are each other's opposite in almost everything: while Veronica is older, richer, and cultivated, Anzola is young, poor (she has only eaten chicken twice in her life), and ignorant. Veronica is an intellectual and is broken down by every experience, Anzola is cheerfully naive (she constantly talks to her favorite saint, Saint Barbara). The ground where they meet is language, narration, and their relationships to words, words that create a game of reciprocation between them. This exchange is forced at the beginning: a woman has another woman in her power. Veronica pays for her need of special care with her storytelling, but this then becomes the basis for a shared destiny. Anzola becomes Veronica's family once Veronica loses everybody she loves; Veronica becomes Anzola's companion when her work at the *lazzaretto* is over and she does not want to return to her convent "da sola," "alone" (78).[6]

Veronica and Anzola are different from each other, yet they represent two similar aspects of female life: both live "secluded" lives, and neither embodies the woman in the traditional role of wife and mother. Although married and with children, Veronica is a "public woman," and Anzola, by becoming a nun, is reserved the part of a cloistered and childless "spouse of Christ."[7] Both personify a specific use of the female body within a patriarchal order. Anzola, as a nun, must forget her body, or better yet, she must mortify it; in fact, she has already done so out of dire poverty. But in reality, she is unfailingly interested in food, and its abundant presence is what fascinates her most in Veronica's recollections of her life before the plague. Veronica's body, on the other hand, is the body of "la più bella cortigiana di Venezia" (31; "the most beautiful courtesan in Venice"). It is a body that must be nourished and beautified in order to be ready for consumption (as when Marco "prepares" Veronica for her meeting with the king of France; 31).

More significantly, both Veronica and Anzola represent the only two female groups that, historically, had access to the territory of writing, although in a limited fashion and under certain conditions. In Maraini's play, writing seems exclusively Veronica Franco's domain; it is not Anzola's, yet Anzola is fascinated by the spoken word, that is, by Veronica's stories. Language is a strategy that allows Veronica to improve her marketability; for Anzola, it is the measure of her ignorance of the world. Moreover, language will become the common link between the two, the instrument that leads to friendship and to an alternative to the two women's cloistered lives. It is the path to potential freedom through their chosen and shared "displacement," the means to subvert the patriarchal system that isolates and silences them.

It is relevant to notice how Maraini depicts differently her characters' verbal exchanges in the play: female language can subvert the preestablished order of things and break the codified limits of the binary opposition between those who are socially powerful and those who are not.

Male speech, on the contrary, tends to establish control over the interlocutor, especially if the latter is female. For example, in her dialogues with both the inquisitor and the king of France, Veronica, whenever possible, reverts to irony to fight their power to constrain her into assuming prescribed roles; both men quickly respond with threats in reaction to Veronica's ironic and "impertinent" replies to their statements. Veronica's talks

Paola Carù

with some of the male characters in the play are marked by animosity and offense: her employee Vannitelli denounces her to the Tribunal of the Inquisition and afterward attacks her with insults when she is acquitted and refuses to have him in her bed. Maffio Venier, the self-appointed "outsider poet" in the patrician Venier family, anonymously circulates satirical invectives against Veronica because she does not welcome him to her house too often (since he does not pay her!), and because she does not share his concept of poetry. Even Marco Venier, the most beloved of her patrons, distances himself symbolically from her: whenever Veronica tries to communicate endearingly with him, he reverts to short and laconic statements.

In Maraini's play, language is used differently by women in their relationship with other women. Not necessarily relaxed, yet respectful, female language acknowledges the other woman as someone with whom contact must be established. Veronica's interactions with Anzola, or with her wet nurse Gaspara (a character that oscillates between a maternal and a sisterlike figure) are sharp at times, but never deeply resentful or offensive.

Maraini's own use of words is intended to highlight Veronica's case of paradoxical female subjectivity, marked by her belonging to a specific gender.[8] In the title of her play, Maraini summarizes Veronica's double (professional and personal) attributes and their unquestionable link to Veronica's body. Maraini uses gendered language: she defines Veronica as a "scrittora," not a "scrittrice," as used in mainstream contemporary Italian.[9]

In the first part of the play, writing is the place where Veronica feels less dispossessed because she can stage within it the play of her desire. Yet, paradoxically, it is through her "dismemberment" that her writing is made possible. Veronica's writing expresses her experience of limits, of "borders." Even within the stringent rules of her status, she asserts her own erotic space; in one of the preludes to lovemaking (to Domenico Venier), Veronica declares: "Me piase il vostro desiderio . . . Me piase zogar" (65; "I like your desire . . . I like playing"). Veronica's relationship to Senator Domenico Venier, the oldest of the three Veniers, reveals this game of challenge to stereotypes on Veronica's part. On the other hand, it states her refusal to be silenced and to camouflage her right to desire. The elderly patrician Domenico Venier is one of the two men

Vocal Marginality: Maraini's Veronica Franco

Veronica admits to having loved. He is intelligent, knowledgeable, and courteous to Veronica, even in public. Moreover, he believes that poetry can transform reality. He is interested in a world where "le montagne sono di seta" ("mountains are silky") and poetry can make language gentler (61). He himself has the ability to manipulate words, and Veronica likes him for it. Thus, Veronica relates to Domenico on a double plane of expression, erotic and literary.

It is important to note the alternating use of Italian and Venetian dialect in the verbal interactions between Veronica and Senator Venier. Dialect, which in Veronica's Venice is both the language of domesticity and the idiom of poetry, marks the moments when Veronica acts as a desiring subject: the phrase "andémo" ("let's go," in dialect) both states the invitation to lovemaking between Veronica and Domenico (65), and seals Veronica and Anzola's final, reciprocal proposal to embark on a common journey, after the end of the plague (78). Dialect represents a domain within the wider territory of language, or better yet, it is a borderland marked as *zona franca,* a free space through which Veronica can step away from the forced silencing of her body and enact her desire. Thus Veronica's shift to dialect, happening at significant moments, and exclusively in her communications with Domenico Venier and with Anzola, signals her need for transgression. Veronica's use of more than one language is a way to overcome the metaphorical boundaries of language. It is a subversion of the social order that lets her reappropriate a space of her own.[10]

Veronica and Anzola's final decision to start wandering together highlights an important motif in Maraini's work. In 1991, a year before *Veronica, meretrice e scrittora* came out, Maraini wrote an introduction to her own poetry collection *Viaggiando con passo di volpe* (*Traveling in the Gait of a Fox*), dedicated to the concept of traveling. Traveling is a way to distance oneself; it is a source of peace. Yet, at the same time, it is a disquieting experience. It is both leaving home and finding oneself at home. It is "[u]na insofferenza insomma, prima di tutto fisica, una urgenza di ciò che è vivo nel nostro corpo" (*Viaggiando* 20; "above all physical impatience . . . the urgency of everything that is alive in our body"; my translation). For Maraini, traveling expresses therefore a need of the soul that is inextricably radicated in the body. It expresses freedom, the painful freedom to be oneself and someone different. It allows one to see one's world from without and from within.[11]

Veronica's setting off together with Anzola symbolically reasserts the presence of the paradoxical factors in their lives. It proves also the possibility of overcoming them: unstructured and unmapped, their journey is the opposite of the courses of their previous lives. The two women's joint departure signals the importance of their bonding and marks the acquisition of a reappropriation of themselves: together they can trespass the boundaries that had kept them forcefully marginalized. It is with their reciprocal invitation to go that Maraini chooses to conclude her "imaginary journey" centered on the figure of Veronica Franco.

Notes

1. For a comprehensive study of the historical Veronica Franco, see Margaret F. Rosenthal's *The Honest Courtesan: Veronica Franco Citizen and Writer in Sixteenth-Century Venice*. Unless otherwise indicated, all translations are mine.

2. On the relationship between women and power in religious contexts, see, among others, *Donna potere e profezia,* edited by Adriana Valerio, and Anna Scattigno's "La retorica della debolezza: esperienza religiosa e percorsi di identità femminile."

3. Veronica's attempts to enlarge her own symbolic space by expanding the borders of her seclusion are a way of "experiencing" and "experimenting." The notion of *esperimentar* was important in Renaissance culture. Usually thought of in relation to men, there exists, in fact, a relevant example that refers to women in the well known anonymous Venetian play *La Venexiana*. Written in the first half of the Cinquecento, *La Venexiana* depicts an amorous game of desire and intrigue that has two women as protagonists, two women that are seen as desiring subjects engaged in pursuing the man they both want.

4. The image of the courtesan as a profane icon and its relationship to the city was, historically, particularly articulated in the case of Venice. Rosenthal points out that: "The representation of the Venetian courtesan in male authors' texts intersects with the virginal civic icon signifying Venetian 'libertà'" (17).

5. See, for example, the end of Maraini's novel *La lunga vita di Marianna Ucrìa* (*The Silent Duchess*), in which the eighteenth-century noblewoman Marianna leaves everything behind and embarks on a journey with Fila, her servant and companion, a poor woman whom she had once saved from death.

6. It is beyond the scope of the present article to analyze the relevance of the nun figures in the writings of twentieth-century Italian women writers, yet one cannot avoid noticing how the nun as a character has intrigued both writers of the older generation, such as Anna Banti and Beatrice Solinas Donghi, and of the younger generation. A representative of the latter group, Silvana La Spina, chooses a nun as the protagonist of her 1995 novel *Un inganno dei sensi malizioso*. Suor Trafitta shares some of the features of Maraini's Anzola.

7. Veronica disapproves of Anzola's definition of Christ as [her] "beloved Lord" ("il mio amato Signore"), the perfect being "who desires only himself" ("che desidera solo se stesso"). Veronica's reply makes a significant point: "Sad is the body that only desires itself" ("Triste quel corpo che desidera solo se stesso"; 49).

8. Rosenthal's study of the documented life of Veronica Franco pivots on a paradox as well: Franco is seen as the "honest courtesan" who questions male stereotypes of "the deceitful whore." Rosenthal discusses how Franco negotiates her position "within Venetian culture to identify herself with other Venetian women as a group and to speak in support of women previously silenced by male authors" (1).

9. Alma Sabatini's *Il sessismo nella lingua italiana* is the first text officially adopted by the Italian government on the issue of sexism in the Italian language. Sabatini accepts the use of *scrittrice* as a regular form to name a female writer (114). Maraini's preference for *scrittora* in the title of her play must be interpreted as a definitely stronger intention to draw attention to the gendered nature of this word (and of writing).

10. Gloria Anzaldúa explores the notion of real and symbolic borderlands and boundary crossing in her work *Borderlands / La Frontera: The New Mestiza*.

11. This is Maraini's answer to the question "What is wandering for you?" in Maraini's interview with Nella Condorelli, "Dacia Maraini: quell'isola che è tra noi " (Dacia Maraini: that island which lies between us).

Works Cited

Anzaldúa, Gloria. *Borderlands / La Frontera: The New Mestiza*. San Francisco: Spinster/Aunt Lute, 1987.

Banti, Anna. *La monaca di Sciangai*. Milan: Mondadori, 1957.

———. *Le monache cantano*. Rome: Tumminelli, 1942.

———. "Joveta di Betania." *Je vous écris d'un pays lointain*. Milan: Mondadori, 1971.

Costa-Zalessow, Natalia. *Scrittrici italiane dal XIII al XX secolo.* Ravenna: Longo, 1982.

Jones, Ann Rosalind. "City Women and Their Audiences: Louise Labé and Veronica Franco." *Rewriting the Renaissance: The Discourses of Sexual Difference in Early Modern Europe.* Ed. Margaret W. Ferguson, Maureen Quilligan, and Nancy J. Vickers. Chicago: U of Chicago P, 1986. 299–316.

La Spina, Silvana. *Un inganno dei sensi malizioso.* Milan: Mondadori, 1995.

Maraini, Dacia. "Dacia Maraini: quell'isola che è tra noi." Interview with Nella Condorelli. *Noidonne* Mar. 1993: 68–69.

———. *La lunga vita di Marianna Ucrìa.* Milan: Rizzoli, 1990. Published in English as *The Silent Duchess.* London: Peter Owen, 1992. New York: Feminist, 1998.

———. *Veronica, meretrice e scrittora.* Milan: Bompiani, 1992.

———. *Viaggiando con passo di volpe: poesie 1983–1991.* Milan: Rizzoli, 1991. Published in English as *Traveling in the Gait of a Fox.* Kingston, ON: Quarry, 1992.

Rosenthal, Margaret. *The Honest Courtesan: Veronica Franco Citizen and Writer in Sixteenth-Century Venice.* Chicago: U of Chicago P, 1992.

Sabatini, Alma. *Il sessismo nella lingua italiana.* Rome: Istituto Poligrafico e Zecca dello Stato, 1987.

Scattigno, Anna. "La retorica della debolezza: esperienza religiosa e percorsi di identità femminile." *Il femminile tra potenza e potere.* Rome: Arlem, 1995. 135–45.

Solinas Donghi, Beatrice. "Tra quelle mura." *La bella fuga e altri racconti.* Milan: La Tartaruga, 1992.

Valerio, Adriana, ed. *Donna potere e profezia.* Naples: D'Auria, 1995.

La Venexiana. Turin: Einaudi, 1965.

Wend, Petra. *The Female Voice: Lyrical Expression in the Writings of Five Italian Renaissance Poets.* Frankfurt: Lang, 1995.

Part 5
Reclaiming the Body in the Construction of Subjectivity

Rodica Diaconescu-Blumenfeld
Body as Will: Incarnate Voice in Dacia Maraini

Gabrielle Cody
Remembering What the Closed Eye Sees: Some Notes on Dacia Maraini's Postmodern *Oresteia*

Pauline Dagnino
Revolution in the Laundry

Áine O'Healy
Toward a Poor Feminist Cinema: The Experimental Films of Dacia Maraini

Rodica Diaconescu-Blumenfeld

Body as Will

Incarnate Voice in
Dacia Maraini

> *They don't know what a body is.*
> Pauline Lermond, on hearing of the violation
> of a young, retarded woman by a group of
> youths with a broomstick.

> Ninnà ninnà bella bambina
> dormi non pensare al tuo futuro
> ti cucirò le labbra con lo spago
> per non avere la tentazione di baciare
> dirai che la tua mamma era una strega
> dirai che la tua mamma era una fata
> ti cucirò la fica con filo di seta
> per non avere la tentazione di chiavare,
> . . . .
> ti cucirò gli occhi col verderame
> per non avere la tentazione di guardare
> dirai che la tua mamma era una strega
> dirai che la tua mamma era una fata
> quando sarai grande vivrai solo fra donne
> diventerai una strega, diventerai una fata.
> Dacia Maraini
> *Dialogo di una prostituta con un suo cliente*

> Ninnà ninnà beautiful baby girl
> sleep, don't think of your future
> I'll sew your lips with thread
> so you won't know the desire to kiss
> you'll say your mother was a witch
> you'll say your mother was a fay

> I'll sew your cunt with silk thread
> so you won't know the desire to fuck,
> ....
> I'll sew your eyes with verdigris
> so you won't know the desire to look
> you'll say your mother was a fay
> when you grow up you'll live only among women,
> you'll become a witch, you'll become a fay.

So tenderly sings Manila, the prostitute mother, at the close of Dacia Maraini's 1978 play *Dialogo di una prostituta con un suo cliente* (*Dialogue between a Prostitute and Her Client*), an apotropaic incantation that can only strike its hearers as image of ultimate violence: the seeling up of the eye, mouth, and vagina of the tiny girl.[1]

How does this fierce emblem of bodily violence come to embody for Maraini the magical act of maternal protectiveness? And what does this protection mean for the woman who sings? Examining the interrelations between penetration, possession, and poetics in the *Dialogo,* we begin to understand how the violent image corresponds to the reality of violation. The mother sings against the violence that will rend her child, entering through the desire that opens her to the world.

Manila has taken up prostitution as a political choice, and her whole manner of conducting business disturbs and dislocates her client, who does not cease to try to assimilate her to his own order of discourse. Particularly notable is a term he twice employs to express his anger at her refusal to conform to his desire. "Porca puttana, mi spoetizzi!" ("Ugly whore, you depoetize me!"), he cries when Manila without euphemism describes their exchange in terms of selling her "fica" ("cunt") "a prezzo ridotto" (*Dialogo* 34; "at a discount"). Neither will she submit to the client's "Facciamo finta" (34; "Let's make believe"), or his elevation of her identity to courtesan and their encounter to adventure. "Ma quante cose vuoi comprare con quei pochi soldi che mi dai?" ("But how many things you want to buy with that little money you're giving me?")—"Perché vuoi spoetizzare tutto?" (43; "Why do you want to depoetize everything?"), he answers. The male character keeps making up stories about the prostitute, trying to renarratize her into some position where he can penetrate "her." She must not be *fica/ meat*, sold by the pound, but the "eminently poetic reality," as Beauvoir puts it (170), that woman is to men. Selfish and sentimental, this phallic fantasy is the male poetics—the alibi of female violation and possession.[2]

Possession, however, *Dialogo* presents also in an alternate mode: as *immedesimazione* ("identification"). Identification can be described as "falling into" or "entry by." The point is a permeation of selves in which the boundary between self and other blurs, a sort of clairvoyant empathy taking place. Several times Manila describes how the act of gazing functions as trajectory of identification: "io guardo, riguardo e poi . . . casco nella cosa guardata . . . questo è il rischio . . . se ad un certo punto guardo ancora mi butto, . . . mi butto dentro la cosa guardata e non ci sono più . . . non sono più io manco per niente, sono quella cosa lì guardata . . ." (*Dialogo* 32; "I look, look again and then . . . I fall into the thing I'm looking at . . . this is the risk . . . if at a certain point I look again I throw myself, . . . I throw myself into the thing and I don't exist any more . . . I'm not me anymore at all, I'm that thing there, the one I'm looking at"). For instance, Manila describes how she "falls into" an old woman on the tram, and through her eyes sees the world "lontano e brutto" ("distant and ugly"), and feels the disgusted gaze of other people on her wrinkled face (53).

The climax of the play is the mutual orgasm of prostitute and client. The forms of possession experientially and textually cohere:

> la cosa tremenda . . . è che ci sto cascando dentro quel corpo sudato, . . . mi faccio lui, timido . . . assetato di latte materno. Apro la camicetta, gli dò da bere il latte mio e lui, cioè io, se ne viene come una fontana. (*Dialogo* 47)

> the terrible thing . . . is that I'm falling into that sweating body, . . . I become him, timid, . . . thirsty for maternal milk. I open my shirt, I give him to drink and he, that is I, come like a fountain.

Most horribly, Manila falls into his own narrative of satisfaction:

> e io divento tutto latte nella gola di mio figlio che sono io e che sputa il seme dolce nel mio ventre che è il suo e io sono

> in lei che è la madre mia e il figlio della madre che si fa latte per il mio amato amore materno. (47)

> and I become all milk in the throat of my son who is me and who spits out sweet seed in my belly which is his and I am in her who is my mother and the son of the mother who becomes milk for my beloved maternal love.

He sucks from her breast the milk of the virgin mother, at whose statue he had wept and masturbated, milk which for him exists as his own tears and sperm. But Manila is penetrated and possessed. And he knows it; on this basis, indeed, he refuses to pay her. It is against this that she wishes to protect her daughter, this penetration and possession, this assimilation to an alien and alienating narrative.

In the prefatory discussion between the author and the women involved in the play's production, the experience of *immedesimazione* is explicitly related to representation: the actress in terms of her roles, Dacia Maraini in terms of writing. Maraini asserts: "for the one who writes it can be a good thing, though exhausting. For a prostitute it is not" (*Dialogo* 9). The problem is not merely one of effort, rather that of existential risk, and here, as in multiple other contexts, we find the suggestion that this possession is the ground of Maraini's poetics—writing the world from the inside.

For Maraini, writing is thus connected to the loss of boundary between self and other, a work of empathy, but, as later becomes clear, also a work of articulation, that is, of distance. This sort of writing is not the writing of a self that transcends other, not a writing of confirmed power (the ultimate meaning of all esotericism), proof against violence. Male poetics, depoetized by the self of an other, can be seen as continuous with the violence that cuts to pieces the body, negating it as self. Manila constructs for her daughter a self locked against violence, a true virgin self, but also of necessity a voiceless subject who can neither taste the world nor speak it. There is no protection for the woman who sings.

The *Dialogo di una prostituta con un suo cliente* shows how the feminism that struggles to order and reorganize exists in tension with the poetics of possession that is affirmation of corporeality. In a world where body is bought and sold, where

Body as Will: Incarnate Voice

meat is mythologized, where women write their continuity to male writing, Maraini's poetics of possession raises profound ethical questions for her readers.

***

It is possible to trace through the corpus of Maraini's writings a mesh of interlacing themes that find unity as constant discourse on the meaning of incarnate voice. One of the most basic insights of feminist theory has certainly been that the gendering of the world extends to culture's most basic dichotomies of interpretation. Mind and matter are dichotomized and gendered. Voice and body are dichotomized and gendered. Maraini has spoken forcefully on the cultural representation of woman as body, voiceless body, and on the need to restore to women their voices ("From the World of Violence—Voices of Women"). Her writing takes this yet further into narratives that reconstitute the concepts, giving body a voice and making voice a body. A will is in the world, a self, an urgent agency, immersed in the wash of wills, of other selves. The body is will, not meat. Maraini is concerned with the integrity of subjectivity, not an integrity that defines or constructs itself as transcendent, as will above body, but a subjectivity that remains agency: the voice to refuse dismemberment.

Manila's body is an open body, exposed at once to pleasure and pain (though mostly she understands its pleasure as pain and degradation). In her song for her infant daughter, she creates a body that is not a body but absolute autism, a body so closed that it cannot experience the world. But Maraini does not argue for a closed body, she does not call for an end to vulnerability: immersion, "falling into" bodies, is what it is to be human and open to the world. In *Lettere a Marina* (1981; *Letters to Marina*), the protagonist-writer Bianca recalls a time of her past when she confused the borders of her body "confini del mio corpo con i confini del mondo" (119; "with the borders of the world"). The self is an effect of overlaying, merging, with other selves, at a level that is at the same time matter and perception.

The idea of a closed body exists in the mother's agonized invocation of total protection, and only as a measure of women's suffering. Manila, like all the female protagonists in Maraini's texts, struggles with the relation between corporeality and subjectivity. Without the open body, subject to other wills, all wills, there is no consciousness. The self finds its possibility in immersion, it others itself in the experience of the world.

In Maraini, making an arc through the course of her texts, from the 1974 *Donna in guerra* (*Woman at War*), to the 1978 *Dialogo,* to the 1981 *Lettere a Marina,* to the 1994 *Voci* (*Voices*), the experience of identification is not constituted by abstract, theoretical, or utopian speculation. Rather, it takes place through the senses, most notably seeing (especially in *Dialogo* and *Lettere*), and hearing (especially in *Donna in guerra* and *Voci*). Hearing seems more likely to produce the presence of the other. Voice cannot be turned off: it invades the perceiving consciousness, it takes up space in it. But gazing/"falling into" is also an invasion, being taken over, since for Maraini gazing is the opposite of distancing and objectification; it is conjoining, commingling of consciousness on a sensual basis. Maraini makes the gaze coextensive with voice, corporeal. The other is not being conjured up, but experienced, not as pure construction, but as embodied subjectivity. In *Dialogo,* Manila falls into *bodies.*[3]

The theme of identification and the blurring of the boundaries of self and other appear with great consistency in the full range of Maraini's texts. Interestingly, these experiences are often characterized by a sense of queasiness or revulsion.

At the end of *Dialogo,* as Manila remembers her immersion in the old woman, she experiences a complex net of desires and resistances:

> ... tenevo una grossa borsa verde sulle ginocchia e ogni tanto andavo a controllare con le dita rugose che la cerniera fosse chiusa .... sotto le braccia sentivo le cosce che si stringevano senza toccarsi, il cuore batteva fiacco fiacco e non mi importava niente di nessuno, volevo solo mangiare una cosa buona, un dolce che tenevo dentro la borsa verde ... sapevo che la mia vita era attaccata a quel dolce e tutto il resto non mi faceva né caldo né freddo. (53)

> ... I had a big green bag on my lap and every so often my withered fingers checked that the catch was fastened. ... Under my arms I could feel my thighs pressing together but not touching. My heart was beating sluggishly and I couldn't

> care less about anybody else, all I wanted to do was eat a lovely cake I had in my green bag .... I knew my life depended on that cake and nothing else mattered. (*Dialogue* 171)

Manila ends her monologue with a sudden return to her own perspective: "che cazzo di vecchia, l'avrei strangolata" (*Dialogo* 53; "fucking old woman, I could have strangled her"). Working within this text are distinct but concomitant lines of desire and repulsion: Manila's empathy with and resistance to the old woman's degraded existence; the old woman's savage indifference to anything but a little piece of cake; the world's and Manila's disgust for the old woman; Manila's fear at having to experience the world through such a body.

The trope of queasiness would seem present in all instances of total immersion/identification. It may be taken to signal the depth of the world. This immersion, at its core empathy and connectedness to others, is incurable. The nausea is incurable. It communicates the submergence of the self in the world, the continuity of body and world. The world is deep and in continuous motion.

The act of "falling into" is already found in *Donna in guerra,* not in relation to a particular individual, rather it is a falling into the deep cauldron of the world of the laundry room. "Casco dentro un sogno afoso e serpentino" (*Donna in guerra* 13; "I fall inside a sweltering and serpentine dream"), states Vannina, the protagonist. This experience is described sometimes as immersion: "ero immersa in un bagno di vapori nauseabondi" (10; "I was immersed in a bath of nauseating vapors"), and "in quell'acqua elettrica e dolce in cui eravamo immerse" (49; "in that electric and sweet water in which we were immersed"); sometimes as entrapment: "ne rimarrò coinvolta ... sarò risucchiata, presa" (135; "I'll remain shut in ... I'll be sucked back in, captivated").

Vannina lives a life of confinement in a regulated time and space, characterized, as Maraini writes elsewhere, by "a docile, bitter attachment, profoundly interwoven with fantasies and daydreams, to [her] own captivity." But, Maraini continues, "underneath it, inside the morbid consciousness which ... confuses pleasure with pain, one feels the existence of a stubborn, delicate will to live" (*La bionda* 155). Vannina's space is traditional (house, courtyard, market), and it structures her day as do her repetitive chores. In slow, repeated movements, through her very familiarity with subjugation, Vannina comes to enlarge the surface of her confinement, until, at the end of the novel, she breaks away from it. Her trajectory from subjugation to freedom is aided by two significant relationships, one with the beautiful, crippled Suna, and the other with the laundry women. While Suna's influence is established through persuasion, logic, and feminist consciousness-raising, the laundry women actualize a very different world for Vannina.

The laundry room in *Donna in guerra* is an early expression in Maraini's work of the incarnate nature of consciousness, where to be incarnate means to be submerged, pushed on every side, as by currents, by other people's desires, wills, fantasies, images, stories.

The laundry women, Giottina and Tota, are in a sense quite mad. Further, they live repressed lives of profound servitude and desperate poverty, causing them, for example, to commit an act of ultimate degradation, the robbing of the dead. Yet toward Vannina they show a degree of concrete, material, generosity: they give her a third of the plunder. They are tragic figures, excluded and abject. But the stories they tell are acts of pure creativity, of narrative genius. The stuff of their stories is sex, pornography, in which folklore and religion mix. Since their stories do not provide any sort of logical categories for interpreting the world,[4] the "feeding" Vannina receives is visceral. The room itself is a viscous body into which she falls. The physical space is a cave, filled with white steam, vapors, heat, and "un odore violento di varechina" (*Donna in guerra* 9; "a violent odor of bleach"). At times the room is bathed in a "luce smorta" (142; "colorless light"), but mostly it is dark and sweltering. As the meetings multiply and the stories grow and make up an increased presence in Vannina's life, the space of the cave becomes indistinguishable from the space of the stories. The adjectives *buio* ("dark"), and *afoso* ("sweltering") are used to describe both the room ("lavanderia buia e afosa"; 134; "the dark and sweltering laundry room"), and the parallel reality of the story-space: "un teatro buio e afoso dove si improvvisano inquietanti giochi dell'immaginazione" (14; "a dark and sweltering theater when disturbing games of the imagination are being improvised").

At the end of Vannina's first encounter with Giottina and Tota, the "nauseating vapors" of the laundry room drive her away. But starting with the second, she realizes that she will return to the laundry women's "giochi rustici, spericolati, pieni di una sensualità agra, selvatica che mi affascina nonostante la nausea" (*Donna in guerra* 14; "rustic, brazen games, full of a harsh, savage sensuality that fascinates me, notwithstanding the nausea"). The feelings of nausea and fascination will be consolidated in all the laundry room meetings: "La nausea mi chiudeva la gola. Avrei voluto scappare. Ma nello stesso tempo ero presa da una strana perversa dolcissima simpatia per le due folli amiche" (122; "Nausea was blocking my throat. I would have liked to run away. But at the same time I was seized by a strange perverse, very sweet sympathy for my two crazy friends").

While *Donna in guerra*'s laundry women can certainly be illumined by Julia Kristeva's discourse of the semiotic, they are not only womb, but also narrative. They draw Vannina into a place where a narrative of desire is constructed, where the pornographic imagination becomes a nurturance in which her sexuality strengthens as will. For themselves, their stories are an aspect of their repression, a form of consolation, but for Vannina they represent the possibility of self-transformation through the invention of other spaces for the body. They generate for Vannina a power of imagining, of creating a different narrative of life.

The distinction of Maraini's discourse from Kristeva's is significant for Maraini's concern for a voiced body that is not only music but also articulate agency. The spatial dimension of the laundry room is, but is not only, a space *in which*. This distinction is further consequential for the relevance of the body as will, the voice as an embodied will, to the problematic of violence.

Those theories, perhaps best exemplified by Kristeva's theory of the semiotic, that emphasize the mother's body as site of a sort of musical nurture, would seem to be participating in the gendered dichotomy of mind and body at another power, thus continuing to conspire against the mother as *subject*.[5] This is not to claim that maternal subjectivity, say in Kristeva, has no place, but rather that the failure to address the mother's body as agency opens it to denial and dismemberment.[6] Adriana Cavarero, in her account, in *Nonostante Platone,* of the symbolic matricide underlying Western culture, at least has shown the links between violence against the maternal body, the refusal of maternal genealogy as immersion in the world, and the problematization of female agency. These are not precisely Cavarero's terms, but they do not falsify her logic. It would seem that the identification of the mother with body has violence against body, specifically female bodies, as concomitant.

Yet violence against the mother is not an attack on inanimate matter. You cannot dismember what is not a whole, nor kill what is not alive. Beauvoir's reading of the Oedipal crisis has the male subject define himself as a transcendent subjectivity (that is, over and against the world) through rejection of the maternal matter from which he has sprung (*Second Sex* 195).[7] We might argue that as this violence cannot be against matter, it is against the occluded subjectivity of the mother. Every murder reduces incarnate subjectivity to matter, makes a body not a body. Do the acts of violence against the bodies of women issue precisely from the inability to knit the sinews of soul and space into a self? They don't know what a body is.

This essay has described a male poetics, as that of Manila's client, constructed in self-referent negation of other. Poetry is not murder, but an identical logic underlies these practices. Both function as operations of fantasized transcendence, though their consequences are not fantasy.

A male poetics continuous with male violence emerges explicitly in *Voci,* a novel about women killed by (their) men, where we also find the continuity of immersion with voice. Michela, the narrating I of *Voci,* is a radio journalist and talk-show host. She works with voices. The voices are the mark of space and time, constructing Michela's world. At the radio station, they are the medium of communication and contact, collapsing distance. At home, objects speak around Michela (*Voci* 13, 127), re-creating motionless physical space into one imbued with life. They also create the spaces of dreams and memory (105). Present and past, they inhabit memory even as they emerge and fade out of a universe that always speaks. Everything around

Body as Will: Incarnate Voice

Michela speaks, sometimes intelligibly, sometimes ambiguously: the women who were killed, those who might be killed, and their killers. Most importantly, in three instances of textual undecidability, other entities speak, with voices that are not voice: the inanimate objects of Michela's house, the slaughtered animals in the butcher's shop, and the silent dance of the cat-woman.

Voices come into Michela's consciousness first as desire: "Sono avida di voci, che siano leggere o pesanti, scure o chiare . . ." (*Voci* 69; "I am avid for voices, be they light or heavy, dark or bright . . ."). As she becomes involved in a project on unsolved crimes against women, the voices shift, expanding the sphere of desire into one where danger, invasion are unequivocal: "Vengo investita da . . . voci . . . . La mia vita sembra ormai fatta solo di voci estranee che cerco di decifrare, di analizzare" (105; "I am invaded by . . . voices . . . . My life seems made only of alien voices, which I try to decipher and analyze").[8] The project becomes an experience of embodied sorrow, and although Michela struggles for the protection of rational knowledge, she is engulfed in a world of "una profonda e lugubre pena" (34; "a deep and dismal pain"), where voices are the subjectivities of dead women. "Fanno un gran chiasso queste morte ammazzate" (85; "They make a great clamor, these murdered women"), Michela notes, and to each she would like to "ridarle la voce" (85; "give her back her voice").

Eager for voices, Michela loves them "per la loro straordinaria capacità di farsi corpo" (*Voci* 69; "for their extraordinary ability to make themselves into bodies"). She listens to them "con attenzione carnale" (69; "with carnal attention"). The concept of voice is synonymous with will or agency in Maraini. Voice is the same as will/agency, and at the same time voice is also body. To say that voice is body is to say that agency is embodied, that body and self are one thing that desires, acts, affirms itself in the world. As in *Donna in guerra* and in *Dialogo,* in *Voci* also Maraini struggles with the dichotomy between will and body, in the attempt to articulate the absolute objectification of women whose voices have been taken away through violence and killing. As long as the dichotomy exists, women will be identified with body that exists for slaughter. Because women are not perceived as voice, they are treated as body and their consciousness is disregarded. But for Maraini, the body is the site of will, the incarnation of agency.[9]

Michela discovers that the mass of murdered women is erased from the "memoria della città" ("memory of the city"), that not "una parola" (*Voci* 84; "a word") of their life is preserved. Yet for her, they are alive; they "continuano a camminare in su e in giù, senza requie, chiedendo un po'di attenzione . . . chiedendo rumorosamente giustizia" (84–85; "keep on walking up and down, without peace, asking for a bit of attention . . . asking vociferously for justice"). So do the women still alive, mothers and sisters of the victims. They all ask to be heard, to be known. But so, for that matter, do their male oppressors. In all of Maraini's texts, and in *Voci,* so does the murderer. All the voices, toward the end of the novel, crystallize in that of Glauco Elia, "una voce circonspetta e studiata, con una intenzione disperata di seduzione" (235; "a circumspect and studied voice, with a desperate intention to seduce"). He too craves Michela's attention, pleading to be understood and not judged. He is the stepfather whose relationship to his stepdaughters, Angela and Ludovica Bari, inscribes itself in the sphere of male poetics. About to be arrested for Angela's murder, he records a cassette—a narcissistic extension of himself—for Michela, in which he protests his innocence even while listing the complex net of forces that brought him from love to humiliation, to rape, and ultimately to murder.[10] He contrives to control Michela's will, as he did his daughters'. He uses the arsenal of manipulations, entreaty, flattery, false confession, miscommunication, and preterition already present in *Dialogo*'s client. He desires Michela's consent, in order to naturalize his alienated narrative, and, in fact, unwilling that anyone should interfere with his self-interpretation, he kills himself. His last words confirm this reading:

> Con questo la saluto sperando che lei mi creda, perché merito di essere creduto e spero che comprenda anche la mia reticenza a farmi analizzare, interrogare, soppesare. Mi sentirei *bétail,* del bestiame da macello . . . (*Voci* 294)
>
> With this I say good-bye, hoping that you'll believe me, because I deserve to be believed, and hoping also that you

Body as Will: Incarnate Voice

> will understand my refusal to allow myself to be analyzed, interrogated, examined, weighed. I would feel as if I were *bétail*, cattle for the butcher . . .

But the word *bétail* establishes a shocking correspondence with an early segment of Michela's story:

> In via San Crisogono mi fermo davanti alla vetrina del macellaio a contare le testine delle pecore morte, appese ai ganci. Lucide come di plastica, le povere orecchie senza pelle, i denti privati delle labbra, gli occhi spogliati delle palpebre, ciondolano contro il vetro sporco . . . . E mi sembra di sentire un mormorio alle mie spalle. Le testine appese sono scosse da risatine sinistre, singulti e squittii. Le voci in questi giorni si sono moltiplicate pericolosamente, hanno toni minacciosi come se una eco dell'assassinio di Angela Bari riverberasse su tutto ciò che avvicino. "Lei conosceva Angela Bari?" dico, come per caso. Il macellaio si ferma con una zampa sanguinolenta in mano. Come sono sicure e allegre quelle mani che strappano, recidono, manipolano la carne morta! (*Voci* 20)

> On Via San Crisogono I stop in front of the butcher's shop to count the small heads of dead sheep hanging on hooks. Glistening like plastic, the poor ears without skin, the teeth without lips, the eyes stripped of eyelids, they dangle against the dirty glass of the shop window . . . . And I seem to hear a whispering behind me. The small hanging heads are being shaken by sinister little titters, hiccups and squeaks. These days the voices have multiplied dangerously; their tone is menacing, as if an echo of Angela Bari's murder reverberated over everything that I come close to. "Did you know Angela Bari?" I ask casually. The butcher stops with a bleeding hoof in his hand. How competent and cheerful they are, those hands that tear, carve, and manipulate the dead meat!

In this passage Maraini articulates a suffering that takes seriously the specificity of the body. The slaughtered animals, medium between the utterly disembodied voices of the dead and the truly inanimate objects, lament the meaning of the body: they never had voices. *Bétail*, meat in the butcher's hands: Glauco cannot accept this lot, and unwittingly enacts the scene of dread and horror that belongs to women. Maraini performs a rhetoric operation that codes the opposition between Michela's and

Rodica Diaconescu-Blumenfeld

Glauco's stories of being in the world, and allows the condensation of an entire symbolic order into a word. Glauco, the killer, the destroyer of the body, does not want to become body.

In *Isolina, la donna tagliata a pezzi* (1985; *Isolina*), the themes of identification and of violence against women intersect at another level, since the *immedesimazione* is not that of a character but of the author herself who puts together through narrative the "pieces" of a young Veronese woman, murdered and hacked apart. In this context we meet again the idea of nausea, here not only a textual but a metaliterary concept, reaffirming the whole constellation earlier located in *Dialogo, Donna in guerra,* and *Voci.* Nausea accompanies the enterprise of analysis, research, and perception of others, which for Maraini is lived experience.

> Scavar nel tempo è difficile e dà un leggero senso di nausea. Come entrare in un mondo di morti che improvvisamente si fanno intransigenti, pettegoli e golosi? Vogliono che tu li ricordi secondo l'idea che loro hanno di sé. (*Isolina* 75)
>
> Digging through time is difficult and gives me a slight sense of nausea. How to enter a world of the dead who unexpectedly become intransigent, chatting and greedy? They want you to remember them according their own ideas of themselves.

The empathetic consciousness is bound to a dynamic of identification and resistance, and writing emerges as the possibility of an empathy that is not final loss of self and of a resistance that is not denial but articulation.

Michela remembers police commissioner Adele Sòfia's advice: "Bisogna dare una forma alle proprie ossessioni, che hanno delle ragioni profonde; non chiuda gli occhi, vada avanti" (*Voci* 274; "One must give form to one's own obsessions, which have profound reasons; don't close your eyes, go on"). To go on means to accept immersion, and it also means to come out again and engage the knowledge of the other in an act of will, agency. For Michela it means not to abandon the victims, to pursue the unsolved crimes, and, perhaps, write a book.

At the end of *Voci,* Maraini is trying to conceive a transcendence that is not an abandonment of experience and of the world:

Body as Will: Incarnate Voice

> Ogni voce ha il timbro della verità, che non sempre coincide con quella logica delle cause e degli effetti cara al giudice Boni e alla commissaria Adele Sòfia. Le voci sono corpi in moto e hanno ciascuna l'ambiguità e la complessità degli organismi viventi; belli o brutti, deboli o forti che siano, sono percorse da vene lunghissime di un azzurro che mette tenerezza, seminate di costellazioni di nei come un cielo notturno ed è difficile metterle a tacere come si fa con le parole cartacee di un libro.
>
> Uscire dalla malia delle voci, come dice Adele Sòfia, ed entrare nella logica geometrica dei segni scritti? sarà un atto di saviezza o una scappatoia per eludere i corpi occhiuti e chiacchierini delle voci? (*Voci* 301)
>
> Each voice has the ring of truth that does not seem to match up with the logic of cause and effect so dear to Judge Boni and to Adele Sòfia, the police commissioner. The voices are bodies in motion, and each has the ambiguity and complexity of living organisms; beautiful or ugly, weak or strong, they are criss-crosses by long veins, of a tender blue, strewn with dark blemishes like constellations in the sky at night, and it is difficult to get them to be silent as one can do with the paper words of a book.
>
> Should I come out from the spell of the voices, as Adele Sòfia tells me, and enter into the geometrical logic of written signs? Would this be an act of wisdom or a sidestep in order to elude the sharp-eyed and chattering bodies of the voices? (*Voices* 247–48; modified translation)

It is not only empathy that entails ambivalence; writing as giving form, insofar as withdrawal from the other, is also ambivalent. There is a violence that subjects one who identifies precisely in that it does not make this subject into matter. At the other pole stands the transcendent subject that does will others into matter out of which self can be constructed. The project of Maraini's writing is through and through feminist in its rejection of this alienated transcendence, this alienated transcendent will. Hers is a writing that struggles to conceive agency and be agent.

Earlier this essay has explored some difficulties implicit in the application of Kristeva's concept of the semiotic to the laundry room in *Donna in guerra*. Taking further this critique, Kristeva's conception of the semiotic entails an emphasis on polysemy (an avatar of dismemberment?), drawing on the theorists preceding her who privilege the polysemic, such as Barthes. But this polysemic ecstasy is surely the privilege of a transcendent subject that can afford to be negated, an author who can afford to be dead.[11] Maraini does not produce polysemic text. Even *Voci,* in its multiplicity of voices, remains a text centered in the agency of Michela who speaks, and in which each voice emerges as a will, even an agonizingly tattered and dismembered will. The heads of butchered sheep make themselves felt to Michela in strange mutters and whistlings that do not reach the level of language.

Maraini configures in language not the dispersion of self, but a self attuned to others. On the one hand, she produces a phenomenology of immersion, articulating identification as experience and interrogating its dangers and its powers. Not only descriptive, however, her meditation on *immedesimazione* has normative implications, functioning as ethical injunction against violence: if you experience the world in a certain way, if you experience a body as a life, as lived subjectivity, violence becomes impossible. And it is through the act of writing that the experience of embodiment described by Maraini is negotiated. Writing becomes a moral paradigm of empathy and individuation. All of Maraini's writing is an indictment of the failure of imagination that creates violence as a mode of mediating difference.

This essay has noted how Maraini shows that self finds its possibility in immersion, others itself in the experience of the world. So also for Maraini narrative is displacement into difference, an othering that must be recuperated into voice.

***

Several times in the novel *Voci,* Michela encounters "la gattara," the homeless woman who cares for the myriad homeless stray cats of the neighborhood. She lives the most impoverished of lives, and she is a wild, demented figure, ranting maniacally (though with a ferocious sort of anticapitalist logic) against the enemies of cats, people and cars. One day, after such a verbal attack on Michela, the cat-woman stuns her with what can only be described as an epiphany:

Body as Will: Incarnate Voice

> Inaspettatamente si mette a saltellare in mezzo alla strada, mandando in alto i piedi chiusi nelle scarpe rattoppate e girando su se stessa con una agilità che non ci si aspetterebbe da una donna della sua età. La guardo sbalordita, poi divertita, ammirata: in quel saltare disperato c'è una grande elegante dignità. (*Voci* 296)

> Suddenly she begins to jump up and down in the middle of the street, kicking up her feet wrapped in patched-up shoes and swinging round and round with an agility one would never expect from a woman of her age. I watch her with amazement, amusement, and then with admiration: there is a great, elegant dignity in that desperate jumping. (*Voices* 244; modified translation)

Voices are bodies in movement. If a voice is a body in motion, then the dance is a voice, the body is precisely voice, but a voice that is not a voice. This is a key event in *Voci,* a contradictory moment that marks the root of the logical construction of embodied subjectivity, of body as will.

In this dance of *Voci*'s cat-woman we may see a sort of counterpart to the song of Manila in *Dialogo*. Manila sings about a closed and speechless body, paradoxically expressing her vulnerability in a song about invulnerability, which while protection is also silence. The cat-woman's dance is speaking that is not speech. She dances. She is expressing will, she is creating herself, flamboyantly and with great power, this powerless woman. She expresses absolute celebratory corporeality, space made self, body as will.

Notes

1. Maraini, *Dialogo* 57; my translation. I have chosen to do my own translations of all except a few passages, which are identified in the text.

2. The majority of male characters in Maraini's work exemplify this male poetics, a master narrative of male self-construction that, unable to compromise itself through empathy, unable to accept a loss of boundaries, sucks up and finally obliterates difference. The pattern of this discourse is not always identical, but certain interpretive motifs emerge with consistency. The moments of this discourse would include domination through seduction/assimilation (the client in *Dialogo,* the headmaster of Vannina's school in *Donna in guerra,* Cusumano's and Glauco's manipulation of the protagonist Michela in *Voci*), through disdain (Giacinto's rape

of Vannina and the headmaster's attack on women in *Donna in guerra,* Cusumano's dismissal of Michela's work in *Voci*), and finally actual destruction (Glauco's killing of his stepdaughter Angela Bari in *Voci*).

3. Two more instances of identification, closely related in style to Manila's old woman, appear in relation to Bianca, the protagonist of *Lettere:* the woman who sells fish (41–42) and the woman who sells vegetables (175–76). Another can be found in *La lunga vita di Marianna Ucrìa* (*The Silent Duchess*), between Marianna and the poor young mother Peppina (240).

4. There is something in the construction of the laundry women's narrative that should not be understood as mere madness or fantasizing; certain things prove to be true (for example, Suna's house really does have a sort of terrace), there is a strange rootedness in what they tell, in the details, their observations, their humor.

5. The baby grows in the mother's body. Maraini's *Un clandestino a bordo* (*Stowaway on Board*) interrogates with subtlety the play of fleshly wills, not falling into a fallacy that demands the one, either one, be made body and the other subject. Here too Maraini attunes herself to the work of identification, the empathies that create and obliterate the self, and in the context of an ultimate violence.

6. For Kristeva's semiotic, see *Desire in Language,* especially the chapter "From One Identity to an Other." For more on maternal subjectivity, see Kristeva's "Stabat Mater" in *Tales of Love.*

7. To give it its most sympathetic reading, the concept of symbolic maternity, as expressed by Luisa Muraro in *L'ordine simbolico della madre,* would be precisely a refusal of identification of maternity with the body, hence a laying claim to the power of a discourse no longer a patriarchal symbolic, and this in an existing world of differences and inequities. That is, it might be read as a particular attempt to heal the will/body dichotomy. Whether Muraro succeeds or falls into a phallicized feminism is another question.

8. In *Il piacere di scrivere,* Maraini describes Michela as a "woman who investigates, who reconstructs events . . . who reasons upon them" (Maraini and Gaglianone 30) trying to understand "the complex relationships between women and their executioners" (31). She at first seems solely the antithesis of the countless female victims whose deaths remain unsolved, and to a certain extent also of Manila and Vannina. But in reality Michela herself experiences a degree of violence through objectification, in her relations with her lover Marco and with Angela Bari's killer, Glauco.

9. For Maraini the concept of the body is of great concern. She traces the source of the importance of the body for women to male codes of oppression through which women were denied access to the word: "female thought has been emptied of meaning and women have been forced to express themselves above all with their body" (Maraini and

Body as Will: Incarnate Voice

Gaglianone 15). That body was then devalued by the very system that produced it. "[T]he locus of male imagination and violence . . . ," the female body, Maraini says, has been historically subject to abuse: "man has tried to control it, possess it, annihilate its tremendous energy. This is the great project of patriarchal culture" (Rossi). Maraini's project, on the contrary, is to turn women's "hyper-corporeality," their confinement to "immanence" (Braidotti 72), into the place of consciousness. The very constraint represents the possibility of "pre-linguistic" resistance, among which Maraini cites anorexia, bulimia, and hysteria (Maraini and Gaglianone 15). And while these are seen as pathologies, something still must be retained, recuperated. Having access to the word should not imply denial of the body. Even in language the woman must "communicate through the body" (16).

10. Glauco describes Angela as "una creatura malleabile e tenera, sensuale e vogliosa di piacere" (*Voci* 285; "a malleable and tender creature, sensual and yearning for pleasure"). If she is dead, it is her own fault, she has invited violence: "il suo corpo era lì a lusingarti . . . era difficile resistere . . . , un corpo talmente arreso e morbido che invitava ad una sorta di cannibalismo amoroso . . . Chiunque di fronte al suo corpo, vestito o nudo che fosse, era preso da una voglia spasmodica di toccarlo, . . . di penetrarlo, perfino di forzarlo, perché lei in qualche modo chiedeva proprio questo, voleva l'urto, la presa di possesso, l'invasione" (288; "her body was there to beguile you . . . it was difficult to resist . . . , a body so surrendered and soft that it invited a sort of erotic cannibalism . . . Anybody who came upon that body, clothed or naked, was seized by a paroxysmal desire to touch it, . . . to penetrate it, even to violate it, because she, in some way, was asking precisely for this, she wanted the harm, the possession, the invasion . . ."). She enticed him with "una sensualità che metteva addosso la voglia di uccidere" (288; "a sensuality that called forth the desire to kill").

11. The point I am making here has been expressed in other forms, as in Alice Jardine's "Woman in Limbo: Deleuze and His (Br)others," which asks whether the deconstruction of the subject can be feminist.

Works Cited

Beauvoir, Simone de. *The Second Sex*. 1952. Trans. H. M. Parshley. New York: Random, 1989.

Braidotti, Rosi. *Soggetto nomade: femminismo e crisi della modernità*. Rome: Donzelli, 1995.

Cavarero, Adriana. *Nonostante Platone: figure femminili nella filosofia antica*. Rome: Riuniti, 1990.

Jardine, Alice. "Woman in Limbo: Deleuze and His (Br)others." *SubStance* 13.3–4 (1984): 46–60.

Kristeva, Julia. *Desire in Language: A Semiotic Approach to Literature and Art.* Trans. Thomas Gora, Alice Jardine, and Leon S. Roudiez. New York: Columbia UP, 1980.

———. "Stabat Mater." *Tales of Love.* Trans. Leon S. Roudiez. New York: Columbia UP, 1986. 234–63.

Maraini, Dacia. *La bionda, la bruna e l'asino.* Milan: Rizzoli, 1987.

———. *Un clandestino a bordo.* 1993. Milan: Rizzoli, 1996. Published in English as *Stowaway on Board.* Trans. Giovanna Bellesia and Victoria Offredi Poletto. West Lafayette, IN: Bordighera, 2000.

———. *Dialogo di una prostituta con un suo cliente.* Padua: Mastrogiacomo, 1978. Published in English as *Dialogue between a Prostitute and Her Client.*

———. *Dialogue between a Prostitute and Her Client.* Trans. Tony Mitchell. *Only Prostitutes Marry in May.* Ed. Rhoda Helfman Kaufman. Toronto, Montreal, and New York: Guernica, 1994. 125–76.

———. *Donna in guerra.* 1975. 2nd ed. Turin: Einaudi, 1984. Published in English as *Woman at War.* 1981. New York: Italica, 1988.

———. "From the World of Violence—Voices of Women." Lecture at Vassar College, 21 Mar. 1996.

———. *Isolina, la donna tagliata a pezzi.* 1985. Milan: Rizzoli, 1992. Published in English as *Isolina.* London: Peter Owen, 1994; distributed by Dufour.

———. *Lettere a Marina.* Milan: Bompiani, 1981. Published in English as *Letters to Marina.* London: Camden, 1987. Freedom, CA: Crossing, 1988.

———. *La lunga vita di Marianna Ucrìa.* Milan: Rizzoli, 1990. Published in English as *The Silent Duchess.* London: Peter Owen, 1992. New York: Feminist, 1998.

———. *Voci.* Milan: Rizzoli, 1994. Published in English as *Voices.*

———. *Voices.* Trans. Dick Kitto and Elspeth Spottiswood. London and New York: Serpent's Tail, 1997.

Maraini, Dacia, and Paola Gaglianone. *Il piacere di scrivere.* Rome: Òmicron, 1995.

Muraro, Luisa. *L'ordine simbolico della madre.* Rome: Riuniti, 1991.

Rossi, Monica. "Interview with Dacia Maraini." July 1995. Unpublished ms.

Gabrielle Cody

Remembering What the Closed Eye Sees

Some Notes on Dacia Maraini's Postmodern *Oresteia*

> The prototypes of drama are hunting, fertility, and initiation rituals .... Rites are staged by older men for the benefit of adolescent boys who frequently are pressed into the leading roles .... Often, the culminating ceremony is circumcision or subincision or some other painful and irremediable body mark.... The father-king-god is overcome/replaced by the son-hero-savior who attains mastery over the family-state-cosmos.... It is the imagination of the adolescent boy that is at the core of theater. It is the celebration of his achieving the status of manhood that is the subject of theater.
>
> Richard Schechner
> *Environmental Theater*

> Through the centuries, woman has looked at the world through a window. Her point of view is from the inside to the outside.... The layers of history belong to our internal house, our soul. I, here, today, feel the experience of our female ancestors: being enclosed, participating in oppression, masochism, and seduction, along with other women.... Madness is not adjusting to the world. ... My play *Clytemnestra* is the story of female madness, of rejection, incongruence, non-relationship with the male world.
>
> Dacia Maraini
> *diacritics*

Gabrielle Cody

The Dreaming and the Undreaming

Whether one believes, as Simone de Beauvoir did, that the *Oresteia* is the mythical rendering of the patriarchal takeover, Aeschylus's trilogy remains a fascinating and disturbing document of what the Greeks were grappling with philosophically during the period of the so-called "birth of tragedy" in the fifth century B.C. The gender agon of the play is rooted in the dangerous and painful passage from one culturally sanctioned symbolic order to another. Aeschylus dramatizes two conflicting life principles, the ancient, but still psychically potent matriarchal worldview governed by *physis,* the irrational, anarchic, and retributive cycle of life and death, *blood lust;* and the emerging patriarchal concept of *nomos,* associated with "civilized," *historic* culture, and judicial law.

The *Oresteia,* literally "Orestes' story," explores the Aeschylean notion of *pathei mathos,* "wisdom through suffering," as the foundation for a new democratic state. Orestes is the body on whom the experiment of the play is enacted, the adolescent male through whom wisdom will emerge at great physical and psychic cost, and whose integration into the society of the Fathers will signal the possibility for the larger culture's evolution. Refracted through a contemporary lens, the play polarizes ancient kinship ties imbedded in the culture's unconscious, and the *homosociality* of Athenian civic consciousness. Presented in a trilogy, Aeschylus's journey is one from darkness to light, recounted myth to actual time, totemic biology to patriarchal science. In the first two plays of the trilogy, prophesies and dreams associated with sacred female kinship are substantive and haunting, convulsive events that would have still been palpably frightening to an audience at a time when theories of the unconscious did not yet exist. By the last play, however, the messy, uncontainable subjectivity of dreams has been replaced by the dangerous objectivity of state-controlled ideology.

The mythical Orestes, like the rest of his family, predates Homer. He is a figure borrowed from ancient Greek legend, the classic Greek mother slayer, pursued by the Furies for violation of matriarchal law (Walker 742). The antiquity of the Furies—ancient goddesses of the night, who condemn Orestes for the *indefensible* crime of matricide—is confirmed by the

Remembering What the Closed Eye Sees

fact that they are summoned against the killers of the female line only. They too are mythical figures from the time when all genealogies were reckoned through women (Walker 327). They take the shape of bloodhounds, horrible beasts whom the Aeschylean Orestes, at the beginning of his quest, deeply fears.

But the mythical stature of Aeschylus's female figures is compromised from the start. Clytemnestra, whose name means "divine wooing" or "sacred marriage," was in ancient myth, the last matriarchal queen of Mycenae. She acted in the traditional right of queens to choose her consort, and have each new lover slay the old one (Walker 172). Yet the moral crisis of Aeschylus's play is precipitated by Clytemnestra's sexual infidelity during Agamemnon's long absence in Troy, an expedition he ostensibly undertook to return Helen to her rightful husband.

In pre-Homeric myth, Helen, also known as Helle or Selene, was worshiped as an orgiastic deity in Sparta (Walker 382). In Homer, she is a beauty who causes men to act irrationally. But in the *Agamemnon*—the first play in Aeschylus's trilogy the *Oresteia*—her anarchic libido is the cause of the costly war in Troy. Equally transfigured is the Artemis-Iphigenia relationship. The chorus of elders, near the opening of the play, tells us that the goddess Artemis placed a curse on Agamemnon that only his daughter's death could lift. Iphigenia's sacrifice allowed the winds to blow again and Agamemnon's fleet to be launched for Troy. However, in ancient myth Iphigenia's relationship to Artemis, goddess of animals, is quite different. Artemis's myths go back to Neolithic sacrificial customs. At Taurus, her holy women, under the high priestess Iphigenia, were said to have sacrificed all men who landed on their shores, apparently nailing the head of each victim to a cross. In her huntress aspect, Artemis led the nocturnal hunt, and her priestesses wore the *masks* of hunting dogs (Walker 58).

Early in the *Agamemnon*, the chorus of elders laments Iphigenia's death, and prays that the Fates of female retribution will be merciful. But they are not. Clytemnestra stages her long-anticipated mise-en-scène of death by having the general walk on the wine-red tapestry, an act reserved for gods, and fall into her trap. His brutal murder is foretold by Cassandra,

Gabrielle Cody

Agamemnon's booty, a concubine from Troy. In earlier legends, Cassandra was a high priestess who placed a curse on Agamemnon's life after he took her prisoner. But Aeschylus has her side with Agamemnon and curse the woman who is about to kill them, for her transgressions as a woman: "No, this is daring when the female shall strike down the male. What can I call her and be right? What beast of loathing? Viper double fanged, or Scylla witch . . ." (*Oresteia* 140).

Clearly, the powerful sexuality and sacred attributes of these mythical figures, once brought into a fifth century B.C. ideological frame, become a distinctly *historic* problem. And so too is the representation of women onstage. The passage from the oral transmission of myths to their embodiment—mimesis—foregrounds the body. But we know that women were approximated by male actors well into the Renaissance. Transvestitism ensured that the female body, and in a sense female biology, sacred in the race's memory, would remain metonymic, in brief, that mimesis would not have a true referent (Diamond 370). The consequences of this erasure are such that the *verisimilitude* of classical Greek drama, and later, in mimetic *realism,* of the female body, "is curiously lost in practice" (Dolan 97).

During the second play of the trilogy, *The Libation Bearers,* it is Clytemnestra who prophesies the future. Guilty for not having given the slain Agamemnon proper burial rites, she dreams that she gives birth to a snake whom she suckles and who draws blood as well as milk from her breast. And indeed, Orestes returns to Argos on cue with his friend Pylades, to avenge his father's death. Urged on by his sister Electra, he kills his adulterous mother. For this crime, he will be pursued by the vengeful Furies. In this sense, the *Oresteia* seriously puts into question the mother's sexual/maternal body and dramatizes a cultural movement from womb worship, to tomb worship. Clytemnestra is murdered, in part, for not having given Agamemnon proper burial rites; Electra is worshiping Agamemnon's tomb when she "recognizes" Orestes. And when Clytemnestra's maternity is denaturalized, Orestes and Electra become children of the city-state.

It is significant that Orestes is psychically rather than physically ambushed by the Furies, who do not manifest physically until the third play, *The Eumenides.* As he puts it, "[t]hese are no fancies of affliction. They are clear, and real, and here: the bloodhounds of my mother's hate" (*Oresteia* 131). When we next encounter Orestes, he is in Delphi, literally, "womb," before the sanctuary of Pythian Apollo. He is there to supplicate the god, after his unthinkable deed. This scene is possibly the most compelling of the trilogy from the standpoint of the religious and cultural shift it dramatizes. First, the Pythia enters alone and gives praise to ancient goddesses:

> I give first place of honor in my prayer to her
> who of the gods first prophesied, the Earth; and next
> to Themis, who succeeded to her mother's place
> of prophecy; so runs the legend; and in third
> succession, *given by free consent, not won by force,*
> *another Titan daughter of Earth was seated here.*
> *This was Phoebe. She gave it as a birthday gift*
> *to Phoebus, who is called still after Phoebe's name.*
> (*Oresteia* 135; emphasis mine)

When the doors of the temple open, and Orestes is revealed, bloody and weakened, surrounded by the loathsome hounds, the pristine Phoebus Apollo stands onstage as Orestes' guide and protector: "I will not give you up. Through to the end standing / your guardian. . . . / . . . I have caught and overpowered these lewd creatures. / The repulsive maidens have been stilled to sleep. . . . / It was because of evil they were born, because / they hold the evil darkness of the Pit below / Earth . . ." (*Oresteia* 137).

Aeschylus, is interested in exploring how the powerful psychic and religious repercussions of matricide can be permanently lifted. His triumph is to make the spectator more psychologically secure over the course of *The Eumenides*. In this final play of the trilogy, he gradually replaces the subjectivities of personal, retributive nightmares with the soothing "objectivity" of rational thinking, the pleasure of suspenseful telos: in this case, democratic justice as happy ending. Similarly, dense narrative has become embodied action, and distant, awesome gods, pleasant, levelheaded dramatis personae.

While Orestes' psychic agony after the matricide constitutes the main dramatic axis of the trilogy, Apollo will absolve him of his malediction. Before taking Orestes' case to the citizen-judges, he attempts to prove Orestes' innocence to the chorus of Furies through a curious science. Apollo exonerates Clytemnestra's murderer by declaring Agamemnon to be the sole legitimate parent: "The mother is no parent of that which is called her child, but only nurse of the new-planted seed that grows. *The parent is he who mounts. A stranger she preserves a stranger's seed, if no god interfere*" (*Oresteia* 158; emphasis mine).

Thus the mother, and the symbolic order informed by her sacred biology, is constructed as the primordial Other. Apollo's proclamation—which can only be viewed as the product of a deep-rooted anxiety about the construction of the symbolic Real—has antecedents in earlier initiatory protodramas that featured male birth-giving. As Barbara Walker suggests, throughout the world, men's initiatory dramas enacted birth-giving to represent the attainment of divine power. "Men or gods began to claim physical fatherhood not so much by an act of begetting, as by a different, ceremonial act designed to imitate the motherly act of birth-giving" (304):

> Since birth-giving was the only true mark of divinity in primitive belief, the first gods. . . . gave birth from their mouths. . . . Hellenic Greeks pretended that their new father Zeus gave birth to the much older goddess Athene from his head. But before he could give birth to Athene, he had to swallow her real mother, Metis (Wisdom), who was pregnant with her at the time. The Hellenes also claimed Zeus gave birth to Dionysus from his thigh; but again, the real mother was the Moon goddess Selene, whom Zeus killed during her pregnancy. As conductor of Souls, Hermes took the six-month fetus from Selene's womb and sewed him up in Zeus' thigh to continue his gestation. A Greek carving showed the god Apollo sitting on a pile of eggs, trying to copy the life-giving magic of his mother Leto who gave birth to the World Egg and hatched it. This World Egg was an Oriental idea. (Walker 106, 107)

It comes as no surprise, then, when Aeschylus's Athene—who proudly states that she is "not of woman born"—makes a final judgment in Orestes' favor, causing a tie vote. Athene then sways the outcome of the vote by persuading the Furies to give up the retributive law of sacred blood-ties and participate instead in the new democracy as goddesses of the home, which is to say, the interior *oikos,* the domestic enclosure from which women will *look out* for centuries.

Flesh, Blood, Milk: The Absent Body's Cry

When Dacia Maraini speaks of the importance of women entering *storia,* "history" (Anderlini 159), she is thinking in Foucauldian terms. Maraini suggests a historicity of the body, an analysis of descent, or genealogy, "situated within the articulation of the body and history," whose "task is to expose a body totally imprinted by history and the process of history's destruction of the body" (Foucault 83). Maraini's drama retrieves female bodies imprinted and destroyed by history, erased by a mimesis without a true referent. *I sogni di Clitennestra* (*Dreams of Clytemnestra*) dramatizes the aftermath of the "story of female madness, as rejection, incongruence, non-relationship to the male world" by exploring "the [female] body [as] the inscribed surface of events" (Foucault 83).

By recasting the *Oresteia* in Catholic, capitalist Europe, Maraini is able to historicize her characters and expose class, gender, and sexual oppression as a continuum in Western culture. She stretches her two-act play across the main events of Aeschylus's trilogy: Iphigenia's sacrifice, Agamemnon's return and subsequent death, Orestes' murder of his mother, his assimilation into patriarchal law. But the eternal subject of theater—the adolescent boy's achievement of his manhood—is recast as a searing parody of the original blueprint. While Orestes is still the center of the play's thematic action, he is no longer the experimental body of the story; Clytemnestra's body is.

Maraini returns the true referent to mimesis by producing a kind of countermimicry, a theater that disrupts and disturbs the model-copy (Diamond 370). Her play conspires against Cartesian telos and clarity, and embraces the subjectivity of dreams in a hilarious rendition of what Luce Irigaray playfully terms "hystera" or "womb" theater (Diamond 369). Maraini writes in the space of what the closed eye sees. Her surrealism is such that our perception is always teased by the phantasmatic projection of the body *as theater.* Maraini constructs Clytemnestra as a stand-in for the absent body's cry. Her character is always

Gabrielle Cody

already aware that, as Maraini puts it, "seduction is above all, a strategy, a game, a fiction and also a form of representation" (qtd. in Mitchell 346). Like Manila, her double in *Dialogo di una prostituta con un suo cliente* (*Dialogue between a Prostitute and Her Client,* an earlier play in which a prostitute/actress/woman dialogues with her client and the audience, Maraini's Clytemnestra exposes the power relations and cultural myths implicit in mimetic representation. She performs a subversive, politically motivated form of psychic striptease. As Maraini says of Manila, "I tried to invent . . . a woman who is aware of what she's doing, and educated, with a degree in philosophy, who decides to sell herself—it's a political decision" (Maraini and Mitchell, "The Future Is Woman?"; qtd. in Mitchell 339). Similarly, the mimetic contract in *I sogni di Clitennestra* is shown to be a process of seduction that Clytemnestra can stop or resume at any moment, an "intelligent" act of prostitution by one who owns her own theatrical means of simulation; unlike her Aeschylean predecessor, she is entirely self-possessed.

In so doing, Maraini disrupts and destabilizes the very foundation of Western philosophy: the "unitary Self-same" of patriarchal ontology. As Elin Diamond suggests:

> Platonic philosophy wants to place man's origins not in the dark, uncertain cave but, instead, in his recognition of the (Father's) light. The philosopher wants to forget—wants to prove illusory—his female origins. But the anarchic effect of that proof . . . is the discovery that his mother is a theatre. (370)

In *I sogni di Clitennestra,* the state-controlled ideology of pre-Christian Democracy is replaced by the repressive sexual morality of modern-day Catholic Italy, the hubris of capitalism. Agamemnon is a businessman; Clytemnestra, a former garment factory worker, who, with her daughter Electra, tries to make ends meet when her husband leaves them to go make his fortune in America. In his absence, she takes a twenty-eight-year-old lover, Aegistus, and when Agamemnon returns, he brings back Cassandra, an American model half Clytemnestra's age. Orestes is a political activist who has been living in Germany. He comes back from self-exile with his lover Pilade.

Maraini opens her play with a prologue in which she dramatizes Clytemnestra as a historicized body, a collective character, the spirit of womanhood conjuring the ancient, sleeping Furies. She is a postmodern figure par excellence, searching for meaning in a godless, indifferent universe. This notion of a collective history is the guiding force and main structuring device of the play:

> ... nell'ora in cui mi abbandonate
> ... mi sento chiamare
> col nome di assassina ...
> ... lo sapete
> vivo sotto il peso della colpa io
> che ho subito ... quel che ho subito,
> e nessun dio si ricorda di me,
> massacrata da una mano matricida.
> Guardate ma col cuore le mie ferite,
> è nel suono che l'uomo vede; di giorno
> i suoi occhi guardano senza luce. (*Sogni* 7)
>
> ... Just as you abandon me for dead
> I hear myself called murderer ...
> ... you know the guilt that
> haunts me, I who from childhood have
> suffered what I have suffered, and no god
> remembers me, slaughtered by a matricidal hand.
> Look, with your heart, at my wounds—
> for man sees in sleep only, by day
> his eyes look without light. (*Dreams* 185)[1]

Iphigenia's recounted sacrifice, here, is made tangible, painfully funny. Sacrificed by her father for a business deal, Iphigenia enters the stage "tied to a bed" (*Sogni* 9 / *Dreams* 189). This literalization of sexual and economic bondage is the first of many eloquent imprints. Similarly, Cassandra's prostituted body is given neo-mythical stature. As described by Electra, "... [è] una che mangia solo rose e carne cruda. E piscia profumato. Balla come una vipera e sotto la veste tiene un bosco ombreggiato che quando lui ci si appoggia la guancia si sente rinascere" (*Sogni* 10; "[t]he only things she eats are roses and raw meat, and she pisses perfume. She dances like a snake and under her dress she keeps cool evergreen that soothes and calms him the minute he rests his head"; *Dreams* 192). In another whimsical literalization, Maraini removes animosity between Cassandra and Clytemnestra. Onstage are three beds, one for each woman and one for Agamemnon, who is asleep. Clytemnestra is only too happy to have her husband's mistress take him off her hands once and for all. By the end of their exchange, "[l]e due donne si addormentano con la mano nella mano" (*Sogni* 21; "[t]he two women go to sleep hand in hand"; *Dreams* 217).

But Orestes' acculturation in *I sogni di Clitennestra* is far more perverse than in the Aeschylean version. At the beginning of the play, we encounter a rebel who is militantly set against state and family. Yet as a result of Electra's efforts to socialize him, he is slowly inculcated into the homosocial pact as a cure for his sexual "division." He murders his mother—who has become pregnant by Aegistus—to punish her for her sexual appetite. The more he accedes to the virility of his cast, the more passionless, and robotic, he becomes. The dialogue between Electra and Clytemnestra preceding her murder epitomizes the dramatic conflict of Maraini's play: the dead morality of the "impersonated" patriarchal body, versus the eroticized body of the female speaking subject:

> *Electra:* È una puttana . . . che ha fatto di questa casa un immondezzaio.
> *Clytemnestra:* Parli come un uomo di un secolo fa. Un uomo vecchio e morto. Tuo nonno, tuo bisnonno. Qualcuno che hai cullato nel ventre per troppi anni.
> *Electra:* È mio padre che parla per bocca mia.
> *Clytemnestra:* Ma tu sei come me, Elettra, sei una donna: hai seno e ventre di donna.
> *Electra:* Io non sono né donna né uomo. Sono la famiglia. . . . La odio, Oreste. . . . Mi ha tradito, ha tradito te, me, tutti. Uccidila!
> (Oreste prende un coltello e uccide sua madre mentre gli altri continuano tranquillamente a mangiare.) (*Sogni* 36)
>
> *Electra:* She's a whore . . . who's turned this house into something filthy.
> *Clytemnestra:* You talk like a hundred-year-old man. Some old, dead man. Your grandfather, your great-grandfather. Someone you've nursed in your gut too many years.
> *Electra:* It's my father speaking through me.

> *Clytemnestra:* But you're a woman, Electra, like me, with breasts and a woman's organs.
> *Electra*: I'm not man or woman. I am the family. . . . I hate her, Orestes . . . . She betrayed me, you, all of us. Kill her!
> (Orestes takes a knife and kills his mother while the others quietly continue eating.) (*Dreams* 258–59)

While each figure is, in a sense, *overdetermined* by her archetypal relation to the Aeschylean version, Maraini's characters have a distinctly Brechtian quality. Her dialectical scenes self-consciously demonstrate the alterable nature of social phenomena. Like Brecht, Maraini creates a kind of "double-seeing," a way for her spectator/reader to understand that ethics and emotions are culturally or economically conditioned. For example, immediately after Clytemnestra's death, Maraini gives the mother-hating Electra a wonderfully unexpected and contradictory response to Clytemnestra's death: "Come ho amato questa madre idiota che ha disubbidito alle regole paterne e ora è morta e glielo posso dire che mi ha fatto patire di gelosia e d'amore come mai un amante mi ha fatto patire" (*Sogni* 38; "How I loved this idiot mother who disobeyed all the paternal rules and now is dead and now I can tell her how she made me suffer from love and jealousy like no lover ever made me suffer"; *Dreams* 263).

The phantasmatic causality of Maraini's distorted realism sends up the notion of mimetically transmittable Truth, by making the cycle of retributive murders psychic—almost psychosomatic—rather than literal. Agamemnon genuinely dies, though he suffers a sit-com style heart attack. His death is farcical, Archie Bunker-like, the result of a misogynist terror of the mythical murder locked in the recesses of his memory. Agamemnon dies, obsessed by the weight of his own myth. And when Orestes kills his mother, she finds herself in a psychiatric ward rather than in Hades. She has gone mad from "rejection, incongruence, non-relationship" to the masculine symbolic (Maraini, qtd. in Anderlini 159). This choice is brilliant on Maraini's part, since the asylum is the quintessential space of female aversion and marginality, a place where libido and intellect have been electroshocked and lobotomized into obedience throughout this and the last century.

Gabrielle Cody

But Clytemnestra never ceases to be the anarchic life force of the play. During most of the second act, she lies in bed, strapped down, yet boldly disobedient, thinking her body and dreams aloud: flesh, blood, milk, memories of hunger, sex, illness, and desire collude in a surreal collage of irrepressible being, while Electra's sad, immemorially closed body continues to mourn the dead Father's absence. Through the mise-en-scène of Clytemnestra's body, Maraini stages the revolt of hystera, the drama of a body that is not containable, the mise-en-scène of a wandering womb (Diamond 375).

Clytemnestra dreams that she is thirteen, and looking for food. She dreams that she seduces her son Orestes, for money. But the supertextual turning point of the play occurs when Orestes has sex with Moira—an aspect of the younger Clytemnestra—the thirteen-year-old apparition/fate who is prostituting herself for food. Through their dialogue, Maraini once again makes material the prostituted condition of the female body, and highlights Orestes' ideological appurtenance to the world of the dead:

> *Orestes:* Guardami: io non esisto. Ho una voce e due gambe. Ma la mia carne non ha consistenza. Non ci sono.
> *Moira:* Non hai neanche qualcosa da mangiare dentro quella valigia?
> *Orestes:* Ma dove ti ho visto io a te?
> *Moira:* Mi avrai sognata.
> *Orestes:* Mille anni fa.
> *Moira:* Vuoi succhiare la mia lingua? (*Sogni* 46)
>
> *Orestes:* Take a look at me: I don't exist. I talk and walk. But you can see right through me. I'm not here.
> *Moira:* Haven't you got anything to eat in your bag?
> *Orestes:* Where have I seen you before?
> *Moira:* In a dream.
> *Orestes:* A thousand years ago.
> *Moira:* Want to suck my tongue? (*Dreams* 279–80)

Orestes dreams that he strangles Moira and that the Furies pursue him for his crime. Like his father, his psyche is contaminated by retrogressive guilt.

Ironically, it is through the dream of his murderous (hetero)-sexuality that Orestes completes his passage into the society

Remembering What the Closed Eye Sees

of the Fathers: he suddenly marries, buys property, and joins the world of business and finance. As Electra proudly declares, "Non sta più con quel disgustoso Pilade. È diventato un uomo normale. . . . Ha comprato due furgoni Ford 150 e va in giro per tutta Prato comprando e rivendendo" (*Sogni* 51–52; "He's dropped that disgusting Pilade. He's a normal man now. . . . He's bought two Ford delivery trucks and goes all over Prato buying and selling"; *Dreams* 296–97).

In the asylum, Clytemnestra tries to seduce her psychiatrist, in vain. He is another impersonated body, "a man of science," the comic stand-in for Athene's paternalistically reassuring presence in the *Oresteia*. A deliberately clichéd figure, he is capable only of binary thinking and Freudian riddles:

> *Clytemnestra:* Sei nato dalla testa di tuo padre.
> *Psychoanalyst:* . . . È una ribellione sterile la tua, perdente. Se stai buona, se impari a parlare pulito, a rispettare gli altri, a fare come dice il medico, esci . . .
> *Clytemnestra:* Faccio il cazzo che mi pare.
> *Psychoanalyst:* . . . La tua aggressività, il tuo parlare sboccato, la tua ossessione sessuale, il tuo infantile esibizionismo, lo sai cosa sono? Invidia bella e buona, invidia della virilità. Tu non accetti la parte femminile di te, la tua dolcezza, la tua passività. Tu vuoi rivaleggiare con l'uomo, col potere e diventi dura, isterica. (*Sogni* 54–55)

> *Clytemnestra:* You were born out of your father's head.
> *Psychoanalyst:* . . . This rebellion of yours is simply sterile, a losing battle. If you're good, if you learn to clean up your speech, and respect others, and do what the doctor tells you, you'll get out . . .
> *Clytemnestra:* I do what the fuck I want.
> *Psychoanalyst:* . . . Your aggressiveness, your filthy language, your sexual obsession, your infantile exhibitionism—you know what they all are? Envy pure and simple, envy of a man's virility. You don't accept the feminine part of yourself, your gentleness, your passivity. You're looking to reevaluate yourself in terms of men and power and you end up bitter and hysterical. (*Dreams* 303–05)

The Furies too visit Clytemnestra's dreams in the ward. But history has taken its toll. The pre-Christian goddesses of the

Gabrielle Cody

night, ancient protectors of blood ties and the rites of women, the hounds of matricide, have become old, tired whores who have betrayed Clytemnestra in exchange for the security and fidelity of the great Christian Father:

> *Clytemnestra:* Mi avete tradita. Avete lasciato andare il mio assassino . . . .
> *Terza donna:* È la scienza che ci ha cambiate. . . .
> *Seconda donna:* Siamo le donne dell'inferno, chiuse dentro la casa del paradiso, per nostra purificazione e gloria. . . .
> *Prima donna:* Siamo state convertite dalle ragioni democratiche. . . . È stato deciso che ammazzare la madre adultera non è delitto imperdonabile.
> *Seconda donna:* È stato deciso che l'uomo nasce dal seme paterno.
> *Terza donna:* È stato deciso che la madre è solo un recipiente.
> *Seconda donna:* La giustizia è passata nelle mani dei tutori delle leggi materne. (*Sogni* 57–58)
>
> *Clytemnestra:* You've all betrayed me. You let the murderer go. . . .
> *Third Woman:* It's science that changed us. . . .
> *Second Woman:* We are the women from hell, shut up in the house of paradise, for our purification and glory. . . .
> *First Woman:* We were converted to democratic logic. . . . It was decided that killing an adulterous mother is not an unpardonable crime.
> *Second Woman:* It was decided that man born is born from a father's seed.
> *Third Woman:* It was decided that the mother is only a recipient.
> *Second Woman:* Justice has passed into the hands of the keepers of paternal law. (*Dreams* 309–12)

Clytemnestra, the ghostly imprint of a distinctly unfunny history, remains alone onstage, having refused psychic and physical domestication. Maraini never lifts her pain or optimistically rigs her future. No wisdom comes from suffering here, as her parting words to us suggest:

> Se morirò sognando forse morirò felice. Ma è un sogno di vita o una vita di sogno? In qualche parte, fra i sogni morti,

io continuerò a vivere, per continuare a sognare. (*Sogni* 58–59)

If I die dreaming possibly I'll die happy. And yet is that a dream of life or a life of dreaming? Somewhere, among dead dreams, I will keep on living, to keep on dreaming. (*Dreams* 314)

From Tomb to Womb: What the Closed Eye/I Sees

The ending of *I sogni di Clitennestra* could be read as politically ambiguous. Clytemnestra's last speech seems to enshrine the intrapsychic power of dreams over social, material change. But as Tony Mitchell has argued, Maraini's work transcends the cultural feminism she is often associated with (Mitchell 332). Maraini believes that language is essentially female. As she puts it, "[t]he mother's body means the flesh and blood and milk of any spoken language" (Mitchell 334). Language becomes male at the point when the symbolic kills the Real. This is when ". . . the mother's body . . . is transformed into the father's body which demands obedience in exchange for security, and fidelity in exchange for grandeur" (Mitchell 334). Maraini recasts the *Oresteia* by locating its drama in a mimesis with a referent, drawing heavily on the Barthian concept that "writing means playing with the mother's body" (Mitchell 334). But her bio-grammar is not reducible to the neo-femininity of *écriture féminine*. Maraini is not merely proposing an alternate myth celebrating the Great Mother. Her countermimicry is aimed at a representational economy and symbolic order in which female *parts*—literally and figuratively—are severed from the body of performance. Maraini asks us to divest the myth of its authority, to interrogate the representational apparatus that has sustained it, and to refuse obedience to the Father's performing body by giving up its security and fidelity.

I sogni di Clitennestra provides an "analysis of descent . . . situated within the articulation of the body and history" (Foucault 83), by gazing back inward into the Impossible-Real of the female symbolic. The subjective action of Maraini's play traces the contours of female absence from the official, legitimate patriarchal symbolic, and dramatizes the *hystera theater* of madness, or "incongruence." Maraini knows that in a very real sense, it would be politically naive to provide an "active" resolution to her play. Clytemnestra's dreams are historicized pockets of irrepressible experience that serve to create a conscious *seeing* of history's destruction of the female symbolic. Maraini leaves her ending in order for the spectator, rather than the character, to potentially take action. The conclusion of *I sogni di Clitennestra* allows for the regenerative opening of what Teresa de Lauretis has termed "a process articulated dialectically on subjective codes and objective realities" (qtd. in Mitchell 339).

This is truly a furious play, one which, like the Furies who attack Orestes' psyche, disrupts, disturbs, and haunts. Perhaps more important, Maraini leaves us with the material reality of the ongoing crisis of the female body in representation. Clytemnestra is left hanging furiously onto dead dreams, knowing only that "the body of a woman who thinks / shakes the scaly back of history."[2]

Notes

1. All translations come from the English edition of the play.
2. Dacia Maraini, "Un corpo di donna," in *Mangiami pure* 52. The Italian reads: "un corpo di donna che pensa / scuote il dorso a scaglie della storia." Modified translation.

Works Cited

Aeschylus. *Oresteia*. Trans. Richmond Lattimore. Chicago: U of Chicago P, 1953. 93–171.

Anderlini, Serena. "Prolegomena for a Feminist Dramaturgy of the Feminine: An Interview with Dacia Maraini." *diacritics* 21.2–3 (1991): 148–60.

Diamond, Elin. "Mimesis, Mimicry, and the 'True-Real.'" *Acting Out: Feminist Performances*. Ed. Lynda Hart and Peggy Phelan. Ann Arbor: U of Michigan P, 1993. 363–82.

Dolan, Jill. *The Feminist Spectator as Critic*. Ann Arbor: U of Michigan P, 1994.

Foucault, Michel. "Nietzsche, Genealogy, History." *The Foucault Reader*. Ed. Paul Rabinow. New York: Pantheon, 1984. 76–100.

Maraini, Dacia. "Un corpo di donna." *Mangiami pure*. Turin: Einaudi, 1978. 51–52. Published in English as *Devour Me Too*.

Maraini, Dacia. *Devour Me Too.* Trans. Genni Donati Gunn. Toronto, Montreal, and New York: Guernica, 1978.

———. *Dreams of Clytemnestra.* Trans. Tim Vode. *Only Prostitutes Marry in May.* Ed. Rhoda Helfman Kaufman. Toronto, Montreal, and New York: Guernica, 1994. 177–315

———. *I sogni di Clitennestra e altre commedie.* Milan: Bompiani, 1981. 5–59. Published in English as *Dreams of Clytemnestra.*

Maraini, Dacia, and Tony Mitchell. "The Future Is Woman?" *Sydney Morning Herald* 18 May 1987.

Mitchell, Tony. "'Scrittura femminile': Writing the Female in the Plays of Dacia Maraini." *Theater Journal* 42 (1990) 332–49.

Walker, Barbara. *The Women's Encyclopedia of Myths and Secrets.* New York: Harper, 1983.

Pauline Dagnino

Revolution in the Laundry

In the early part of Dacia Maraini's novel *Donna in guerra* (*Woman at War*)[1] the heroine, Vannina, travels with her husband from the everyday social reality in Rome to an island holiday somewhere off the coast of Naples. On this island she makes new friends and eventually decides to spend time in Naples without her husband before returning home. Among these new friends are Giottina and Tota, two women Vannina regularly meets in the laundry. Although these characters make only a minor appearance in the novel as a whole, I would like to suggest here that their presence is essential to the development of the heroine and serves to mark Dacia Maraini's importance as a feminist writer.

Donna in guerra was first published in 1975 during a shifting focus in the European feminist movement. While it is true that the relationship of women to both history and culture has always been subject to debate, in Europe in the late sixties this debate took the form of open militancy that in turn was replaced by the "post militant" feminism of the eighties and nineties. With their intense political activity, the European women of 1968 sought a place for themselves in a predominantly male world but this activity itself marked a break from established traditions and gave rise to a new generation of feminists who felt themselves different from the others. This later generation began to be aware of itself as having an experience that was "different" from that of men and endeavored to find articulation for this experience.[2] Whereas in the sixties and early seventies gender was seen as sexual difference, from the mid-seventies onward the question of difference became the problem of articulating women's different experiences.

Like the feminists themselves, a feminist writer may also be classified by generation. Critical readings of *Donna in guerra* have linked the work with the militant generation of feminists, suggesting that the act of war carried out in this novel is the militancy of its female protagonist who demonstrates that she is no longer content with the space of silence and absence designated for her by the male-dominated social structure.[3] The development of the heroine of this novel from a traditional position of learned passivity to one where she is able to take control of her own life and power over her own body has generally been seen as the militant feminist act that demonstrates the political basis that much personal experience is built upon. Robin Pickering-Iazzi summarizes "Vannina's journey to authentic being" as one that "expands the possible meanings and forms of women's existence" (336), while Carol Lazzaro-Weis concludes that *Donna in guerra* unmasks "the illusion that political fact could be separated from private life" (304).[4]

In these readings, the heroine's achievement of autonomy is described as a movement that somehow traverses a terrain from private to public, or from the space of silence and absence to a privileged vantage point. From just such a reading, the private is still defined from the point of view of the public and the silent, absent space from the position of privilege. Notions of identity are still grounded exclusively in male perceptions and experience of self. There has been no identification of the articulation of women's different experiences, which is the concern of the feminist writers of the post militant generation.

The articulation of women's experience of difference is itself problematic. To write about women, it is not enough just to be a woman who writes. As Anne Cranny-Francis notes, "many writers work conscientiously within the dominant ideologies of gender, race and class; after all, that is the best way to make a living" (1). The skills and traditions involved in the production of literature have been devised according to the needs and interests of men. Traditional narrative forms and conventions have supported and perpetuated the cultural norms that have worked to define women in relation to masculinity. Through reading within these forms and conventions, a woman reader more often than not is required to learn to consider herself in relation to others. Conventional plot structures for women have progressed toward the heterosexual relationship and marriage where man has been the active agent of courtship, seduction, or proposal and woman the passive object. The countless women who end up marrying the heroes of fairy tales do so only after their passivity is tested during a period when they have been chained to a rock or confined in a tower.

Many women who write have had to acquire skills and learn about traditions that have been kept from the experiences of women. Those women who have become important in the literary tradition of the dominant culture have done so because they have learned the traditions of representation devised for those who write for men and as men. But access to the male-dominated culture has often brought with it the alienation of the "feminine" inheritance nurtured in silence and isolation away from the public eye. The strategies representing women only in relation to men have permitted the presence of a suppressed subculture of female experience that is in excess to the represented experience. When discussing the small part of women's lives that have been made visible in literature through the representation of women only in relation to men, Virginia Woolf comments:

> Suppose, for instance, that men were only represented in literature as the lovers of women, and were never the friends of men, soldiers, thinkers, dreamers; how few parts in the plays of Shakespeare could be allotted to them; how literature would suffer! We might perhaps have most of Othello; and a good deal of Antony, but no Caesar, no Brutus, no Hamlet, no Lear, no Jaques . . . (80)

Many feminist studies have exposed oppositional practices employed by women writing within the conventions of culture. An example of the working of oppositional practices within traditional discourse can be seen in Marie Maclean's investigation of women's traditional narrative. Her study of the folktale, traditionally seen as working to reinforce conservative social structures and patriarchal values, highlights the fact that these tales can be seen also from a maternal perspective inasmuch as the oppositional practices they contain aim at a special relationship with a female audience. She identifies these oppositional practices as the inversion or negation of male values and masculine self-satisfaction, and the creation of heroines who either speak bi-vocally from a traditional female position, seeing man as Other, or reverse the traditional tale, where the female is the object of the active hero, by taking the active role with the man as object.

Oppositional practices correspond to the activities of the early generations of feminists as they strive for a place for women in a predominantly male world. The expression of an oppositional pose within the convention has been described by Cranny-Francis as a compromise. She states that her own interest as a feminist is in the fiction of women who write not within but against these conventional structures. These texts, she feels, not only tell different kinds of stories, they function differently as well (1). Taking an oppositional pose often brings with it a consolidation of gendering by ignoring the history of women's oppression and the position of difference assigned to a woman within the social body. A woman writer who succeeds in writing against the conventional forms, succeeds, like the post militant generation feminist, in articulating the female experience in its relationship to culture. The focus on the relationship to culture is stressed by Anna Nozzoli in the specific context of contemporary Italian women's writing. In her prescription for future feminist endeavor, she envisions a focus that includes "an investigation of the underlying roots, the contradictions and ambiguities which characterize the relationship between women and cultural production" (Nozzoli 46).

Feminist theory proposing an alternative to the formation of female identity from a relationship to masculinity relies on reworkings of specific areas of psychoanalytic and narrative theory. For it is here, in both the psychoanalytical discussion of the individual's recognition of identity and the discussion in narrative theory of the mechanics of representation by which we establish and accept values and institutions, that the construction and acceptance of gendering can be demonstrated.

In psychoanalytic and narrative theory, the social reality of the definition of woman in relation to masculinity is illustrated through the familial metaphor. In a patriarchal culture the family unit provides the first points of reference for a representation of the developing individual. From the first relationship within this nuclear configuration, a developing individual seeks and finds in an external shape a representation of his or her inner desires.

Within the patterns of interaction told in the family story it is possible to find an intersection of social and psychological reality and narrative representation. The pattern of socialization described in the Oedipal family story has often been described as the basis of all social and narrative development. Oedipus's killing of his father and marriage with his mother highlights the struggle between father and son over the body of the mother, emphasizing the masculine line of descent and the silencing of the female story.

Feminist theorists working in this area have sought to expand the family story to include the voices of female members silenced by the privileging of the masculine. In particular French feminists Julia Kristeva, Luce Irigaray, and Hélène Cixous have posited an alternative to the patriarchal tradition in the pre-social, pre-Oedipal area where a different relationship governed by a connection to the mother is possible. Maraini's reworking of the family story in *Donna in guerra* provides a reassessment of the mechanism for the socialization of women through the characters Giottina and Tota, who function in the novel in much the same way as the pre-social area that Kristeva has defined as the semiotic.

The formation of female identity from a relationship to masculinity has been responsible for leaving undisclosed a vast area of potential female individuality. Able to recognize and be influenced by only the narrow range of images of women circulating in the male-dominated culture, the developing female has been unaware of the potential identity lying outside this range. The development of Vannina includes a recognition of the socially disruptive nature of this potentiality. The negated femininity is able to be identified and used to dislocate the ordering of the social body in the same way that, according to the theories of Julia Kristeva, the semiotic, or representations of our precultural experiences, is able to challenge the symbolic, or representations of our cultural experiences.

In Kristevan theory, Jacques Lacan's explanation of how we become sex-gendered people through entering the symbolic order and language is expanded to allow for the presence of an articulation of our earlier cultural experiences. According to Lacan and Kristeva, the development of the speaking subject and entry into the symbolic are made through a process of separation. The developing individual becomes aware of itself as an entity when it can distinguish an outside—the position of another that appears to reflect itself. This stage of development is referred to by Lacan as the mirror stage. Socialization follows with the individual's acceptance of culture and entry into the language system.[5] Kristevan theory has endeavored to underline the presence of the precultural stage of human development. John Lechte sees Kristeva's difference from Lacan as the intent to show the importance of the semiotic without denying the importance of the symbolic (130).

In positioning the existence of semiotic discourse alongside the discourse of the social body, Kristevan theory permits the articulation of those female experiences that have been negated by culture and, at the same time, this articulation shows them in the very act of being left out. In *Donna in guerra,* the negated femininity is exposed through Giottina and Tota, whose characters and actions link them to categories implicit in the Kristevan semiotic.

Vannina's meetings with Giottina, a cleaner, and Tota, a laundry woman, take place regularly in a launderette, a long, dark room carved out of the rock. The menial jobs of the two women and the underground location of their meeting place suggest a position within the social body that is also marginalized and unobserved from the center of power. Kristeva has referred to the semiotic continuum by the term *chora*[6] from Plato's use of the term with the meaning of receptacle. The description of the chora as a container together with its link with the mother/child symbiosis associates it with the maternal womb. The confines of the laundry, the long, dark room carved out of rock, create such a receptacle.

The meeting place is linked with the idea of the semiotic through the use of the image of the sea. The laundry is dripping with moisture. Vannina's clothes stick to her body. It is a place where the rhythms match the rhythms of the sea. The "tonfo regolare del ferro da stiro" (14; "regular thumping of the iron"; 14) matches the "ritmo gioioso e ondulato" (13; "joyful and undulating rhythm"; 13) of their voices. The image of the sea expresses the idea of the totality associated with the semiotic, where the identity assumed upon entering the symbolic exists alongside all the other possible identities that were left out in the formation of this one identity. The sea has a volume that is infinite. Its crisscrossing of currents complements the regularity of the tides. It is governed by both the sun, with its evening and morning tides, and the moon, with its high and low tides.

Like the undifferentiated merging bodies of the semiotic, the two women in the laundry have no clearly defined identities—they seem to merge into each other: "Giottina assomiglia a Tota! Ha il corpo come un fagotto. Le braccia corte, forti, abbronzate; la faccia senza età, gli occhi grandi languidi" (9; "Giottina looks just like Tota! Her body is a bundle, she has short, strong, suntanned arms, an ageless face and large, listless eyes"; 9). These merging bodies are the bodies of women without a sense of subjectivity: the undifferentiated community of women that have been left out of the socially constructed identity.

Within the semiotic, existence is experienced as a continuum. The child exists in a continuity with the body of the mother. This continuum Kristeva describes as dominated by primary processes, a body crisscrossed by a flow of impulses or drives, primarily anal and oral, which are simultaneously dichotomous.[7] Similarly, simultaneous yet contrasting drives seem to dominate the relationship in the laundry. Giottina and Tota seem governed by impulses that are both simultaneous and dichotomous. The two women are able to fight and make up so spontaneously that there seems no division between the two opposing actions. As Vannina says:

> Tota mi è venuta incontro battagliera, una cicatrice sul labbro, una grossa macchia blu sotto l'occhio sinistro.
> — Mi voleva ammazzare la cornuta, ma io l'ho conciata peggio, le ho strappato un pezzo di carne così dal collo.
> — Allora la vostra amicizia è finita?
> È scoppiata in una risata brusca, i due denti d'oro luccicanti fra le labbra esangui, come due stelle.
> — Ora lo sai che facciamo?
> Mi ha preso per un braccio, complice e autoritaria.
> — Compriamo delle paste e andiamo a mangiarle giù al negozio.
> Così abbiamo fatto. (26)

Revolution in the Laundry

> Tota came up to me looking like a prize fighter with a scar on her lip and a large blue bruise under her left eye.
> "She tried to kill me, the bitch. I did worse to her, though, I ripped a piece of flesh this big from her neck."
> "So your friendship is over, is it?"
> ... She gave a sudden sour burst of laughter, her two gold teeth sparkling between her bloodless lips like two stars.
> "Guess what we'll do now?" She dragged me by an arm, with an air of complicity.
> "Come on, we'll buy some cakes and eat them in the shop." So that's what we did. (26)

Within this relationship, the impulses seem to relate to the oral and anal drives characteristic of the mother-child symbiosis. The women are perpetually eating and feeding each other:

> Tota ha preso la pasta e gliel'ha messa sotto il naso. Giottina continuava a storcere la bocca. Tota, con due dita asciutte e rugose, si è aperta un varco fra le labbra serrate dell'amica. Le ha dischiuso i denti con le unghie e poi le ha premuto la pasta sulla lingua. Giottina si è arresa: a occhi socchiusi ha preso a succhiare la crema. Poi ha affondato i denti nella crosta molle, lenta e ingorda, immusonita. (122)

> Tota picked up a cake and put it under her nose. Giottina kept on twisting her mouth up. With two rough dry fingers Tota opened a gap between her friend's tightly shut lips. She separated her teeth with her nails and pressed the cake on her tongue. Giottina gave in: with half-opened eyes she started sucking up the cream. Then still frowning she sank her teeth into the soft crust, slowly and greedily. (122)

In the laundry, Giottina and Tota engage in storytelling. Theirs are the stories of a female experience that is outside of a society divided into male and female, where male is opposed to and superior to female. Their stories are from outside the heterosexual arrangements that are privileged in a patriarchal culture; beyond the genital arrangements of male and female. They tell of a female singing star, Purea Willey, who has something weird about her body. She is half man, half woman, with a "pesce frollo che le pendeva fra le gambe" (48; "limp worm dangling between her legs"; 48). Another story of the Villa Trionfo tells of the maid and the mistress who engage in an all-woman sexual encounter that leaves the man totally excluded: "Isso non fa niente, il marito, meschinello, rimane così vestito e le due serpente si baciano, si baciano, si strusciano, e lui rema" (13; "The man doesn't do anything, poor sod, just stays still, all dressed up like that, and the two serpents kiss each other, pet, rub against each other, and he rows on"; 13).

The storytelling of the women brings a vocal element to the novel and allows for the presence of sound through which the semiotic can be discerned. For Kristeva, the presence of the semiotic can only be detected through sounds; through the rhythmicity produced by repeated alliterations, displacements, and condensations. For the semiotic, which is "antecedent and subjacent to representation . . . admits of analogy only with vocal and kinetic rhythm" ("Subject" 22).

According to Kristeva, the presence of sound within the text is able to rearrange signification. Sounds are able to organize themselves into a network of semantic values that are not necessarily those given by the morphemes and lexemes.[8] Because they speak from the semiotic, this sound permits a dissolution of the socially constructed symbolic self. As Jean Wyatt remarks:

> We respond to words as we did in infancy, when we registered the sound, rhythm, music of words rather than their significance. The position of detached analytic reader structured by the conventions of the realistic text disappears, and we become semiotic, responding to words with what is left out of the socialized "I": fluctuating, instinctual responses. (122)

As sound, the laundry women have this same function of rearranging signification. In their stories, the socially constructed self, polarized into male or female where male is privileged over female, dissolves. Meaning is no longer phallocentric. In one of the stories, the male seed is implanted into the maid by the mistress (*Donna in guerra* 137). In another the phallus is left dangling, like the tie of the man, as the two women kiss each other in the boat. The man is no longer the subject of the action. It seems as if he now has to contend with a force coming from the semiotic. He is now an alienated linear motion contending with the power of the conflicting currents in an endless sea where he never gets anywhere; he just rows and rows (13).

In Kristevan theory the sounds of a language have, by their ability to open the text to the semiotic chora, the possibility of rearranging signification but also of opening up the text to meaning that is infinite. Sound does this because it makes connection with all that has been left out of language as it is constructed into a system of meaning. In "Phonetics, Phonology and Impulsional Bases," Kristeva writes:

> While still conserving the phonematic function in order to assure the symbolic-commutative function of language (*langage*) the phonemes reacquire what the sounds lost in becoming the sounds of a given language (*langue*): they reacquire the topography of the body which reproduces itself in them. (34)

Like the sounds in Kristevan theory, the laundry women make sounds by telling stories and gossiping about life on the holiday island. These sounds have several elements that suggest incantation. They occur regularly in the story as a background to events in the home and in the piazza and contain their own rhythms through the patterns of the interchange of voices and the repetitions of key words and ideas. The rituals associated with incantation often suggest contact with a magic or spiritual existence that is invisible or not easily recognized in the everyday social reality. The voices of these laundry women also serve to suggest a connection with all that has been left out of the social structure and language.

Aside from telling stories, the laundry women take Vannina on a short trip to look at the body of a dead tourist that they have found in a hut in an out of the way corner of the island. Accompanying their storytelling, this action can also be associated with a rearrangement of signification. In the male-centered social structure where the female is defined from the masculine perspective, much female identity has remained repressed. Because it has not found recognition in the social structure, this repressed experience can be viewed as unlived or dead experience. The laundry women's action in taking Vannina to view the body of a dead woman has the same function as the Kristevan sound that works to show meaning that is infinite. Giottina and Tota show Vannina meaning that is infinite by taking her to see all that has been repressed; all that has been left out of society as it constructed itself into a system defined by man—a woman who is not living.

Vannina's look at the body of the dead American woman is an act that symbolizes that she is able to recognize the repressed femininity excluded from representation in the male-centered culture. Vannina's look is one that has to focus on female sexuality as the clothes are stripped off and the nude body of the American woman is displayed: "La donna non portava mutande. Il sesso bruno è apparso improvvisamente nudo e pallido in mezzo al ventre abbronzato e magrissimo, rugoso" (77; "The woman wasn't wearing panties. Her genitals, naked and brown, appeared suddenly in the middle of a tanned, skinny, wrinkled belly"; 78). As a sexual being, woman has been considered in relationship to male sexuality as object of male sexual desire. The female sex has been unrepresented in culture because it has been appropriated into male sexuality. Hélène Cixous sees this appropriation in terms that can be linked to the body of the dead American woman when she says it is as if woman's body had been confiscated from her, "turned into the uncanny stranger on display" (250).

Vannina is required to piece together the identity of the dead woman by translating letters found with the body. The letters are from the dead woman's son and describe the repression of his wife, her death as a woman: "'Dice che l'ho rovinata, che l'ho portata via dal sud per farla vivere in questa orribile città nebbiosa, che l'ho sposata solo per avere una che mi cucina mentre io dipingo'" (80; "'She says I've destroyed her, that I've dragged her away from the South and made her live in this horrible foggy city, that I married her just to have someone to cook for me while I'm painting'"; 81).

Whatever the actual reason for the American woman's death, she lives only in the son's letters, which describe another woman's death—in the discourse of a man. Cixous comments on the definition of women by men with a similar image when she writes: "Woman has always functioned 'within' the discourse of man, a signifier that has always referred back to the opposite signifier which annihilates its specific energy and diminishes or stifles its very different sounds" (257).

For Vannina, the journey to look at the dead stranger has two outcomes. It represents her recognition that there is more to woman than the role constructed for her by the society built on the male model. There is an unused or unexpressed area of female existence lying as if dead, that which has been left out of the social construct, a residue. More importantly for *Donna in guerra,* the residue of femininity, like the Kristevan phoneme that reacquires what the sounds lost when they became the sounds of language—the infinite possibility of sound—carries with it the possibility of infinite renewal. It enables Vannina to introduce an element of change into her life. After her return from the hut, Vannina's socially constructed identity becomes more fluid. She begins to question her socially constructed role as Giacinto's wife and is able to consider a few days in Naples without him. In her meeting with the laundry women, Vannina learns to recognize the negated female; the woman as undifferentiated being. Cixous often seems to suggest that the female is permanently "Undifferentiated, unbordered, unorganized . . . incoherent, chaotic." Kristeva on the other hand, seems to suggest the semiotic as a point of departure for self-development; anything more permanent would be like an underwater dive followed by emergence where nothing of the underwater experience remains as the diver returns to the surface.[9] The laundry women are recognized as the semiotic mode but used to suggest the possibility of a repositioning through an expanded viewpoint that includes both semiotic and symbolic. A representation of female existence without this expanded viewpoint is like staying permanently in the laundry, where the atmosphere is nauseous and "il mondo fuori dai vetri gocciolanti sembrava un fondale marino, assolato, fresco, irraggiungibile" (142; "through the dripping glass the world outside looked like a sunny, fresh, unattainable seabed far beyond our reach"; 146).

Notes

1. The translations used in this paper are taken from the English edition of the novel, *Woman at War,* prepared by Maria Benetti and Elspeth Spottiswood.

2. Julia Kristeva discusses the different generations of feminists in her article "Women's Time" 18–20.

3. See Carol Lazzaro-Weis, "Gender and Genre in Italian Feminist Literature in the Seventies"; Bruce Merry, *Women in Modern Italian Literature: Four Studies Based on the Work of Grazia Deledda, Alba De*

Pauline Dagnino

Céspedes, Natalia Ginzburg, and Dacia Maraini; Augustus Pallota, "Dacia Maraini: From Alienation to Feminism"; and Robin Pickering-Iazzi, "Designing Mothers: Images of Motherhood in Novels by Aleramo, Morante, Maraini, and Fallaci."

4. See also Merry 213.

5. Kristeva discusses this development in *Revolution in Poetic Language* 46–48.

6. For an elaboration of the Kristevan conception of the chora, see Kristeva, *Revolution* 28–29.

7. For a description of the semiotic, see Kristeva, "Subject" 21–23.

8. Kristeva discusses the semiotic presence in language in her article "Phonetics, Phonology and Impulsional Bases."

9. Jean Wyatt (124–25) discusses these differences in the theories of Cixous and Kristeva.

Works Cited

Cixous, Hélène. "The Laugh of the Medusa." *New French Feminisms: An Anthology.* Ed. Elaine Marks and Isabelle de Courtivron. 1980. Amherst: U of Massachusetts P, 1989. 245–64.

Cranny-Francis, Anne. *Feminist Fiction: Feminist Uses of Generic Fiction.* Cambridge: Polity, 1990.

Kristeva, Julia. "Phonetics, Phonology and Impulsional Bases." *diacritics* 4.3 (1974): 33–37.

———. *Revolution in Poetic Language.* Trans. Margaret Waller. New York: Columbia UP, 1984.

———. "The Subject in Signifying Practice." *Semiotext/e* 1 (1975): 19–26.

———. "The System and the Speaking Subject." *The Tell-Tale Sign.* Ed. Thomas A. Sebeok. Lisse, Neth.: De Ridder, 1975. 47–55.

———. "Women's Time." *Signs: Journal of Women in Culture and Society* 7 (1981): 13–35.

Lazzaro-Weis, Carol. "Gender and Genre in Italian Feminist Literature in the Seventies." *Italica* 65 (1988): 293–307.

Lechte, John. *Julia Kristeva.* London: Routledge, 1990.

Maclean, Marie. "Oppositional Practices in Women's Traditional Narrative." *New Literary History* 19 (1987–88): 37–48.

Maraini, Dacia. *Donna in guerra.* Turin: Einaudi, 1975. Published in English as *Woman at War.*

———. *Woman at War.* Trans. Maria Benetti and Elspeth Spottiswood. Brightlingsea, Essex, UK: Lighthouse, 1984.

Merry, Bruce. *Women in Modern Italian Literature: Four Studies Based on the Work of Grazia Deledda, Alba De Céspedes, Natalia Ginzburg, and Dacia Maraini.* Townsville, Austral.: James Cook U of North Queensland, 1990.

Nozzoli, Anna. "La donna e il romanzo negli anni ottanta." *Empoli: rivista di vita cittadina.* Ed. Sergio Gengini. Empoli: Comune di Empoli, 1983. 45–53.

Pallotta, Augustus. "Dacia Maraini: From Alienation to Feminism." *World Literature Today* 58 (1984): 359–62.

Pickering-Iazzi, Robin. "Designing Mothers: Images of Motherhood in Novels by Aleramo, Morante, Maraini, and Fallaci." *Annali d'italianistica* 7 (1989): 325–40.

Woolf, Virginia. *A Room of One's Own.* London: Granada, 1984.

Wyatt, Jean. "Avoiding Self-Definition: In Defense of Women's Right to Merge (Julia Kristeva and Mrs. Dalloway)." *The Female Imagination and the Modern Aesthetic.* Ed. Sandra M. Gilbert and Susan Gubar. New York: Gordon and Breach, 1986. 115–26.

was to "say" things in an expressive medium that still seemed alien to her ("Tema" 62–63). Her subsequent assumption of a different cinematic language was articulated through a kind of filmmaking that finally afforded her "the pleasure of looking, touching, and understanding" the image in her own terms (63). This, she tells us, occurred almost by accident, with a change of technical format. Having bought a super-8 camera to document a feminist protest march, Maraini was immediately struck by its convenience and portability, in sharp contrast to the heavy instruments of commercial filmmaking. Moreover, super-8 technology offered the unique possibility of filmmaking "in the first person," through a direct involvement in all phases of production from shooting to editing, by taking advantage of a cinematic practice that did not depend on the technical cooperation of large crews, production companies, and institutions. The principal appeal of this kind of "poor cinema," she tells us, was that it allowed her finally to appropriate the gaze, to stake out a place in a world (i.e. the world of cinema) that, historically, she had no right to inhabit[3] (59).

Maraini's short essay "Tema," which was written after the completion of her first super-8 film *Mio padre amore mio* (My father my love), reveals how her serendipitous discovery of super-8 and the subsequent experience of shooting a film in this format provoked an evolving reflection on the possibilities of feminist cinema ("Tema" 58–64). In terms that seem to echo the writings of feminist theorists and filmmakers in the U.S.A. and U.K. during the same period, Maraini identifies her task as the appropriation of filmic expression for women. The essay suggests that she conceived of her venture into experimental filmmaking primarily as an attempt to deconstruct the patriarchally inflected stereotypes of mainstream filmmaking. But she also saw it as an effort to explore the issues of female subjectivity and desire, thus investigating through formal experimentation the terms of a female imaginary.

Though "Tema" is written in an informal, almost anecdotal, style without reference to other writing on the subject of women's cinema, it resonates with arguments made in more elaborate terms by feminist theorists writing in English during the mid-1970s. Like Claire Johnston and Laura Mulvey, Maraini expresses her interest in the possibilities of women's cinema as part of the feminist struggle to appropriate the means of signification. In terms not dissimilar to those articulated in Johnston's essay "Towards a Feminist Film Practice," Maraini asserts that women's filmmaking must challenge dominant cinema whose instruments of signification are tied to a patriarchal ideology that constitutes sexuality in a manner that is destructive to women. Johnston observed that one of the problems that face feminist theorists and filmmakers was the lack of adequate symbolization for the feminine in the dominant culture, which tends schematically to construct woman as "other" ("in the asymmetry of patriarchal culture . . . woman is defined as other, *as that which is not male*"; 322). Similarly, Maraini notes that within the limiting terms of phallocentric representation—which dominates mainstream cinema and culture—there is no possibility for the recognition of women's "difference," apart from the kind of difference understood as the negative or "other" of man ("Tema" 58).

In her awareness of the gendered quality of the cinematic gaze, Maraini's comments also resonate with Mulvey's argument in "Visual Pleasure and Narrative Cinema" that the gaze in dominant cinema is fundamentally male and thus constructs a male spectator. Given the persistence of the patriarchal paradigm and women's resulting lack of cultural identity, Maraini briefly wonders if women can have any access to the gaze. She notes how women have for centuries endured the negativity of the male imaginary, where the fear of castration has inspired the creation of imaginary monsters, and men's horror of seduction by women has led to the construction within representation of witches, sirens, and spells. She also points out that the focus of men's expressive world is the female body, which, in representation, vacillates between a figure of terrifying threat and a seductive trap ("Tema" 59).

Maraini's essay nonetheless affirms that one of the principal goals of the journey undertaken by a radical, feminist cinema is the "recognition" of the bodies of other women, bodies that must be reconfigured cinematically in a manner no longer inflected by male fears and fantasies ("Tema" 59). Another, related aspiration of women's cinema, she claims, is to explore through the camera lens the territory of female desire, and to express fears, fantasies, and beliefs that are different from those

Áine O'Healy

of men. According to Maraini, in the new wave of women's filmmaking there must be no rules, no restrictions, no dogma, but a multiplicity of voices and styles.[4] In this all-embracing approach, her attitude contrasts with that of Mulvey and others, who, in taking an oppositional stance against narrative illusionism in favor of formalist experimentation, denounced the practice of realist filmmaking and the pursuit of conventional narrative pleasure, which they perceived as rooted in patriarchal ideology.[5]

I will now examine the three super-8 films that Maraini produced in the late 1970s in the light of her declared interest in creating an alternative women's cinema. Placed within the historical context of feminism in the late 1970s, these film texts reveal points of contact and contrast with the work of other women filmmakers, with Maraini's writings, and with the ongoing debates within feminism regarding sexual difference, subjectivity, and discourses of the body. The three films *Mio padre amore mio* (1976/1979),[6] *La bella addormentata nel bosco* (1978; Sleeping Beauty) and *Giochi di latte* (1979; Milk games) explore, in quite different ways, the symbolic effects on women of familial relations. This meditation is articulated lyrically, through subjective, dreamlike imagery, rather than through conventional narrative strategies. All three were shot as silent films. A sound track with nondiegetic music and minimal sound effects was added in post-production.

Mio padre amore mio, the earliest and most complex of Maraini's super-8 films, is an autobiographically inspired meditation on a woman's phantasmatic relation to her father, alternately resented and adored. The narrative is framed in the dressing room of a theater. Here, in the film's opening shot, we see the protagonist—a young actress—seated before the mirror as she begins the process of painting on a clown's face for her role in a performance. Repeatedly the film returns to this scene, recording each phase of the woman's make-up, and ending at the moment that the process comes to completion.

Most of the action in the film occurs at a different diegetic level, in scenes corresponding to the woman's memories and fantasies as she paints her face at the mirror. Throughout her methodical application of the clown's mask, the scene shifts back and forth between images of her father as remembered from childhood, and fantasies or memories of her more recent past, where father and lover are fused into the person of the same actor. It is a story of love and resentment, violence and *jouissance,* dependency and willed separation. Most of all, it is a story of obsessive repetition, of the father's ineluctable return to the woman's consciousness, despite her imagined efforts to kill him again and again.

Fragments of disjointed narrative evoke childhood summers at a villa in the country. Here, two characters appear on-screen, the protagonist as a little girl and her father as a young man in a white suit and Panama hat. In the earliest memory, she sees herself being rocked happily in a hammock by the father. In a play of concealment and retrieval, the image cuts back and forth between the father's face, half-hidden under his Panama hat, and the child who almost vanishes from sight as she is rocked within the fold of the swinging hammock. Later, as the two play together in the sunlit garden, they splash each other with the garden hose. Drops of water glisten on their tanned and almost naked bodies and peals of laughter are heard on the sound track. The child offers her father a cool slice of watermelon, which they share with each other. He plays at blind-man's-buff as the girl rides on his shoulders, her blue dress masking his eyes. Finally, as they sit together under a tree, the father reads to her from a picture book.

These images of edenic innocence are intercut with more troubling and ambivalent scenes where the daughter, now a young woman, continues her intense involvement with the father/lover in a bond that vacillates between moments of *jouissance* (which rhyme visually with the games of childhood) and fantasies of murderous resentment. Armed with a gun, she spies on him as he dances inside a window with another woman. Later, she approaches him in a distant field. She fires one shot, then another, and the man falls dead to the ground. This scene is repeated in several variations, and each time the father/lover inexplicably returns to life.

If the father does not die, his image must nonetheless acquiesce to the daughter's staging of his injury and disempowerment. Following one of her acts of "murder," the adult

Áine O'Healy

daughter visits his body in the mortuary. Using white greasepaint she covers his face with a deathly pallor and traces a blood-red wound on his temple, supposedly where the fatal bullet entered his head. She then unbuckles his belt and gently extracts his lifeless penis, holding it tenderly to her cheek. Thus marked by injury and mortality, and deprived of its resplendent phallic potency, the body of the father/lover becomes the object of the daughter's tender care.

The scene in the mortuary is a pivotal one, introducing the intertexual links with Giuseppe Verdi's *Rigoletto* that play an important part in the contrapuntal movement of the film's signifying strategies. As the woman leans over the body of the father/lover, we hear a tender exchange from Verdi's opera, where Gilda, beloved daughter of Rigoletto, greets her father with words that clearly inspired the chiasmatic title of Maraini's film: "Mio padre! . . . Oh, quanto amore, padre mio!" In response, Rigoletto sings of his great love for Gilda: "A te d'appresso / trova sol gioia il core oppresso" ("Only with you does my heavy heart find joy").[7] Rigoletto assures his daughter that she means more to him than life itself: "Mia vita sei! / Senza te in terra qual bene avrei?" ("You are my life. Without you, what would I have on earth?"). In Verdi's opera, however, this passionate declaration of paternal love masks a possessiveness that will ultimately contribute to the daughter's destruction.

"Dead women, dead so often," Catherine Clément observes in her study of opera, a medium devoted to narratives that stage the "infinitely repetitive spectacle of a woman who dies, murdered" (47). Italian melodrama is full of women who love too much, and who die of this excess. Gilda meets her death in *Rigoletto* partly as the result of paternal love gone awry. Caught hopelessly between the constraints imposed by a possessive father and the heartbreak meted out by her suitor, the Duke of Mantua, she allows herself to be murdered in order to prevent the death of her beloved.

The voice of Gilda's suitor is also heard on the sound track of *Mio padre amore mio* in a sequence that features Maraini's adult protagonist. We now see the young woman sharing a slice of watermelon in a scene of erotic play with the father/lover, as the treacherous Duke of Mantua sings seductively of his love for Gilda: "È il sol dell'anima . . ." ("It is the sunshine of my soul . . .")· Gilda, who has fallen in love with the Duke while still a virtual prisoner in her father's house, responds to his words with heartbreaking naiveté: "Ah, de' vergini sogni son queste / le voci tenere sì care a me!" ("Ah, these are the tender, longed-for words I have heard in my maiden dreams!"), while on the visual track we see a flock of lambs, perhaps on their way to slaughter. In this, the longest musical sequence invoked in *Mio padre amore mio,* Gilda's refrain confirms the obsessive, delusional quality of romantic love. Simultaneously, Maraini's deployment of the same actor in the roles of both father *and* lover/s suggests how this passionate emotion is nothing other than a phantasmatic restaging of the daughter's desire for the father.

A third excerpt from *Rigoletto* is invoked in the film in a scene where Maraini's protagonist says good-bye to her father/lover at a train station. Here a blue filter sets the melancholy mood of their farewell, and, as the young woman boards the train, a poignant duet between Rigoletto and Gilda begins: "Ah, piangi! fanciulla . . ." ("Ah! Weep, my child"). The melodramatic power of the operatic excerpt is radically undercut in the film, however, by the fact that Maraini's protagonist, in preparation for her departure by train, has painted a dark tear on the man's face, signaling the emotion that she wishes to observe in him at the moment of their separation. The act of painting the father's face within the diegesis signals to the spectator that the young woman who is articulating these memories and fantasies in the present tense of the film's narration is not devoid of a sense of agency. Acknowledging her participation in the family romance as a performance, she also insists on the performative quality of the father's role in the same drama and her own complicity in that performance, thus claiming some distance from his phantasmatic power.

Further clues of the protagonist's self-conscious resistance to the father's power are offered throughout the film. In the present tense of the narration we watch this woman reinvent herself in the mirror, not by taking on the traditional masquerade of femininity but, rather, by assuming the ludic mask of the clown. Significantly, just as she is about to complete her makeup, the scenes featuring the father/lover come to an end, and there is a brief sequence showing a torch-lit feminist demonstration, suggesting the protagonist's active involvement in the women's movement. Finally, as she adds the last touches to her clown's face, we see images of the mime show that she is now about to perform. In conjuring up these images, she begins to smile, and, in observing her own grin in the mirror, she laughs again at her reflection.

In concluding with the image of the laughing jester, *Mio padre amore mio* highlights its ironic intertextuality with Verdi's *Rigoletto*. It is the daughter, not the father, who plays the jester in Maraini's film. Moreover, it is the father, not the daughter, who "dies" in the course of this narrative. And, unlike Rigoletto, servant of the Duke of Mantua, the female jester is the servant of no one, and her story ends with laughter rather than terrible grief. Gilda and Maraini's protagonist, however, have one striking attribute in common: they both appear to be motherless daughters. In the first exchange between Gilda and Rigoletto, which is heard on the sound track of the film, Gilda begs her father to tell her about her dead mother, to which she receives the peremptory reply: "Padre ti son, e basti" ("I am your father, let that suffice"). The denial of the daughter's need for the mother through the father's insistence that the daughter is his alone recalls the Greek myth of Persephone, who was snatched away from her mother Demeter and taken to live in Hades, the realm of her father.

In contrast to Gilda's nostalgic plea, the figure of the mother is not explicitly invoked in *Mio padre amore mio*. She is simply absent from the narrator's memories of childhood and youth, where the daughter's all-absorbing involvement with the father seems to preclude the possibility of attachment to a maternal figure. There is, however, one fleeting glimpse of a female rival (a woman seen dancing with the father/lover through the window of the villa), and it is this incident that apparently sets off the protagonist's fantasies of murderous revenge. In the light of this early scene, the introduction toward the end of the film of the sequence suggesting the woman's involvement in the feminist movement is particularly interesting. So, too, is the mime sequence presenting a carnivalesque enactment of female jealousy, which appears to trigger the protagonist's cathartic laughter. Thus, at the film's conclusion, the images of feminist activism and those of a liberating self-awareness achieved through creative performance suggest the possible conditions for the creation of a female imaginary. In this imaginary the mother will no longer be eclipsed and the daughter no longer exiled to the realm of the father.

The deployment of the film's narration as an interaction between the narrator and her specular image provides an interesting subversion of Jacques Lacan's theory of the mirror stage. According to the Lacanian paradigm, the young child, sometime between nine and eighteen months of age, takes on an integrated form, a cohesive identity, through the mediation of its own reflection in the mirror. The sight of its apparently solid and well-defined body, clearly separate from the Other, comes as a surprise to the child's sense of its hitherto uncertain boundaries and shaky motor skills. For Lacan, this alienation, or misrecognition, in the constitution of the self later serves as the basis for the alienation of the specular self in the social self, which he describes as a "paranoic alienation, which dates from the deflection of the specular *I* into the social *I*" (5). Luce Irigaray and other feminist philosophers, however, have questioned the status of the exteriority of this constituting shape, and the "phantoms" it leaves behind. Irigaray is interested in exploring what is excluded or not properly contained by the necessity of constituting a well-ordered, presentable self (*This Sex* 116–17).

Maraini's protagonist disrupts the apparent stability and solidity of her identity in the mirror by replacing her familiar facial features with the absurd mask of the clown. In the process of making herself strange, replacing symmetry with asymmetry, the human face with the absurd mask, she reverses the impression of mastery and cohesion supposedly glimpsed by the child in the mirror phase. But in this deliberate dissolution of a fixed identity, she experiences a kind of therapeutic release, a carnivalesque laughter. The images that are summoned up as she contemplates her altered features are especially interesting in this regard. In visualizing the comic routine soon to be performed, she observes her wobbly, clownish movements; the staging of a jealous fight with another female clown while a tall, male figure presides over the scene; and her eventual assault at the hands of the other woman, who wields a papier-mâché sword. The threat of this absurd injury, of bodily fragmentation, inspires laughter rather than terror in the protagonist in the present tense of the film's narration, since she appears to have already securely reinvented herself through the collective imaginary of the feminist project.

In Lacanian psychoanalysis, the constitution of identity through the misrecognition of the specular self as ideal ego in the mirror phase marks the inception of the imaginary (one of Lacan's the three psychic registers, with the symbolic and the real). This process provides the basis for all later identifications, and cannot be reduced to something that pertains only to the mirror phase of early childhood. Lacan envisioned the imaginary as sexless or genderless, since its inception precedes the entry into the symbolic, the order of language, culture, and the Law of the Father. The Lacanian symbolic, initiated after the completion of the mirror phase and, like the imaginary, effective throughout the life of the subject, is, instead, predicated on the acknowledgment of the phallus as transcendental signifier. Since the imaginary and the symbolic are interdependent, however, the imaginary cannot be said to remain untouched by the phallic bias of the symbolic order. For Irigaray, Lacan's conception of both the imaginary and the symbolic is based on a hom(m)osexual (or monosexual) model of subjectivity, that is, on the phallic illusion of sameness and the denial of sexual difference.

Since the late 1970s, feminist theorists in France, Italy, and elsewhere have argued that women must begin to define the terms of a female symbolic and a female imaginary. For Irigaray, a female symbolic depends on a female imaginary, and vice versa. She points out that the imaginary is, in fact, an effect of the symbolic, since it is the symbolic that structures the imaginary (*Speculum* 84). Noting that while the female imaginary can be understood as the underside of the dominant (masculine) symbolic order, she asserts that it could also be understood as something still to be created. This would entail a collective restructuring of the imaginary by the symbolic.

Along with Irigaray, the Italian philosophers of the Diotima group and the Milan Women's Bookstore Collective began in the 1980s to express concern regarding the unsymbolized nature of the mother-daughter relationship. What is meant by unsymbolized is that there is a lack of linguistic, social, cultural, iconic, mythical, or other representations of that relationship. This does not mean that there are none, but that existing representations are inadequate, allowing a woman "too few figurations, images, or representations by which to represent herself" (*Speculum* 71). In other words, there is no maternal genealogy. This awareness has led a number of feminists to attempt a theoretical delineation of the mother-daughter relationship, thus proposing an alternative symbolic order predicated not on the phallus but on the power of the maternal figure. Luisa Muraró, one of the foremost exponents of the necessity of a female symbolic order, has explained her own journey from the critique of patriarchy to the theorization of the maternal symbolic as follows:

> What I gained from the critique of patriarchy was a level of self-awareness, but not the ability to signify freely the greatness of the feminine. During the early months and years of my life I had encountered and fully recognized this greatness in the person of my mother, and later sadly lost sight of it, almost to the point of denying its existence. (21)

According to Muraro, while feminist discourse has produced a convincing critique of patriarchy and the cultural systems supporting its dominion over women, the merit of this critique will vanish in a couple of generations if women do not create a movement to affirm the symbolic power that is held in woman's relationship with the mother.

Maraini's 1979 film *Giochi di latte* predates most of the theoretical discourse on the necessity for a female symbolic order. Nonetheless this twenty-minute film, articulated around the image of lactation as a symbol of maternal power, resonates with the thrust of the subsequent theoretical project, while at the same time coming close to the risk of essentialism. The film begins as a pregnant woman and a little girl—presumably her daughter—walk hand in hand through a city park. The woman tidies the child's hair, smiles at her warmly, and draws her close to her pregnant body. This moment of socializing discipline and affirming embrace sets the stage for the "lesson" that the child will learn in the sequence that follows. Coming upon a path lined with classical sculptures, mother and daughter observe that one of these statues, a dilapidated stone goddess, has begun to excrete milk from its breast.

Áine O'Healy

The remainder of this long, central sequence abandons the realistic register of the framing scenario (the walk in the park) to weave a montage of images, mostly shot in close-up, that celebrate symbolically the power of the mother. The milk that springs from the breast of the statue flows over the rim of the pedestal and falls onto the grass, eventually forming a great river of abundance that appears to cover the entire landscape. This magical spectacle is intercut with scenes corresponding to the child's projections or fantasies, in which the woman gently expresses milk from her naked breast. The girl holds up an empty bowl, and milk pours into it. As the milk continues to flow, it rains down on all living things, including the skin of a naked man who lies, face downward, in a garden. The woman offers her breast to the man, and he suckles in her arms like an infant. Later, seated together at a table, the man and the woman feed each other from a spoon. The man spreads milk on his face, and appears to weep tears of milk. The woman also places drops of milk on her face, then contemplates her reflection in the mirror. Throughout the film, it is the gaze of the child in the framing sequence that mediates the fantasy of maternal nurture for the spectator. Meanwhile, the daughter's vision is facilitated diegetically by the mother, who holds her hand in the park and seems to speak to her of this nurturing abundance.

In the quest to posit the terms of an alternative symbolic order, it became clear that feminist discourse must avoid creating a simple substitute for the phallus as transcendental signifier. The image of the breast ran the risk of appearing too rigid, too readily associated with the phallus and its binary signifying system. Maraini's image of milk provides a fascinating, fluid alternative. Discourses of the body had begun to achieve prominence in Italian feminist debates of the late 1970s, shifting away from the social or egalitarian emphasis of the earlier phase. Yet linking female subjectivity too closely to discourses of the body, and particularly the maternal body, was seen as a perilous enterprise, given the long-standing patriarchal tendency to equate the feminine with the corporeal.

Giochi di latte, it must be observed, does not focus on the maternal simply as a figure of bodily nurture. Rather, its principal emphasis is on the mother-daughter relationship. Here the daughter discovers, through the mediation of her mother, that she is positioned within a genealogy of the powerful, nurturing feminine. In the fantasy that is generated from this perspective, the male figure is devoid of phallic connotations, and takes on a quasi-fraternal relation to the observing daughter. In fact, the centrality of the mother in feminist discourse is quite different from the emphasis on the mother in the patriarchal system, where woman and mother are one and the same, and where daughters are generally configured in relation to the father. Maraini's film leaves room for the awareness that while not all women are (or wish to be) mothers, all of them are daughters-of-mothers, in an infinite reverse progression that goes back to our living origins.[8]

La bella addormentata nel bosco, the third super-8 film produced by Dacia Maraini during the late 1970s, reiterates her critique of the condition of women in patriarchy. In its deployment of a straightforward chronological narrative, it is less innovative on the formal level than either of the other films. Combining a realistic, almost ethnographic, recording of a woman's household chores with the subjective articulation of her daydreams, the film charts a day in the life of a woman who seems to have no identity beyond her function as housewife and mother. Like *Jeanne Dielman* (1975), Chantal Akerman's more famous feature film made just a few years earlier, *La bella addormentata nel bosco* highlights the mind-numbing monotony of the protagonist's routine and hints at the violence that this drudgery exerts upon her spirit. But, unlike Akerman's protagonist, Maraini's character seems to find small intervals of pleasure in the execution of her tasks. As she prepares and cuts the food for cooking, for example, the camera lingers in sensuous close-up on the color, shape, and texture of the ingredients, and the practiced, rhythmic motion of the woman's gestures.

At other moments, however, she is less at ease in her world. Her teenage son and daughter appear, disappear, and reappear at the table expecting to be served. They invade her space with loud music ("I Can't Get No Satisfaction" is heard blaring on the sound track as the son places his transistor radio on the kitchen table). Neither adolescent shows any interest in the mother beyond her function as provider of food.

When she finds herself alone with her tedious tasks, the woman takes refuge in daydreams. Two daydreams are articulated

Áine O'Healy

in the course of the film, both of them variations on the tale of Sleeping Beauty. The first fantasy begins as she prepares a pail of suds to wash the floor. To the sound of Baroque trumpets she imagines herself clothed in regal finery, walking through the fields toward a ruined castle. This is the woman's first excursion outside her home, and, like the subsequent outing, it occurs only in her imagination. Meanwhile, somewhere in the distance, Prince Charming (the *principe azzurro* of Italian popular tradition) comes riding through the landscape, wearing a plumed hat and blue velvet tunic. The woman sits at the window of the castle, waiting. As she begins to fall asleep in the empty chamber, bushes and weeds appear to engulf the ruined building. Finally, the prince arrives and forces his way through the overgrowth to enter the castle. On approaching the sleeping woman, the young man briskly searches under her dress and extracts a small box that contains a single red flower. Then, as he kisses her, she begins to wake up, returning his embrace. Removing the young man's mask, the woman expresses surprise, since the prince's face, shown in the reverse-shot, bears the features of her own teenage son.

The theme of sexual violation that is usually repressed in popular versions of the Sleeping Beauty fable is foregrounded here, unsettlingly, as part of the woman's phantasmatic desire. Her romantic rescue is thus overlaid with the connotation of masculine violence. And the repetition of this ambivalent scenario down through the generations is suggested in Maraini's casting of the same young actor in the role of teenage son and princely seducer.

Another daydream is set in motion as the woman takes a break from her chores and sits down to drink a glass of liqueur. In this fantasy sequence she is witness rather than participant in a drama of heterosexual seduction and violence. Walking through the wood in summertime she observes, from a distance, that a young woman and man are engaged in what appears to be a flirtatious game. As she watches, however, the protagonist realizes that the man has begun to attack the girl, assaulting her with a crude weapon until she falls on to the ground, apparently unconscious or dead. When the aggressor has left the scene, the protagonist advances toward the younger woman, moving with difficulty through the trees. In a gesture that evokes the *pietà* motif, the older woman takes the girl's mortally wounded body in her lap, offering her breast in an attempt to nurse the girl back to life. The fantasy sequence concludes with a close-up that discloses the identity of the young girl as the woman's own teenage daughter.

Thus in the second daydream the woman assumes the active role of rescuer, casting herself not as the object of seduction by the prince/lover/son, but as the nurturer and comforter of another woman, her daughter. As she returns to the reality of her daily routine, however, it becomes clear the protagonist is still invested in the fantasy of Sleeping Beauty, which provides her with enough illusory expectation to endure the completion of her tasks. Thus, having finished her chores, she takes a bath, paints her toenails, applies makeup before the mirror, and changes into fresh clothes and sandals. Then, as she sits alone in the living room facing the television set, ready for the arrival of a non-existent prince, she finally falls asleep with exhaustion. It is in this concluding tableau that the "true" story of Sleeping Beauty is ultimately revealed.

At a distance of twenty years, the three experimental films made by Dacia Maraini in the late 1970s offer a clear, passionate statement of a deeply felt commitment to women's politics at a specific moment in the evolution of feminist consciousness. The films have a striking lyrical coherence. Though uneven in their technical merits, they reveal a complex conceptualization, foregrounding the constructedness of representation, the illusoriness of identity, the performative quality of intersubjective relationships, and the necessity of new modes of feminine expression. Sadly, given the lack of technical support for the screening, processing, or restoration of super-8 technology that has resulted from the widespread availability of video, these fascinating film texts are likely to remain the least-known aspect of Maraini's creative work.[9]

Notes

1. *L'amore coniugale* (1970), starring Thomas Milian and Macha Meril, was produced by Delta Films. It is no longer commercially available, and has never been released on video. Maraini claims that the film's critical and box-office failure "saved" her from falling into the trap of a career in mainstream cinema.

Contributors

Rodica Diaconescu-Blumenfeld is an associate professor of Italian Studies at Vassar College. She is the author of *Born Illiterate: Gender and Representation in Gadda's* Pasticciaccio. She has published articles on Marco Risi, Lina Wertmüller, and Gianni Amelio. She is co-editing (with Áine O'Healy) a collection of essays on representations of the Balkans in recent European cinemas and is currently working on a manuscript on the politics of cultural repression in classic and contemporary Italian cinema.

Corrado Federici is an associate professor of Italian at Brock University, St. Catharines, Canada. He has published articles on Luigi Pirandello, Eugenio Montale, Camillo Sbarbaro, Giorgio Bassani, Lamberto Pignotti, Dino Buzzati, and Umberto Eco, as well as on contemporary Italian poetry. He is also the author of articles on hypermedia and multidisciplinary approaches to the study of language. A translation of a collection of essays on aesthetics by Luciano Nanni is forthcoming.

Giancarlo Lombardi is an assistant professor of Italian at CUNY / College of Staten Island. He has published articles on Alba De Céspedes, Elena Ferrante, Susanna Tamaro, and Margaret Atwood. His book *Rooms with a View: Feminist Diary Fiction, 1952–1994* is forthcoming. He is currently writing another book on fictional representations of Italian terrorism.

Maria Ornella Marotti is an independent scholar in comparative literature and women's studies. She has taught at the University of Rome, La Sapienza, and the University of California, Santa Barbara and Santa Cruz. She is the author of *The Duplicating Imagination: Twain and the Twain Papers*, the editor of *Italian Women Writers from the Renaissance to the Present: Revising the Canon*, and co-editor of *Identità e Scrittura: saggi sull'autobiografia nord-americana*, and of *Gendering Italian Fiction: Feminist Revisions of Italian History*.

Elisabetta Properzi Nelsen is an assistant professor of Italian at San Francisco State University and coordinator of the Italian Program in the same university. She has published on Elsa Morante and Italo Calvino. At present she is working on a book on Baroque poetry, which has been her first literary passion since her years at the University of Florence.

Áine O'Healy is a professor and chair of the Department of Modern Languages and Literatures at Loyola Marymount University in Los Angeles. The author of *Cesare Pavese,* she has also published articles on Italian literature, cinema, and feminism in *Romance Languages Annual, Feminist Studies Review, Italica, Annali d'italianistica, Cinefocus,* and *Spectator.* She is currently working on a study of the discourses of gender and nation in recent Italian cinema, and is co-editing with Rodica Diaconescu-Blumenfeld the above-mentioned anthology.

Virginia Picchietti is an assistant professor of Italian at the University of Scranton, Pennsylvania, where she is also director of the Italian Studies Program. Her fields are gender studies and Italian, and she has published articles on Dacia Maraini and Federico Fellini, and is currently working on a book on Dacia Maraini.

Ada Testaferri is an associate professor of Italian and women's studies at York University, North York, Canada. She has published on issues of feminism and politics, Boccaccio, and contemporary Italian women writers. She is the editor of *Donna: Women in Italian Culture* and the co-editor of *Feminism in the Cinema.* Currently she is working on a study of Boccaccio and the Italian short story of the thirteenth, fourteenth, and fifteenth centuries.

Index

abortion, 8, 96n9, 123, 135, 138, 139–41
Aborto: parlano le donne. See Maraini, Dacia: *Aborto: parlano le donne*
Aeschylus, 216–21, 225. *See also* Oresteia
aesthetics, 61
affidamento ("entrustment"), 48, 105–07, 108–12, 113–15, 116n4, 131
agency, 12, 199, 203–06, 209–11. *See also* subjectivity; will
Age of Malaise, The. See Maraini, Dacia: *L'età del malessere*
Akerman, Chantal: *Jeanne Dielman,* 259
Aleramo, Sibilla, 78
Alexander, Marguerite, 152–53, 162
A memoria. See Maraini, Dacia: *A memoria*
amore coniugale, L'. See Maraini, Dacia: *L'amore coniugale*
Anabasi, 116n6
Anderlini, Serena, 15n9, 151, 154
Anderlini-D'Onofrio, Serena. *See* Anderlini, Serena
Andersen, Hans Christian, 160
androcentrism, 42
animals, 31–33, 49, 63, 65, 70, 207, 210
Anzaldúa, Gloria, 191n10
alibi, 43, 56n11
archetype, 64, 65, 69
Ariosto, Ludovico, 180
articulation, 232–33, 236, 237
assassin, 43, 48, 50
authority, 63, 65, 69

autocoscienza ("consciousness-raising"), 81, 105, 106, 107, 114, 115–16, 116n4 and n6, 117n7 and n11
autonomy, 233

Bachelard, Gaston, 61, 62, 68, 71
Bagheria. See Maraini, Dacia: *Bagheria*
Banti, Anna, 78, 191n6
Barilli, Renato, 163n2
Barthes, Roland, 13, 29, 229
Beauvoir, Simone de, 104, 204, 216
Beckett, Samuel, 152–54, 163
bella addormentata nel bosco, La. See Maraini, Dacia: *La bella addormentata nel bosco*
Bersani, Leo, 154
bildungsroman, 44, 53
Birnbaum, Lucia Chiavola, 62, 94, 135
birth-giving, 13, 220
Boccia, Maria Luisa, 116n3
body, 10–11, 44, 51, 58n25, 169–71, 184, 187, 195–211, 218, 221, 223–24, 226–30
 body politics, 171
 of the father, 229
 of the mother, 13, 29–30, 203–04, 212n7, 218, 228–29
 patriarchal, 184, 187, 229
 of performance, 229
 as theater, 221
 and writing, 10, 27, 81, 127
Braidotti, Rosi, 15n9, 116n3
Brecht, Bertolt, 225
Brooke, Gabriella, 178n10

Calderón de la Barca, Pedro, 162–63
Cannon, JoAnn, 168, 177n5

Index

canon, 3–4, 7–10, 14nn3–4, 42, 44
capitalism, 221–22
castration, fear of, 249
Cavarero, Adriana, 10, 178n10, 204
chauvinism, 41
child abuse, 125, 126
Chodorow, Nancy, 116n2
"Cinque donne d'acqua dolce." *See* Maraini, Dacia: "Cinque donne d'acqua dolce"
Cixous, Hélène, 10, 77, 86, 87, 96n8, 236, 242, 243
clandestino a bordo, Un. *See* Maraini, Dacia: *Un clandestino a bordo*
class, 171, 174–75, 177n2 and n7. *See also* Foucault, Michel
Codice Rocco, 125
Colonna, Vittoria, 180
community, 103, 105, 108, 112, 114, 116
complicity, 105, 113, 115
Conrad, Joseph, 42, 46–49, 56n13 and n14, 57n21
The Secret Sharer, 42, 46–49
consciousness-raising. *See autocoscienza*
constructed images, 64–66, 67, 70
Controparola, 132
courtesan, 181–82
  in Venetian society and culture, 181, 190n4, 191n8
creativity, 44, 49, 57n19
crime, 41, 43, 45, 48, 50, 51
criticism, literary, 3, 7–8, 21, 25, 30–31, 33, 35
  feminist, 234–35
  and women's writing, 21, 35
Crudeltà all'aria aperta. *See* Maraini, Dacia: *Crudeltà all'aria aperta*
cultural legacies, female, 103, 105, 112

Dagnino, Pauline, 118n15
daughter, 108–09, 112–14, 116n3. *See also* mother-daughter bond
De Benedetti, Antonio, 33–35
de Certeau, Michel, 165
de Lauretis, Teresa, 11, 61, 230
Demau, 116n6
"Demetra ritrovata." *See* Maraini, Dacia: "Demetra ritrovata"
democracy, 216, 219–20, 222, 228
Derrida, Jacques, 12, 16n12, 95n4
desire, 236, 242
detective, 41–45, 48, 50, 55n9, 56n11
detective fiction, 42–45, 50, 54n2
  genre, 42, 45, 49
  novel, 41–43, 48–49, 53–54, 54n5
  story, 42, 44, 45, 50, 55n9
Devour Me Too. *See* Maraini, Dacia: *Mangiami pure*
Dialogo di una prostituta con un suo cliente. *See* Maraini, Dacia: *Dialogo di una prostituta con un suo cliente*
Dialogue between a Prostitute and Her Client. *See* Maraini, Dacia: *Dialogo di una prostituta con un suo cliente*
Diamond, Elin, 218, 222
difference, 53, 54n1, 105, 108, 112, 116
Dimenticato di dimenticare. *See* Maraini, Dacia: *Dimenticato di dimenticare*
Diotima, 131, 256–59
Dolce per sé. *See* Maraini, Dacia: *Dolce per sé*
Donna in guerra. *See* Maraini, Dacia: *Donna in guerra*
donna perfetta, La. *See* Maraini, Dacia: *La donna perfetta*
Donne in poesia (Women poets), 77, 95

270

Index

Donne mie. See Maraini, Dacia: *Donne mie*
Doppelgänger, 46–49, 56n13, 56–57n14
doppia militanza ("double militancy"), 117n7
double, 46, 47, 49, 54
double militancy. See *doppia militanza*
drama, 215–30
  Greek, 218
  iniatory, 215, 220
  male, 215, 218, 220
dream, 216, 221, 226–27, 229–30
Dreams of Clytemnestra. See Maraini, Dacia: *I sogni di Clitennestra*

écriture féminine, 12, 16n13, 81, 86, 229. See also female writing; *scrivere donna;* writing
emancipation, 64, 71, 127
entrustment. See *affidamento*
esotericism, 9, 198
età del malessere, L'. See Maraini, Dacia: *L'età del malessere*
euphemism, 24, 32
ex-centric, 42, 44, 53
exclusion, 171
existentialism, 152–54
exploitation, 65, 66, 67, 70, 72

fairy tales, 140–41, 144n8, 234, 260–61
family, 44, 45, 53, 56n11, 58n23, 67, 89, 103, 106–07, 113, 115
family story, 235, 236
Fare teatro. See Maraini, Dacia: *Fare teatro*
father, 45, 56n11, 58n23, 125–27, 226–29. See also body: of the father

fear of castration, 249
female cultural legacies, 103, 105, 112
female friendships, 103–08, 110–12, 115–16, 131
female genealogy, 106. See also female cultural legacies
female imaginary, 256
female kinship, 216
female protagonist, 233, 235
female symbolic order, 169, 256–57. See also symbolic: female
female writing, 22, 25. See also *écriture féminine; scrivere donna;* writing
feminine, the, 45–46, 49, 51–53, 58n24
feminism, 3–5, 10–11, 13, 36, 41, 45, 53, 56n10, 58n24, 61, 62, 69, 71, 72, 94–95, 166, 173–74, 232, 235
feminist film theory, 248–50
feminist reading position, 233–34
feminist writer, 93–95, 233–35
feminization, 167
  of culture, 167
  as emergence of the feminine, 167, 176
  of society, 175–76
film theory, female, 248–50
Foucault, Michel, 95n4, 165, 174, 221
Franco, Veronica, 179–92
Freud, Sigmund, 156
friendships, female, 103–08, 110–12, 115–16, 131
Furies, 216, 218–20, 223, 226–28, 230
Fusini, Nadia, 10, 25

Galli De' Pratesi, Nora, 24
Gallop, Jane, 126
Gauthier, Xavière, 10
gaze, 197, 200
  in cinema, 249–50

271

Index

gender, 61, 67, 69–70, 168
  in the Renaissance, 179, 181
genealogy, female. *See* female genealogy
genre, 43, 50
Giochi di latte. See Maraini, Dacia: *Giochi di latte*
Ginzburg, Carlo, 165
Ginzburg, Natalia, 78–79
gods, Greek, 217, 219–20, 227. *See also* Furies
Grosz, Elizabeth, 12
Gugliemi, Angelo, 35
"gynealogy," 169

hermeneutics, 61
Highsmith, Patricia, 57n15
historical novel, 166, 168, 177n5
historicity
  of the canon, 8
  and Maraini's writing, 11–12
history, 36, 44, 45, 53, 56n11, 65–67, 70, 151, 165, 167–68, 179, 218, 223, 227, 229–30
History of Sicily (Mack Smith), 167, 174, 177n2 and n6
Holiday, The. See Maraini, Dacia: *La vacanza*
homosociality, 216, 224
honor
  in Mediterranean societies, 124, 125
  in patriarchal society, 125
Hume, David, 170–73
  Treatise on Human Nature, 172
hystera, 221, 226, 229. *See also* womb
hysteria, 227. *See also* hystera

identification, 44, 47, 55n8, 57n14, 57n15, 197–201, 208–10, 212n3
identity, 46, 103, 104, 107, 235–36, 238, 241, 243

ideology, 62, 71, 75
imagery, 61–66, 68, 71, 73
imaginary, female, 256
imagination, 24, 26–27, 61, 62
immedesimazione ("immersion"), 197–201, 208–10, 212n3. *See also* identification
immersion. *See immedesimazione*
incantation, 241
incest, 45, 125–27, 131
Irigaray, Luce, 11, 81, 94, 96n8, 114, 117n10, 221, 236, 256–57
Isolina. See Maraini, Dacia: *Isolina*

Jeanne Dielman (Ackerman), 259
Johnston, Claire, 248–49
  "Towards a Feminist Film Practice," 249

Kemp, Sandra, 10
kinship, female, 216
Kristeva, Julia, 81, 88, 92, 96n8, 203, 209–10, 212n6, 236, 237, 241, 243

Lacan, Jacques, 236, 237, 256
Laing, R. D., 153, 163n4
La Maddalena, 135
language, 26, 29–30, 229
  bonding through, 186
  dialect, 189
  female, 188, 229
  male, 187–88
  sexism in, 191n6, 192
  as subversion, 187
Lazzaro–Weis, Carol, 117n8
Leclerc, Annie, 10
lesbian love, 97n13
"Lettera sull'aborto." *See* Maraini, Dacia: "Lettera sull'aborto"
Lettere a Marina. See Maraini, Dacia: *Lettere a Marina*

Index

Letters to Marina. See Maraini, Dacia: *Lettere a Marina*
liberation, 103, 106–08, 109–11, 116n1
Lonzi, Carla, 116n6, 123, 125
Lotman, Juri, 61
lunga vita di Marianna Ucrìa, La. See Maraini, Dacia: *La lunga vita di Marianna Ucrìa*

Mack Smith, Denis, 174
  History of Sicily, 167, 174, 177n2 and n6
madness, 153–54, 215, 225
Mangiami pure. See Maraini, Dacia: *Mangiami pure*
manifesto, Il. See Maraini, Dacia: *Il manifesto*
Maraini, Dacia, vii, 3–7
  Aborto: parlano le donne (Abortion: women speak out), 247
  A memoria (By heart), 149–64
  L'amore coniugale (Conjugal love), 246, 261n1
  Bagheria, 125–26, 169, 177n4
  La bella addormentata nel bosco (Sleeping Beauty), 250, 259–61
  "Cinque donne d'acqua dolce" (Five sweetwater women), 115–16
  Un clandestino a bordo (*Stowaway on Board*), 46, 127, 128. *See also* Maraini, Dacia: "Lettera sull'aborto"
  Crudeltà all'aria aperta (Cruelty in the open air), 63, 64, 66, 68, 77
  "Demetra ritrovata" (Demeter regained), 109, 262n8, 205, 206, 211, 222
  Dialogo di una prostituta con un suo cliente (*Dialogue between a Prostitute and Her Client*), 195–200, 222
  Dimenticato di dimenticare (Forgot to forget), 63, 74
  Dolce per sé (Sweet by nature), 7, 126–27
  Donna in guerra (*Woman at War*), 42, 77, 78, 80, 83, 88–92, 93, 103, 107–12, 115, 117n8 and n10, 118n12, 122–24, 128–31, 200–03, 205, 208–09
  La donna perfetta (The perfect woman), 135–36, 138–43, 144nn6–8
  Donne mie (Women of mine), 63–65, 67, 68, 70, 77
  L'età del malessere (*The Age of Malaise*), 77–78, 80, 82–83, 88–91, 93
  Fare teatro (Making theater), 135
  Giochi di latte (Milk games), 250, 257–59
  Interviews, 16, 19, 20, 134, 144, 145, 163, 164, 214, 230, 231
  Isolina, 42, 68, 208
  "Lettera sull'aborto" (Letter on abortion), 123 (*see also* Maraini, Dacia: *Un clandestino a bordo*)
  Lettere a Marina (*Letters to Marina*), 103, 112–15, 118n14 and n16, 199–200
  La lunga vita di Marianna Ucrìa (*The Silent Dutchess*), 124–25, 129, 131, 165–78, 190n5
  Mangiami pure (*Devour Me Too*), 63, 65, 69, 71, 73
  Il manifesto (The manifesto), 103, 105, 106–07, 115, 116n6, 135–38, 139, 141–43, 144nn2–5, 144n9
  Memorie di una ladra (*Memoirs of a Female Thief*), 77, 80, 84, 91

273

Index

Maraini, Dacia *(continued)*
  Mio padre amore mio (My father my love), 250–56, 262n6
  Ritratti di donne africane (Portraits of African women), 247
  I sogni di Clitennestra (*Dreams of Clytemnestra*), 215, 221–30
  "Tema" (Composition), 248–49, 262n4
  La vacanza (*The Holiday*), 41
  Viaggiando con passo di volpe (*Traveling in the Gait of a Fox*), 63, 64, 68, 71–73
  Voci (*Voices*), 41–60, 122, 127, 131, 204–11
Marchese, Angelo, 61
marginality, 55n9
marginalization, 68, 74, 169
matriarchy, 216–17
matricide, 216, 219, 223, 228
Memoirs of a Female Thief. See Maraini, Dacia: *Memorie di una ladra*
Memorie di una ladra. See Maraini, Dacia: *Memorie di una ladra*
memory, 36, 151, 226
menstruation, 83–84
Merry, Bruce, 66, 68
metaphor, 61, 63, 64, 65, 70–72
Milan Women's Bookstore Collective, 15n9, 105, 116n3, 256
mimesis, 218, 222, 225, 229
Mio padre amore mio. See Maraini, Dacia: *Mio padre amore mio*
mirroring, 43, 47, 48, 54. See also *rispecchiamento*
Mitchell, Tony, 229
Montini, Ileana, 155
Morante, Elsa, 78, 96n10
Moravia, Alberto, 41, 82, 96n7
Morra, Isabella di, 169, 177n3

mother, 108, 111, 113, 114, 115, 116n3, 118n12, 216, 220–21, 225, 229, 236. *See also* body: of the mother; mother-daughter bond
mother and child, 238, 239
mother-daughter bond, 104, 108–09, 113, 116n3, 195–96, 198, 256–59, 262n8
Mulvey, Laura, 248, 250
  "Visual Pleasure and Narrative Cinema," 246–47, 249, 262n5
Muraro, Luisa, 212n7, 257
  L'ordine simbolico della madre, 178n9
murder, 43, 44–46, 50
murderer, 42–45, 48–50, 52, 55n9, 56n11
Murders in the Rue Morgue, The (Poe), 42, 49–52
mystery, 50–53
mythology, 66, 68, 69, 216–30

naturalism, 33–35
Neera (Anna Radius Zuccari), 96n10
neorealism, 41
nouveau roman, 151–52
nuns, 179
  and writing, 187

objectification, 63, 68
obscenity, 23–25
  Maraini's trials for, 23
obscurity 152–53
Oedipus, 236
oppositional practices, 234–35
oppression, 62, 63
ordine simbolico della madre, L' (Muraro), 178n9
Oresteia (Aeschylus), 216–22, 224–26, 230

Paolucci, Gabriella, 104, 105
Papetti, Viola, 10

Index

Pascal, Blaise, 172
Pasolini, Pier Paolo, 31
patriarchy, 42, 45, 49, 56n11, 62, 75, 128, 173, 179, 181, 222, 228–29
perception, 10–11
Percovich, Luciana, 114
Petrarchism, 180
phallocracy, 42, 46
phenomenology, 61, 71, 72
Pickering-Iazzi, Robin, 118n12
plot structure, 233–34
Poe, Edgar Allan, 42, 49–52, 56n12 and n14, 58n22, 58n23
  The Murders in the Rue Morgue, 42, 49–52
poetics, 196, 198–99
  male, 197–98, 204, 206, 211n2
  of space, 61
polysemy, 210
"poor cinema," 248, 262n3
Porta, Antonio, 67
possession, 196–99. *See also immedesimazione*
power relations, 174–75. *See also* Foucault, Michel
pre-Oedipal sphere, 108, 109, 112, 113. *See also* mother-daughter bond
prostitution, 222, 226, 228
protagonist, female, 233, 235
psychoanalysis, 5–6, 153–54, 158

quest, 44, 49

Radius Zuccari, Anna (Neera), 96n10
rape, 45, 124–25, 128–30, 170, 173, 260
Raymond, Janice, 116n3
readers, female, 27–28
Real, the, 220, 229
religious references, 136–38, 141–43

Renaissance Italian women poets, 180
representation, 43, 44, 45, 53, 63, 66. *See also* mimesis
  dramatic, 222, 229
  of women, 218, 234–35, 236, 242–43
resistance, 49, 55n7
Rigoletto (Verdi), 252–53, 254
rispecchiamento ("mirroring"), 105, 113, 115. *See also* mirroring
Ritratti di donne africane. See Maraini, Dacia: *Ritratti di donne africane*
Rivolta Femminile, 116n6
Robbe-Grillet, Alain, 152, 163
romance, demystified, 81, 93
Rosenthal, Margaret, 180, 181, 190n1 and n4, 191n8
Rossanda, Rossana, 104

Sarraute, Natalie, 152, 163
scrivere donna, 25. *See also* female writing
Secret Sharer, The (Conrad), 42, 46–49
semiotic, the, 236, 237, 238, 240, 243
semiotics, 61, 72
sexed voice, 4, 7
sexual difference, 11, 14, 15n9, 169, 232–36, 239
sexuality, 44
Sicily, 165
  aristocracy, 167, 171, 177n2 and n7
  cultural and economic backwardness, 167
  eighteenth-century, 165–66, 174–75
  feudal, 167, 172, 177n2
  history, 166, 168
  idiom, 166
  society, 129, 174–76
signature, 4, 11–12

275

Index

signification, 240, 241
Silent Dutchess, The. See
    Maraini, Dacia: *La lunga vita di Marianna Ucrìa*
sisterhood, 105, 109. *See also* female friendships
Sleeping Beauty, 260–61
society, 45, 50, 53
sogni di Clitennestra, I. See Maraini, Dacia: *I sogni di Clitennestra*
sound, 240–41
space. *See also* poetics
  hostile, 68, 71
  of self, 188
Stampa, Gaspara, 180
stereotype, 69, 70
Stowaway on Board. See Maraini, Dacia: *Un clandestino a bordo*
style, 12–13
subjectivity, 9–10, 27, 44, 82–83, 109, 112–14, 199–200, 203–05, 209–10, 221, 224. *See also* agency; will
Sumeli Weinberg, Grazia, 66, 144n5
symbolic, 220, 228–30
  female, 228, 230 (*see also* female symbolic order)
  masculine, 225
  order, 236, 237, 243
  patriarchal, 229
symbolic mediation, 104, 105, 108, 109, 116n3

Tamburri, Anthony, 97n14, 117n8
"Tema." *See* Maraini, Dacia: "Tema"
theater, 221, 229. *See also* drama
  hystera, 221, 229
thriller, 43
Tian, Renzo, 136
"Towards a Feminist Film Practice" (Johnston), 249

tragedy, 216. *See also* drama
traveling
  imaginary, 179, 183
  as self-discovery, 189–90
Traveling in the Gait of a Fox. See Maraini, Dacia: *Viaggiando con passo di volpe*
Treatise on Human Nature (Hume), 172
Tropics of Discourse (White), 165, 168

vacanza, La. See Maraini, Dacia: *La vacanza*
Vegetti Finzi, Silvia, 10, 112
Venexiana, La, 190n3
Venice, 180–85, 187, 189, 190n1 and n4
Verdi, Giuseppe: *Rigoletto,* 252–53, 254
Viaggiando con passo di volpe. See Maraini, Dacia: *Viaggiando con passo di volpe*
Vico, Giambattista, 176
victim, 41–43, 45, 47, 48, 50, 51
victimization, 45, 48
violence against women, 41, 50, 51, 121–24, 130, 196, 203–04, 208, 212n5 and n8, 212–13n9
Violi, Patrizia, 10
Virgin Mary, 154–55, 157
"Visual Pleasure and Narrative Cinema" (Mulvey), 246–47, 249, 262n5
Voci. See Maraini, Dacia: *Voci*
voice, 195–211
Voices. See Maraini, Dacia: *Voici*
vulgarity, 23–24

Walker, Barbara, 216–17, 220
Way of the Cross, 136–37, 143. *See also* religious references
White, Hayden: *Tropics of Discourse,* 165, 168

Index

will, 198–99, 203–06, 209–10. *See also* agency; subjectivity
Wittig, Monique, 10, 96n8
Woman at War. See Maraini, Dacia: *Donna in guerra*
womb, 218–19, 221, 229. *See also* hystera
Wood, Sharon, 10
Woolf, Virginia, 234
writer, feminist, 93–95, 233–35
writers, female, 21–22, 25, 28–31, 35

Italian women poets in the Renaissance, 180
writing, 10, 26–28, 198–99, 209–10. *See also* body; *écriture féminine;* female writing; poetics
 as empowerment, 185
 as erotic space, 188
 gendered, 26
 and prostitution, 179
 as transgression, 183

DISCARDED